Long Range Shooting Handbook

Ryan M. Cleckner, Esq.

Published By:

North Shadow Press, an imprint of Cleckner, LLC
5543 Edmondson Pike
Nashville, TN 37211

To order additional copies of this book,
products discussed herein, or to learn about
additional books and projects, please visit
the author's website at
www.RyanCleckner.com

ISBN-13: 9781538028025

Photography, Illustration, and Design by: Ryan M. Cleckner
Edited by: William Keller and Iain Harrison

DISCLAIMER: This publication contains content intended to educate readers about long range shooting principles and theories as well as assist readers in safely handling and shooting firearms. Readers are responsible for their own firearm safety. The publisher and author assume no liability for the careless handling of, or misuse of, firearms.

Ryan is a firearms attorney who helps and represents FFLs all across the country. He's also started a new project to help people get their own FFLs:

RocketFFL is the premier resource for getting your Federal Firearm License (FFL), becoming an SOT (Class 2 or 3), and learn about firearm compliance. Learn more at https://www.RocketFFL.com

Get Your Own FFL - Use our online guide to help you get your very own Federal Firearm License (FFL) and start buying and selling guns, or even make your own firearms, fast! Complete step-by-step guide makes it easy.

Become an SOT - If you already have your FFL, becoming an SOT will allow you to start dealing in or making Silencers, Machine Guns, Short Barreled Rifles and Shotguns, and more!

Learn About Firearms Compliance - Getting your FFL is just the first step – now you've got to comply with the MANY rules and regulations! Our online training courses make it easy!

Courses available:

Get Your FFL:
http://courses.rocketffl.com/courses/get-your-ffl

Become an SOT:
http://courses.rocketffl.com/courses/become-an-sot-class-3

Compliance Training:
http://courses.rocketffl.com/collections/compliance-courses

DEDICATION

I dedicate this book to the memory of the Ranger heroes who made the ultimate sacrifice during the Battle of Takur Ghar:

SGT Bradley S. Crose

SPC Marc A. Anderson

CPL Matt A. Commons

CHAPTERS

Application 171

Appendix 277

TABLE OF CONTENTS

Fundamentals   109

Appendix   277

ACKNOWLEDGMENTS

I am particularly grateful for the assistance and support from my family.
To my wife, thank you for helping me finish this book.
To my kids, thank you for distracting me and
keeping me from finishing this book.

Additionally, I'd like to thank everyone who advised or encouraged me
along the way. Specifically, a special thanks is owed to:

Iain Harrison
Colby Donaldson
Tony Shankle
Robert Farago
Chris LaValley
Trevor Wilson

1 FIREARM SAFETY

Firearm safety is paramount. The fact that I included this section before any others should be a testament to my belief in its importance. I wrote this book because I enjoy passing along the information I have learned and I enjoying seeing people fall in love with shooting like I have. I want you to be able to take the information in this book and apply it out on the range. But, I only want you to do so if you are safe. If you are not safe with firearms and choose to disregard this chapter, please pass this book along to someone else. I want to grow a community of responsible shooters.

Just as there are many techniques and theories to shooting, there are also many versions of the rules of firearm safety. While I do not believe that any of the published rules by other entities are bad, I do believe that they are often too dense. If firearm safety is not tangible to a new shooter, then it won't be followed. My personal rules of firearm safety are heavily based on the rules of firearm safety from a legend of firearm instruction, Col. Jeff Cooper.

There are 4 basic rules of firearm safety. The first three rules apply to handling firearms and the fourth rule applies to the use of firearms while shooting. I segregated the rules for handling firearms to help remind you that they apply every time you are around a firearm – not just while you are at the range.

1.1 Safe Firearm Handling

Rule #1 – Treat all firearms as if they are loaded

If there is a most important rule, this is it. I teach this rule to new shooters like this: "Never do anything with a firearm while using the excuse, 'don't worry, it's not loaded.'" If you treat every firearm with respect and you treat every firearm like it was loaded, then you'll never break the other rules.

Take note that keeping a firearm's safety "on" until you're ready to shoot is not part of these rules. This is because mistakes can happen when shooters rely on a gun's "safety" as a safety device. Firearm safeties are mechanical devices that can fail. Also, reliance on a safety often encourages shooters to break one of the other rules. For example, "don't worry, the safety is on" is an unacceptable excuse for poor firearm handling.

Rule #2 – Never point a firearm at anything you are not willing to shoot

I teach new shooters to treat the firearm like it always has a laser pointing down and out the barrel. If they are always conscious of where the imaginary laser is pointing and they never let the laser's dot appear on anything they aren't willing to shoot, then they'll be following this rule.

Rule #3 – Keep your finger off of the trigger until you are ready to shoot

"Ready to shoot" means that the firearm is oriented towards the target and you are about to shoot - it does not mean that you have showed up to the range and you are ready to go to the firing line and shoot.

This rule is easiest taught with a training device/non-firearm. Have the new shooter repeatedly pick up and handle the non-firearm until they can demonstrate that they can keep their finger not only off the trigger, but also positively aligned with the firearm's frame. My favorite restatement of this rule is… "Keep your booger hook off the bang switch."

1.2 Safe Firearm Use

Rule #4 – Be sure of your target, what is around it, in front of it and behind it.

Every bullet that leaves your firearm is your responsibility - regardless of where it travels. Once you fire a bullet, you can never bring it back. Always ensure that you have an appropriate backstop and always think about where your bullet may travel if you miss your target.

2 HOW TO USE THIS BOOK

In an effort to organize the information in this book, I have divided this book into three sections: 1) equipment, 2) fundamentals, and 3) application. These sections should help you understand 1) what each piece of equipment is and how it works, 2) the core principles of long range shooting theory and technique, and 3) how to apply what you've learned. I believe that this "what it is, how it works, and how to use it" system is the best way to guide you through this information. After all, you won't be able to use it properly if you don't know how it works and before you know how it works, you need to know what it is.

2.1 Format

This is supposed to be a *handbook*. This means that I expect you to carry this book with you while you are learning and refer to it as often as needed (I made the cover orange so that it is easy to find in your gear at the range).

That said, this book can easily be read front to back by someone brand new to long-range shooting. And before you start jumping around from section to section, I do recommend reading through this book at least once.

Also, please refrain from rushing out and purchasing any equipment until you have made it all the way through the book at least once. There is some information that I cover later in the book that might help guide your purchasing decisions.

2.2 Website/Supplemental Information

For your benefit, I have created a section on RyanCleckner.com for this book at https://ryancleckner.com/long-range-shooting-handbook/.

On this book's webpage, you will find additional information that accompanies the information covered in each chapter of this book. For example, in *Section 20.4.1* of this book, I discuss appropriate cleaning equipment. In the section of the webpage for Chapter 20, I have provided links to where you can find and purchase some of this equipment.

Also for your benefit, when mentioning another online resource inside this book, instead of including the link herein (which might become outdated   / difficult to hand-type into your internet browser), I have included the links in the respective chapter's section of my website. This way, I can update links on the website without your copy of this book being out of date and you can follow links and view YouTube videos without typing long and completed URLs into your browser.

Throughout this book, I make recommendations for particular equipment. I think it is important to note that I am not affiliated with, nor sponsored by, any of the referenced companies (although, I'm happy to accept gear for testing . . . ahem).

2.3 Feedback

My website, www.RyanCleckner.com, also has a section where you can contact me with questions, leave compliments, or complaints about the book.

Because I have decided to primarily offer this book for sale through Amazon.com, I appreciate any reviews you leave there.

I do understand, however, there's a good chance you disagree with some of the information I have in this book. This is because some of my techniques and theories are a bit unorthodox. I believe that my unique methods and way of looking at things are what make my instruction effective - of course, you may disagree.

This is, in part, because this book is not a restatement of standard sniper manuals or teaching. Instead, it is my unique take on the theories and techniques described.

If you think I'm dead-wrong about something or you disagree with my approach, feel free to contact me through this book's website. I learn something from every course I teach - I view this book as a course and I might just learn something from you!

I'll make you a deal - if you reach out to me and correct an error in this book or help me explain something in a better way, I will include your edits in the next edition of this book and, with your permission, I'll give you credit in the book.[1]

I hope this approach will do two things. 1) I hope it makes us all a community of shooters striving to make each other better instead of tearing each other down. 2) I hope it keeps the internet comment/ forum "I'm more tactical than you" pissing contests to a minimum.

2.4 Sections

2.4.1 Equipment

This part of the book is the "what it is/how it works" section. In this section, we'll cover the terminology, function, and selection considerations of equipment for long range precision shooting. This section includes the following chapters:

- Ammunition
- Rifles
- Aiming Systems

---

[1] Thank you to TJ Sanner, Erich Sagers, Paul Bandy, Eden Neary, David Durra, Travis Jones, and Jacob Hall who each accepted this offer and read this book critically enough to find a couple typos which have since been corrected!

- Accessories
- Selecting the right Rifle, Scope, and Ammunition

2.4.2 Fundamentals

This part of the book is the "basics of long range shooting"/ classroom section. I normally teach these topics with a whiteboard or chalkboard. This section includes the following chapters:
- Fundamentals of Marksmanship
- Units of Measurement
- Ballistics
- Environmental Effects

2.4.3 Application

This part of the book covers how to put the first two parts of the book into practice. You may not like the techniques introduced in this section. All I ask is that you try them. If you don't like them, you don't have to use them. I teach the "toolbox method." Take a tool I'm showing you and try it out. It may not be useful in all circumstances but you should learn it and keep it in your "toolbox." Who knows, someday the technique may prove valuable. At the very least, you'll find a method you don't like - sometimes that's just as important as finding a method you do like.

This section includes the following chapters:
- Scope Mounting and Setup
- Shooting
- Spotting
- Zeroing Your Rifle
- Alternate Positions
- Estimating and Adjusting for Target Distance
- Estimating and Adjusting for Wind
- Estimating and Adjusting for Angles
- Cleaning Your Rifle

Equipment

Generally, a great shooter with a mediocre gun can outperform a poor shooter with a great gun. This is because good performance is more often a product of skill - "it's the Indian, not the arrow." Although that aphorism is generally true, a good shooter's performance can be held back by sub-standard equipment when it comes to precision shooting.

An expert long range shooter can shoot up to the performance capability of a rifle. For example, a rifle system (rifle, scope, ammo, etc.) that can shoot no better than a 5 inch group at 100 yards while bolted into a vise will not magically shoot better because an expert shooter holds it while it is fired - contrary to what Hollywood shows us. In fact, the shooter is the least accurate part of a system when quality equipment is used - a high-end precision rifle is more accurate without us.

You should think about each part of the system, including yourself, as potentially adding variability and decreasing accuracy. I argue that any particular piece of equipment doesn't actually make a system more accurate. Instead, good equipment can just help minimize inaccuracy.

Although this might be too abstract of a concept for an introductory book, I think it is important to think about. Unlike with a race car, for example, where a certain part, like a turbo-charger, has a direct effect in increasing the car's performance, consistency is

> Consistency is the key to accuracy

the key to accuracy in shooting. For example, if the barrel on a rifle is so bent that it shoots bullets at a 45 degree angle, it can still be an incredibly accurate rifle as long as it does it the exact same way every time.   The turbo-charger on a car isn't about consistency, it is all about maximizing output.   A faster car is the goal.   Quality equipment in rifle shooting isn't necessarily about performance, it's about consistency shot after shot

Match-grade ammo, for example, isn't necessarily any faster or more powerful than hunting ammo. A comparison of specs might actually show that the hunting ammo is "higher performance." All that matters for match-grade ammo is that it does the exact (or close to it) same thing every time - even if what it does isn't that spectacular.

If you think about your rifle system as starting with a baseline of capability, and realize that every other variable can interfere with its consistency and make it more inaccurate, then you'll be on the right track. For example, a quality barrel locked into a vise is the most accurate baseline. Putting that barrel into an action in a poor stock will decrease its accuracy while putting it into a quality stock will help it retain most of its accuracy. The good stock didn't give any accuracy to the barrel, it just minimized the variability and therefore minimized the inaccuracy it introduces.

The same can be said for a shooter. A good shooter won't make the rifle more accurate. Instead, the good shooter just reduces the amount of inaccuracy that can be introduced by having the rifle operated by a human.

Having the proper equipment is clearly important.   I strongly recommend, however, spending your money on training with serviceable equipment, rather than purchase the best equipment possible and not know how to use it. With $4,000, a novice shooter can purchase an $800 rifle, a $1,200 scope and have $2,000 left for training, ammunition, and some recommended accessories like a sling and shooting bag. That shooter will be a better marksman and more capable with their rifle than someone who purchased a $4,000 rifle and has no idea how to use it.

These chapters will explore and explain suitable equipment for long range shooting. Some topics will be saved for later in this book or for the sequel to this book, *Advanced Long Range Shooting*.

3 AMMUNITION

Each functional part of a rifle has a purpose and a function related to how ammunition is handled and fired. Heck, the entire purpose of the rifle is to shoot ammunition, so it is obviously difficult to discuss rifles without first understanding ammunition.

Ammunition is the assembled combination of the following components: a projectile (the bullet), propellant (the gun powder), a case, and a primer. The primer ignites the powder. The powder burns and expels gas. The gas builds pressure which pushes the bullet out of the firearm. This assembled unit is called a cartridge (or a "round" of ammunition). Technically, U.S. federal law treats each individual component of ammunition as ammunition itself.

The size, shape, and power of ammunition all affect the classification of the cartridge or chambering. Only the ammunition for which a rifle is chambered should be used in that rifle.

The terms caliber and chambering are often interchanged even though they refer to different things. The chambering, or cartridge, is the entire package. A specific chambering has certain dimensions for its case and overall length, a certain bullet diameter and weight

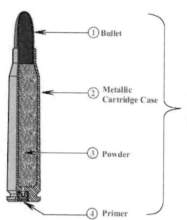

Source: ATF

range, and a certain pressure limit. Caliber, on the other hand, refers only to the nominal bullet diameter.

A complete round of ammunition or any enumerated sub-component is ammunition as defined.

For example, 308 Winchester (308 Win) and 300 Winchester Magnum (300 Win Mag) are two different cartridges. The 300 Win Mag has a bigger case (length and diameter), and therefore has a larger case capacity to hold more powder, its headspace is measured off of a rim around its base instead of its case's shoulder like the 308 Win, and it operates at a higher pressure. Despite the differences in the overall cartridges, they are both .30 caliber because they both have bullets that are .308 inches in diameter.

Although caliber and chambering are two different things, I will sometimes use the term "caliber" to describe both aspects of a cartridge because it is the common/every-day use of the term. When someone comes up to you at the range and asks what caliber your rifle is, they almost always are wondering what cartridge it is chambered for. They are expecting an answer like "308 Win" or "300 Win Mag." They'll look at you funny if you answer with ".30 caliber" even though it is exactly what they asked.

3.1 Bullets

The bullet is the projectile which is fired from the rifle - it is not the entire cartridge. The primary purpose of a firearm is to transfer energy from the firearm to a target.[2] The bullet is what transfers the

---

[2] The exception to this, of course, is when you are shooting paper targets where the intent is solely to make holes in paper.

energy.

The energy that a bullet can potentially transfer to a target is calculated by multiplying half of the mass of the projectile by its

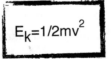

$$E_k = 1/2mv^2$$

velocity squared. This translates to a fast heavy bullet having more energy than a slow light bullet. It also means that speed is more influential than mass when calculating energy. *(see Chapter 10 - Ballistics)*.

3.1.1 Bullet Design

A whole book could be dedicated to bullet design and function. In fact, some have been. But remember, this is a handbook for beginners so we will only be briefly discussing bullet design.

Shape

The shape of a bullet has a direct effect on its ability to travel through the air and transfer its energy to a target. An aerodynamic pointed bullet can fly through the air easier, maintaining a higher speed which results in more available energy. A blunt-faced bullet, however, doesn't travel through the air as easily and will slow down more due to wind resistance.[3]

It should be noted, however, that although the blunt-faced bullet may have less available energy by the time it reaches the target, its blunt face may help it transfer more of the energy to the target. Think about it like this: a pointed bullet passes through things easier - this includes both the air and targets. A blunt bullet generally resists passing through things, both the air and targets, and therefore transfers more of its energy to whatever it is passing through.

Bullets come in all shapes, including flat front, hollow point, and even round balls, to name a few. For the purpose of this book, the

---

[3] Actually, "air resistance" or "drag"

only bullet shape we'll discuss is the spitzer, or pointed, shape due to the desire to use aerodynamically efficient bullets for long range shooting. *(see Chapters 9 - Units of Measurement and 10 - Ballistics).*

Weight

The weight (actually, the "mass") of a bullet has a direct effect on its performance. Bullet weight is typically measured in "grains." 7,000 grains equal one pound. *(see Chapter 9 - Units of Measurement)*

Heavier bullets require more energy to get up to speed (and therefore "kick" more), but they better maintain their speed while flying through the air and are less affected by wind (compared to a lighter bullet at the same speed).

As a result of the need for more energy to get them up to speed, heavier bullets in a particular cartridge generally leave the rifle at a slower velocity than lighter bullets. This is the trade off in the energy calculation of a bullet.

For some people, it is difficult to believe that heavier bullets can maintain their velocity better than lighter bullets. As a rudimentary thought experiment, imagine throwing a ping pong ball and a golf ball across your back yard. The ping pong ball will probably leave your hand faster, but the heavier golf ball will maintain its speed longer and travel further. When shooting long range, heavier bullets generally travel farther. The exception, of course, is a light bullet that can be shot at such a high speed that it still stays supersonic at the range you are shooting. *(see Chapter 10 - Ballistics)*

Heavier bullets can be affected less by the wind as compared to a lighter bullet at the same speed. Note that this comparison is made for bullets traveling the same speed. If one bullet is traveling faster, then the faster bullet will not be exposed to the wind for as long and will therefore experience less of a shift than a slower bullet. Whichever variable you are focusing on, mass or speed, it is important to note that they both have an effect and attributing a change to only one variable when both have changed (for example, lighter bullets generally start out traveling at faster speeds) may lead you to an incorrect conclusion. Of course, the shape of the bullet also has a significant effect on its drift but that topic is discussed later.

Size

The diameter of the bullet determines its caliber. For example, 30 caliber bullets are nominally .30 inches in diameter and many different chamberings can use the same 30 caliber bullet. For example, 300 Blackout (BLK), 308 Win., 30-06 Springfield (Sprg), and 300 Win Mag can all use the exact same 30 caliber bullet.

3.1.2 Parts of a Bullet

The basic parts of a bullet are the tip, the head (or ogive), the bearing surface (shank / body / sides), and the tail (or base).

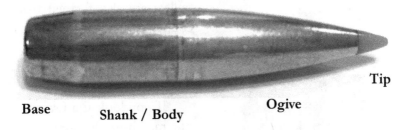

Tip

Base   **Shank / Body**   **Ogive**

Tip

The tip of the bullet is its forward facing point as it flies through the air. The tip of a bullet for precision long range shooting is usually one of three types: full metal jacket, open tip, or polymer tip.

Full metal jacket (FMJ) bullets are rare in precision shooting. They are durable and easy to manufacture and are, therefore, the most common bullet style in economy-priced ammunition. In addition to being durable while they are handled and fed into the chamber, FMJ bullets are also known for their ability to penetrate without expanding compared to other styles of bullets. This is not desirable when hunting, and as such, FMJ bullets are usually banned for hunting purposes.

FMJ bullets are rare in precision shooting because of their manufacturing process. It is difficult for the manufacturer to ensure consistency when making FMJ bullets because the process is designed for economy of scale; cheap but not very consistent. These bullets are made by forming a cup of copper around a lead core, leaving the base of the bullet open.

Open tip bullets, also called open tip match (OTM) bullets, have been the standard precision rifle bullets for a long time. These bullets are not considered "hollow point" (HP) bullets because the opening in the tip of the bullet is a byproduct of the manufacturing process and it is not designed to expand on impact like true HP

bullets are. Like FMJ's, OTM bullets are also formed from a copper cup, but in this case the opening is at the top, which is what causes the open tip, called the "meplat."

If you look at a few rounds of match-grade ammunition with OTM bullets, you'll likely notice how imperfectly they're shaped. It always amazed me that bullets with such jagged-edged and inconsistent tips could fly so well.

The reason OTM bullets are so accurate is not necessarily because of their tip, but rather how they're constructed. These bullets are accurate despite their inconsistent tips because of the extra care given to quality in the important parts of the manufacturing process.

Some people argue that the meplat creates a small bubble of air at the nose of the bullet which helps the bullet fly through the air without undue turbulence.   There may be something to this argument, but polymer tipped bullets don't have this feature and they sure don't seem to need it.

Some match shooters choose to modify the meplat on OTM bullets to make them more uniform. This can be done by trimming the tips or by squeezing them into a finer point. I've never modified the tips of my bullets (but I'm also not a world-class bullseye target shooter).

Polymer tipped bullets are a more recent trend in bullet design.   A polymer tipped bullet has a larger opening than an OTM bullet and the opening is filled with a plastic tip during the manufacturing process. These polymer tipped bullets can have all of the manufacturing advantages of an OTM bullet but can also have much better consistency in tip shape.

By looking at the bullets, you might think that the polymer tips are the most accurate because their tips have nice aerodynamic and uniform points.   Despite this, match shooters, especially those that are winning, are still mostly using OTM bullets.   I believe it is only a matter of time until polymer tipped bullets start to dominate.

Standard polymer tips can be easily deformed due to rough handling and it was recently discovered that they may be melting at high velocity thereby changing their efficiency as they travel down-range. Hornady has just come out with a new tougher polymer tip material that better withstands the heat from friction through the air. So far, results with these new "ELD" bullets have been great - I'm interested to see where they lead our industry.

Ogive

The ogive of the bullet is the part of the bullet that gradually gets wider from the tip to the shank (or bearing surface or sides) of the bullet. The shape of the ogive has a lot to do with a bullet's efficiency.

The ogive is measured by its radius (curve) and is generally either a tangent ogive or a secant ogive. Some newer bullets are a hybrid of both tangent and secant ogives.

To keep it simple, I'm going to explain the difference in a simple way. If you want an in-depth discussion on bullet shape, please look up Bryan Litz (he's probably forgotten more about bullet design than I know). The good news is, unless you're designing bullets, you don't need to know much about bullet design either - you can just do like I do and choose the most efficient ones, then spend lots of time practicing shooting them. In the military, snipers don't get a choice of which bullet to use and they seem to be able to do their jobs just fine.

Imagine drawing a football profile on a piece of paper. The pivot-point is where you could pick the ball up by its sides with two fingers and have it balance itself. If that's where the curve of the bullet stopped, it would be a tangent ogive. If instead, the curve of the bullet stopped sooner, then it would be a secant ogive.

Tangent ogives are common on most bullets. They are not as efficient as secant ogives but they are less sensitive to their position in the chamber when firing (free-bore jump). This is why

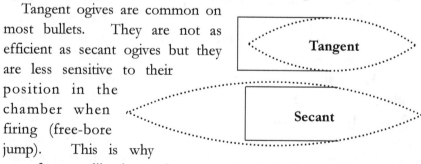

manufacturers like them - they can make the bullets and be confident that they will perform well in almost every rifle, regardless of how each individual consumer's rifle is head-spaced, or where their rifling starts. *(see Chapter 4 - Rifles)*

Secant ogive bullets can have less than desirable results if they're not in the exact right position with respect to the start of the lands and grooves. Reloaders who are knowledgeable can set the bullets properly for their rifle during the hand-loading process, but a manufacturer can't possibly know how every consumer's rifle will be chambered.

Hybrid bullets, available only from Berger Bullets (as far as I know), combine the efficiency of secant ogives with the stability and generous free-bore requirements of tangent ogives. It is no wonder that hybrids are starting to be the bullets that are winning competitions. It might also have something to do with the fact that Litz is Berger's chief ballistician!

Shank / Body

The shank or body of the bullet is the full-diameter sides of the bullet which make contact with the rifling in the barrel. This section is also sometimes called the bearing surface. The diameter of this section dictates the bullet's caliber.

Some bullets have a band in this section called a "cannelure." The cannelure is usually a small ribbed band that provides a place for the lip of the case to be crimped into. This is especially desirable on bullets in auto-loading rifles. Without a crimp, the rough loading

process in an auto-loading rifle can sometimes push a bullet back into a case. This can decrease the internal capacity of the cartridge which can then lead to dangerously high pressures and can cause the cartridge not to feed or function properly. Also, bullets can come loose prematurely and fall out of a case. This is especially true in high recoil rifles and heavy bullets. The inertia of a heavy bullet in a rifle's magazine makes the bullet want to stay in place while the case is yanked rearward under recoil.

To prevent a bullet from being pushed back into or pulled out of a case, the lips of the case are slightly crimped into the bullet, with or without a cannelure, to help the case hold the bullet in position. This is generally not as desirable for precision rifle work, as the crimp is just one more thing that might introduce an inconsistency.

Base

The base of the bullet is more important than one might think.   Economy bullets typically have flat bases while precision bullets typically have a so-called  "boat-tail" bases that taper in slightly at the bottom of the bullet.

Boat-tailed bullets allow the air to gently glide off the back of the bullet without creating disturbing turbulence at the bullet's base. The easiest way to describe this is to ask you to imagine a bicyclist's "time trial" helmet which tapers back to a point.   The same principle applies with bullets.

This is also a reason OTM bullets can be more accurate than FMJ bullets.   Bases on OTM bullets usually have a boat-tail.   In fact, another common name for an OTM bullet is "HPBT" which stands for hollow-point (not that kind), boat-tail.

3.1.3 Components of a Bullet

Bullets are generally made up of just two components: the core and the jacket. Exceptions to this are polymer tipped bullets which have a polymer tip, monolithic bullets which are made out of one solid piece of material, and armor piercing bullets which often have an additional material in the core to help them penetrate.

Jacket

The jacket of the bullet is the outer coating which protects the core. Although some bullets are bare lead and don't have jackets, these bullets aren't suitable for long range precision work.

Jackets are typically made out of copper. Copper is ideal because it is strong enough to form a protective shell around the core but it is soft enough to be deformed by the rifling in the barrel. This deformation is a good thing - it's what allows the rifling to spin and thereby stabilize the bullet in flight.

Some precision rifle bullet jackets are coated in a dry lubricant called molybdenum disulfide (moly-b or moly). These bullets have a slightly transparent (depending on the thickness of application) black coating. The moly-b coating helps to lubricate the bullet and keep the copper jacket from fouling the barrel. Some shooters swear by, and will only shoot, moly-b coated bullets.

Core

Source: Hornady

The core of the bullet is, well, the core. It's the center of the bullet and what makes up most of its mass. For precision shooting, cores are mostly made of lead. Lead is ideal because it is cheap, heavy, and it is deformed easily (both in the rifling of the barrel and also in the target).

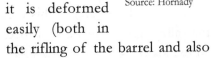

In monolithic bullets, there isn't really a core - the entire bullet is made out of the same material. In most cases, this material is copper. I see a lot of advantages to solid copper bullets. They hold together better when hunting and I don't have to deal with lead.[4]

A potential down-side to solid copper bullets is their light weight. Because copper is less dense than lead, a copper bullet needs to be longer (it can't be fatter without jumping up to a different caliber) than an equivalently weighted lead bullet. Also, the majority of competitive target shooters still use lead core bullets - there must be a reason.

[4] It is important to note that hunting with lead is safe

The shape of the core and how it interacts with the jacket can change how well a bullet performs. For example, some bullets have cores that are chemically bonded to the jacket to help them hold together better upon impact. Also, other bullets have designs where the jacket mechanically locks into the core to hold the two together better.

3.2 Powder

Powder is the component of ammunition responsible for accelerating the bullet down the barrel and out of the firearm. The powder is also the source of energy (chemical energy) that is transferred to the target by the bullet (kinetic energy).

Detonation is the supersonic (faster than the speed of sound) combustion of a material propagated through sound waves. **Deflagration** is the subsonic (slower than the speed of sound) combustion of a material propagated through heat transfer.

Modern gun powder does not detonate, it deflagrates. This means that although it can be classified as an explosive under U.S. law in some rare circumstances, it doesn't explode in the typical sense of the word. Instead, it burns rapidly and builds pressure. The rapid burn of the powder in a cartridge's case releases gas which builds pressure behind the bullet.

There are two main types of powder used in rifles: black powder and smokeless powder.

3.2.1 Black Powder

Black powder is the original gun powder and is generally used in antique firearms and muzzle-loading rifles. Black powder doesn't really belong in a discussion of long range precision shooting. I've included it in this book solely to let you know that black powder and smokeless powder are very different and should never be interchanged.[5]

3.2.2 Smokeless Powder

Modern gun powder is called "smokeless powder." That doesn't mean that there isn't any smoke when a firearm with smokeless powder is fired, but rather that there is MUCH less smoke than when compared to the original black powder.

Just like with bullets, gun powder is measured in "grains." The unit of measurement doesn't refer to each individual piece, or grain, of powder, but instead refers to the weight (actually, the mass) of the powder. *(see Section 9.3.1)*

Smokeless powder can be divided into two main categories, single-base and double-base, and then further divided into shape.

Single-base powder is made from nitrocellulose and double-based powder is made from nitrocellulose and nitroglycerine. The differences between the two types include burning temperatures, velocities, cleanliness, and sensitivity to temperature. It is difficult to say which is better overall because of effects that the variations in shape and chemical additives have on each powder. Single-base powder generally burns cleaner and double-base powder burns hotter. It is enough to say that both are widely used and a deeper discussion is best saved for another book.

As mentioned above, smokeless powder, unlike black powder, does not "explode" if it's ignited in the open. I put explode in quotes because smokeless powder doesn't explode in the detonation sense of the term. Instead, it

---

[5] Except in extremely rare cases where recommended by the manufacturer

deflagrates (burns incredibly fast).

Be careful when shipping powder or ammunition. It's perfectly legal and safe if it's done the right way. But, it may require special hazardous material fees and considerations. Also, the storage of smokeless powder should be done properly - not only to obey the law but also to be safe.

Smokeless powder comes in three main shapes: ball (spherical), extruded (cylindrical), and flake (flat). I'll briefly discuss each, because if you are just getting into long range shooting, you are likely purchasing your ammunition already loaded.

Ball Powder

Ball powder is the worst possible shape for powder. When it is first ignited, it has the most surface area it will ever have. The greater the surface area, the more material is available to be burned. As the balls of powder are burning, they are getting smaller and smaller, thereby resulting in much less surface area. This means that ball powder generally starts with a big burn and pressure spike and then gradually gets weaker and weaker.

This problem is magnified by the fact that the pressure spike comes when the volume (internal space) of the combustion area is the smallest because the bullet is near the chamber. As the bullet travels down the barrel it creates more space to fill and therefore more gas volume is needed to maintain pressure - this is when ball powder is at its weakest.

However, if you are reloading, ball powder can be the easiest to run through the powder measure because it flows the easiest and can be started and stopped with a moving gate without being chopped into smaller pieces. This powder measures (meters) very well through reloading machines and I have had good performance results with it.

There is a variation on ball powder which appears to be slightly squished balls.

Extruded Powder

Extruded powder is the most common powder used in precision ammunition. This type of powder takes the shape of tiny cylindrical sticks. It may not appear as consistent as ball powder, but the accuracy results obtained by using it have proven otherwise.

My favorite powders, H4895, H4350, and Varget, are all extruded.

Flake Powder

Flake powder is generally found in shotgun and pistol ammunition. It's easy to manufacture and can burn quickly. Quick burning powder is needed in both shotguns and handguns - often they use the exact same powder. For example, my favorite powder for 45 ACP handgun loads is Winchester Super Target (WST), which is sold as a shotgun shell powder.

3.3 Case

The cartridge case, also sometimes called "brass" due to the material from which it's usually made, is what holds all of the components of ammunition together. It's also what's handled by the parts of a rifle during its cycle of function. *(see Chapter 4 - Rifles)*. The feed lips of a magazine hold the round by the case, the bolt face feeds the round by pushing on its base, the case is extracted by its rim, and the case is ejected by pushing on its base.

Ammo is sometimes loaded in steel or aluminum cases. Even though these cases aren't made of brass, you wouldn't be looked at sideways for calling them "brass." But if you're shooting a precision rifle for accuracy, you shouldn't be using steel or aluminum ammunition. Of course, as with all things in life there are exceptions.

Hornady's Steel Match ammo is one, providing very good accuracy and consistency.

Most recently, polymer cases are starting to be used, which is an interesting development. Polymer cases are lighter than brass and with the proper care in manufacturing, polymer cases also can have more consistent internal capacity than brass. This means that they can be made more consistently, and therefore more accurately. Also chamber heat may not affect the powder as quickly (a concept we'll explore in *Chapter 11 - Environmental Effects*) in a polymer case which could lead to better consistency. The downside to polymer cases is that you can't reload them (yet).

Mouth

Lip

Shoulder

Rim

The case holds the bullet in the "mouth" at the top of the case and it holds the primer in the "primer pocket" at the bottom of the case. The edge around the mouth is called the "lip" and if there's an angled portion of the case that gets narrower toward the mouth, it's called the "shoulder."

At the base of the case is a rim. The rim is used to aid extraction and it is normally recessed into the side of the case. Some cases have rims that extend beyond the case but these are typically found in older rifles or revolvers, which use the rim to keep the round from falling through the chamber.

Belt

The headspace of the cartridge, as discussed next in *Chapter 4 - Rifles*, is usually measured from the base of the case to the shoulder. If the case doesn't have a shoulder - common on handgun ammunition - the headspace is measured from the base to the lip.

Some magnum cartridges have a "belted" case. This belt was designed as a method to strengthen the least-supported part of the case while it's fired, and to provide a spot to measure headspace on rounds that didn't have a distinct shoulder. 300 Win Mag is an example of a belted magnum.

3.4 Primers

Primers are responsible for igniting the powder inside the case. The firing pin (or striker) strikes the center of the primer (we're not discussing rimfire ammunition which is struck on the rim) and crushes the cup of the primer against a small anvil inside. Between the cup and anvil is a chemical mixture, usually a lead-styphnate base, that ignites when it is crushed.

Anvil   **Cup**

As you can see by the name of the chemical, primers usually contain lead. This burning lead is the most toxic part of the expanding gasses when firing ammunition. Even if your bullets aren't made of lead, your risk of lead exposure comes from the primer. Always shoot in a well ventilated area and wash your hands after shooting!

Primers are held in the primer pocket by friction alone in commercial ammunition. Military ammunition has primers which are crimped and then glued/sealed into place. Because of the friction-only hold in commercial ammunition, primers can sometimes come out of the primer pocket during firing. This is due to the pressure on the primer while the powder is burning.

The primer cup can deform when there's too much pressure in the cartridge because the material needs to be soft enough that it can deform when struck by a firing pin. A tell-tale sign of too much pressure in a cartridge can be seen by looking at the primer of a fired cartridge case. If the primer is squished back into the firing pin hole, its edges are flattened, or if it is blown-out completely, there is probably too much pressure.

3.4.1 Types of Primers

Center-fire primers come in two styles: Berdan or Boxer. Ironically, Berdan primers were invented in the United States. but aren't typically used in the United States. Boxer primers, which were invented in England, are the most common type of primer in the United States.

Berdan

Cartridge cases for Berdan primers have two holes in the primer pocket in the bottom of the case through which flame from the primer travels to ignite the powder ("flash-holes").

Boxer

Cartridge cases for Boxer primers have a single flash-hole in the center of the primer pocket. Because of the central location of the flash-hole on Boxer-style cases, they are much easier to reload. If you are shooting modern American ammunition, it's going to have Boxer primers.

4 RIFLES

According to U.S. law at the time of this printing, a firearm is "any weapon . . . which expel[s] a projectile by the action of an explosive."[6] A rifle is a type of firearm which has a rifled barrel and is designed and intended to be fired from your shoulder.[7] From these definitions, we know that a pellet gun/air-rifle is not a "firearm"

---

[6] Gun Control Act (NFA) of 1968, *18 U.S.C. 921(a)(3)(A)*. A discussion about the other definitions of a firearm (*id. (3)(B-D)*) or whether all objects which expel projectiles by an explosive are weapons is best saved for another book.

[7] *id. (A)(7)*

because it doesn't use an explosion to launch a projectile. Also, we know that if a firearm with a rifled barrel was designed and intended to be fired from your forehead, it isn't a rifle.

Once a firearm falls into the definition of a rifle, it must have a barrel that is at least 16 inches long and and its overall length must be at least 26 inches in order to be treated as a "standard" rifle and avoid certain extra regulations. If either the barrel or the overall length of the rifle are too short, then the rifle is a "short barreled rifle" (SBR) and is subject to National Firearms Act (NFA) taxation and registration. SBRs are generally unsuitable for long range shooting and won't be discussed here.

4.1 Types of Rifles

The two main categories of rifles for the purposes of this book are manually operated rifles and automatically operated rifles.

Manually operated rifles require some manipulation by the shooter in order to "cycle the action" whereas auto-loading rifles generally

use some of the energy from the previously fired round to cycle the action. The action is the combination of parts of a rifle's mechanism by which the rifle is loaded, fired, and unloaded.

Examples of manually operated rifles are: bolt-action rifles, pump-action rifles, lever-action rifles, and break-open rifles. The vast majority of manually operated precision rifles are bolt-action rifles. This book will not cover the other types of manually operated rifles.

Examples of automatically operated rifles are: gas-operated and recoil-operated rifles. Gas-operated rifles use the expanding gasses from the burning gunpowder during firing to cycle the action, whereas recoil-operated rifles use the rearward force generated by the bullet's travel to cycle the action. Gas-operated rifles can be operated by either direct impingement whereby gas is redirected down a tube and pushes directly on the bolt or bolt carrier or by a piston whereby gas is redirected and then pushes on a piston head which is connected to the bolt or bolt carrier. Direct impingement rifles (like the classic AR-15) are lighter and simpler, but their actions become dirtier faster because the exhaust gasses from firing are vented directly back into the action.

Automatically operated rifles can either fire one cartridge for every pull of the trigger (semi-automatic) or continuously fire

multiple cartridges as long as the trigger is depressed (fully-automatic, full-auto, or machine-gun). Do not confuse "automatic operation" with "full-auto firing." The vast majority of automatically operated precision rifles are semi-automatic rifles. Full-auto rifles will not be covered in this book.

Cycling the action generally refers to unlocking the action, extracting and ejecting the case of a fired round of ammunition, re-cocking the firing mechanism, feeding and chambering the next round of ammunition, and then re-locking the action in preparation for firing the rifle.

4.1.1 Cycles of Function

Each step in the process of a firearm's operation is part of the eight "cycles of function" common to almost all firearms. Each step of this process is important to understand as it will help you learn how your rifle works and diagnose malfunctions. When a rifle doesn't function properly, it is not simply a "jam" but rather a specific failure to feed, extract, eject, or any other step in the cycles of function.

You should commit the 8 cycles of function to memory - they are helpful in understanding how most firearms work.   I have a mnemonic[8] that helps me remember these which starts by taking a date out to dinner (feeding) before bringing her back to your place (chamber), but I'll spare you the rest.   Suffice it to say that inappropriate mnemonics are the easiest to remember - just ask anyone who can rattle off the mnemonic for the 5 principles of patrolling faster than the principles themselves (Ranger inside joke).

8 Cycles of Function
1. Feeding
2. Chambering
3. Locking
4. Firing
5. Unlocking
6. Extracting
7. Ejecting
8. Cocking

The bolt (rifle/shotgun) or slide (pistol) [1] feeds a round from the magazine as it travels forward, pushes the round into the [2] chamber, [3] locks the action as it goes into battery (closed position ready to fire), then the round is [4] fired, the bolt or slide [5] unlocks, [6] extracts the empty shell casing out of the chamber, [7] ejects it out of the firearm, and then it [8] cocks the firing mechanism and starts the cycle from the beginning.

A failure to feed can happen when the bolt or slide fails to strip a round out of the magazine. A failure to chamber or lock happens when something prevents the firearm from going into battery. A failure to extract happens when the empty shell case is not removed from the chamber. A failure to eject happens when the shell case is removed from the chamber but it is not "kicked" out of the firearm.

Each one of these failures is unique. If you just say that you had a jam, it is difficult to diagnose the problem. If however, you say that you had a failure to extract, then we could start by looking at the extractor on the bolt or slide face. When discussing a failure, always refer to the actual symptom so that it is easier to diagnose the problem.   For example, a failure to extract will likely also cause a failure to feed. After all, the next round can't be fed into a chamber which still contains the un-extracted brass from the previous round. Don't call this malfunction a failure to feed, or your gunsmith will be looking at your magazine and feed ramp and not your extractor.

---

[8] For my Marine readers, this is a trick or device people use to help remember something.

4.1.2 Bolt-action Rifles

Manually operated rifles, such as bolt-action rifles, can be made to be more accurate than most semi-auto rifles. This does not mean that all bolt-action rifles are more accurate than every semi-auto rifle. In fact, many high-end semi-auto precision rifles outperform most stock bolt-action rifles.

> Consistency is the key to accuracy

As I'll repeat often in this book, consistency is the key to accuracy. The less complicated rifle with fewer moving parts is easier to make uniform, making the bolt-action rifle a more consistent rifle than a semi-auto.

Bolt-action rifles typically come in three action lengths: short, long, and magnum. Short action bolt-action rifles typically can accommodate cartridges up to 2.8 inches in overall length. The most common short action rifle cartridge for precision shooting is the 308

Common Cartridge Bolt Face Diameters and Action Sizes

	0.384"	0.470"	0.540"	0.585"
Short Action	17 Rem. 204 Ruger 223 Rem.	22-250 Rem. 243 Win. 260 Rem. 6.5 Creedmoor 308 Win. 338 Federal	7mm Rem. SAUM 7mm WSM 300 WSM	
Long Action		240 Wtby Mag. 6.5-284 Norma 270 Win. 30-06 Sprg.	264 Win. Mag. 7mm Rem. Mag. 300 Win. Mag. 338 Win. Mag.	
Magnum Action			300 RUM 375 H&H 458 Lott	338 Lapua Mag. 416 Rigby 460 Wtby Mag.

Figure 4.1-1

Winchester (308 Win). Long action bolt-action rifles typically can accommodate cartridges up to 3.34 inches in overall length. The classic long action rifle cartridge is the 30-06 Springfield (30-06 Sprg) and a popular long action precision shooting cartridge is the 300 Winchester Magnum (300 Win Mag). Magnum length bolt-action rifles can typically accommodate cartridges up to 3.75 inches in length such as the 375 Holland and Holland (375 H&H) and a popular extreme long range cartridge, the 338 Lapua Magnum.

Many different cartridges share common bolt face diameters. In fact, most rifles, whether short, long, or magnum length action, come with one of four bolt face diameters: 0.384", 0.470", 0.540", or 0.585".

Of the four, the most common are the two middle sizes (0.470" and 0.540") with the largest and smallest sizes used only for a few cartridges on the extreme ends of the scale. *See Figure 4.1-1.*

Another reason bolt-action rifles can be so accurate is because they can have truly free-floating barrels. A free-floating barrel does not touch any part of the rifle other than where it attaches to the receiver. This is important because the barrel moves during firing due to harmonic vibration, sometimes called "barrel whip," that occurs while the bullet is traveling down the barrel. By keeping the barrel from touching anything, the barrel is free to flex/vibrate/whip consistently, without interference.

Often, a free-floating barrel will be demonstrated by showing that a dollar bill can pass between a rifle's barrel and stock fore-end all the way back to the receiver. This is not an accurate test necessarily. Often, the barrel will touch the stock during firing/use even though there is a gap between the

If there is too much of a gap between the barrel and the stock, debris can get in the gap. Cleaning out stuck debris can be difficult in the field. A neat method I've seen to clean out the gap is to leave a small piece of cord between the barrel and stock up against the receiver. Then, when you need to clean out the gap in a hurry, you can grasp both ends of the cord and pull it forward.

barrel and the stock while the firearm is at rest. If a stock is too flexible, it can touch the barrel if enough force is applied. Also, if the gap between the barrel and stock is too small, the barrel can strike the stock during firing because of barrel whip.

A better way to confirm that a barrel is not touching a stock is to take the action and barrel out of the stock and inspect the barrel after it has been used a bit. If the barrel is striking the stock, you should see evidence of contact in the finish on the barrel.

4.1.3 Semi-auto Rifles

With modern manufacturing, semi-auto rifles have become viable platforms for long-range shooting. As mentioned, some semi-auto rifles are more accurate than most bolt-action rifles.

As an example, I had many (too many) rifles issued to me while I was in the military. I had two 5.56mm semi-auto rifles, two 7.62mm bolt-action rifles, one semi-auto 7.62mm rifle, one bolt-action 300 Win. Mag rifle, and one semi-auto 50 BMG rifle. One of the two 5.56mm semi-auto rifles was a highly accurized AR-15-style rifle called the Mk12 SPR. I'm known for loving the simplicity and purity of a bolt-action rifle and also for not being a big fan of the AR-15 platform. In fact, I still believe that a bolt-action rifle in the proper hands can out perform a semi-auto rifle (even during rapid engagements). The Mk12 SPR, however, was the most accurate rifle I had and, therefore, I often carried this amazing performer on combat missions. If I could've kept one rifle as a parting gift from leaving the military, it would've been that Mk12 SPR.

I've included some photos of a younger me and my Mk12 SPR

from Asadabad and Gardez, Afghanistan. In order, the photos below show me and a local in Gardez (this guy was an amazing man), two photos taken on mountains in Asadabad, the suppressor of my rifle sticking out from underneath some camouflage (look for it in the center of the picture pointing left and away), and a photo of my rifle next to my backpacking stove while making some tea in the mountains.

Although some semi-auto rifles have free-floating barrels, the barrel on a gas-operated semi-auto is never truly free-floated like it can be on a bolt-action rifle because it's inevitably attached to a gas-tube or piston. The gas tube is usually made of a different material than the barrel, and it heats up and cools down at a different rate. Because of this, the gas tube can cause inconsistent pressure on the barrel. Piston systems introduce a moving part (the piston) within the piston tube attached to the barrel. Although the bullet should have left the barrel before the piston really starts moving, the system introduces more parts and variables into an area where less is better than more.

4.1.4 Bolt vs. Semi

All else being equal, semi-auto rifles have some advantages over bolt-action rifles. The biggest advantage is that a semi-auto rifle can shoot multiple rounds quicker than a bolt-action rifle, and it can do so without the shooter having to adjust his position. When extreme accuracy is required, however, a bolt-action can be employed just as well as a semi-auto rifle.

Some scenarios don't require extreme accuracy. For example, in combat situations a rifle which can engage close targets quickly may be more useful. Also, running the bolt on a bolt-action rifle requires

the shooter to move whereas a semi-auto rifle allows a shooter to stay in the exact same position from shot to shot. That is, of course, until it is time to reload the rifle. Additionally, semi-auto rifles produce a less-felt recoil than similarly weighted and chambered bolt-action rifles.

Reloading can be another advantage to using a semi-auto rifle. Many semi-auto rifles are fed from a box-style detachable magazine whereas many bolt action rifles are loaded one round at a time through the top of the action with the bolt in the open position. Removing an empty detachable box magazine and inserting another with ammunition is surely faster than loading additional rounds one at a time. However, magazine fed systems are only faster while there are loaded magazines available. Once there are no more loaded magazines, it can be faster to use one hand to drop a single round into a bolt-action rifle and push the bolt forward than to use both hands to reload an empty magazine, then insert it into a rifle and close the bolt.

AR-style semi-auto rifles can't get as low to the ground as bolt-action rifles with standard rifle stocks. This is because the pistol grip on an AR-style rifle and the detachable magazine both protrude down below the action. As I'll mention later in this book, the lower you can get to the ground, the more stable you'll be. The more stable you are, the more accurately you can shoot.

Another potential negative to AR-style semi-auto rifles is the requirement to mount a scope higher than is necessary on standard bolt-action rifles. This is because the hand guard on an AR-style rifle will usually interfere with a scope's objective lens. The higher the scope is mounted, the higher the rifle's cheekpiece will need to be in order to shoot the rifle accurately and comfortably. High cheekpieces may not be an option on AR-style rifles because of clearance needed for a standard charging handle.

The differences in loading time, ability to get low to the ground, and scope mounting height between semi-auto and bolt-action rifles are lessened by the fact that many bolt-action rifles are now being made with (or converted to) pistol grips, AR-style hand guards, and the ability to accept detachable magazines.

4.2 Common Parts

Although the parts described below are unique on different rifles, each rifle has at least one of each of these parts and are common to all rifles.

4.2.1 Receiver

The receiver is the part of a rifle that serves as a base to which other parts are attached. Effectively, a firearm receiver is like the frame of an automobile. By U.S. law, the receiver is the only individual part of a firearm that is treated as a firearm. To lawfully purchase a receiver from a manufacturer, you must acquire the receiver from a Federal Firearm Licensee (FFL) and complete a Form 4473 and a background check, if applicable. Every other part of the firearm, however, may be purchased directly from the manufacturer and delivered straight to your home.

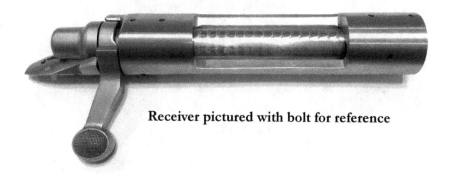

Receiver pictured with bolt for reference

Some firearms have more than one receiver. For example, AR-15 type rifles have an upper and a lower receiver. In these instances only one of the receivers is determined to be the firearm by the Bureau of Alcohol, Tobacco, Firearms and Explosives (ATF). For AR-15 type rifles, the lower receiver is considered the firearm and in some other rifles, such as the Bushmaster ACR, FN FAL, and the Sig Sauer 556, the upper receiver is considered the firearm. If you're not sure which part of your firearm is the receiver, look for the serial number. If there's only one serial number on your rifle, then the serialized part is probably the receiver.

On bolt-action rifles, the receiver is the central part of the rifle to which the barrel, trigger group, bolt, scope and stock attach. On semi-automatic rifles that have two receivers, the lower receiver generally houses the trigger group, magazine, grip, and butt-stock.

The upper receiver generally houses the bolt and is the part to which the barrel, hand guard, and scope attach.

4.2.2 Barrel

The barrel is the tube through which the bullet travels. Just as the receiver is the main part of the rifle for legal purposes, the barrel is the main part of the rifle for accuracy purposes. A good rifle with a bad barrel will not shoot accurately. Conversely, a poor-quality rifle with a good barrel can shoot accurately.

Chamber

The part of the barrel closest to the receiver is the chamber. The chamber is shaped to house the specific cartridge that the rifle is intended to shoot. During the normal operation of a rifle, the cartridge of ammunition is pushed into the chamber, typically locked into the chamber, fired in the chamber, and then the cartridge case is extracted from the chamber. Because the chamber must contain the energy of the ammunition as it is fired, it is usually the strongest part of a firearm.

Often, a rifle is said to be "chambered" for a certain cartridge. For example, a rifle that is made to shoot 308 Win. cartridges is "chambered" for 308 Win. The dimensions of the chamber are very important. If the chamber is too tight, a cartridge may neither reliably fit in nor be extracted from the chamber. If the dimensions are too loose, the cartridge may not be supported properly during firing and the cartridge case may rupture.

Another important dimension in a firearm is the "headspace." Headspace is the measurement from the bolt-face to a particular spot on a cartridge. Rimmed cartridges like 45-70 Govt. and 22 LR have a headspace which is measured off of the front of their rim. Rimless straight walled cartridges like 30

> **Headspace:** the measurement from the bolt-face to a particular spot on the cartridge.

Carbine and 50 Beowulf have a headspace which is measured off of the front edge of the case. Rimless bottlenecked cartridges like 30-06 Sprg. and 223 Rem. have a headspace which is measured off of a precise point of their shoulder. Rimless belted cartridges such as 300 Win. Mag. and 375 H&H Mag. have a headspace which is measured off of the front edge of their belts.

The headspace of a rifle is generally set by how far the barrel is screwed into the receiver on most bolt action rifles or the barrel extension on most semi-automatic rifles. If the chamber is cut too deep, the barrel may not be able to be set in deep enough and the headspace will be too long. If the chamber is cut too shallow, the barrel may not be able to be screwed in enough to support the cartridge case. It is important to have the headspace of your rifle set by someone who is knowledgable. A rifle with an improperly set headspace can be dangerous.

Rifling

After the chamber ends, the rifling begins. Rifling is the spiral grooves in a barrel which cause the bullet to spin. Projectiles are typically spin- or fin-stabilized. Examples of spin-stabilized projectiles are bullets and spiral-thrown footballs. Examples of fin-stabilized projectiles are rockets and arrows. There is also a method to stabilize a projectile by drag, such as by using a streamer, but that method is not relevant here.

There are two main types of rifling, standard and polygonal. Standard rifling is a series of alternating high and low spots, called lands and grooves, whereas polygonal rifling is in the shape of a polygon. In order for rifling to work, it needs to be small enough in diameter that the bullet must be deformed slightly in order to pass through the barrel. The fit is so tight that a bullet which is stuck in a barrel can not be pushed out by hand.

Just as the chamber of the barrel is dependent on the specific cartridge, the diameter of the rifling is dependent on the caliber. For example, 308 Win., 30-06 Sprg., and 300 Win. Mag. are all different cartridges but they all fire 30 caliber bullets. Therefore, rifles for each of the cartridges will have chambers unique to each cartridge but their rifling will all be the same diameter for the same 30 caliber bullets.

Twist Rate

The rate at which the rifling in each of the above rifles twists, however, may be different. Faster or slower twists are required to stabilize different weight, size and speed bullets. The twist-rate of rifling is measured by how many inches a bullet will need travel in order to make a complete revolution. The twist-rate of a barrel

> **Twist-rate:** the speed at which a bullet rotates measured by the number of inches a bullet travels for each complete revolution.

is denoted as "1:x" where x is the number of inches required for a full revolution.   1:7 twist rifling is faster (tighter twist) than 1:10 rifling because a bullet will make a complete revolution in 7 inches in the 1:7 twist barrel whereas it will take 10 inches for a complete revolution in the 1:10 twist barrel.

As a general rule, heavier bullets in the same cartridge need to be spun faster in order to properly stabilize. For example, 55 gr. bullets fired from a 223 Rem. work well in 1:9 twist barrels. In order to accurately fire 75 gr. bullets from a 223 Rem., however, a faster 1:8 or 1:7 twist barrel is needed. *See Section 10.2.7.*

Contrary to what you may hear, the twist rate has no direct relationship with barrel length. Twist rate is based on bullet size, weight, and speed only. Although a barrel's length can affect a bullet's speed, it is not necessary for the bullet to exit the barrel after a complete revolution. For example, a 1:10 twist barrel does not need to be 20 inches long so that the bullet has two complete revolutions. Instead, a 1:10 twist barrel can be any length. As a note, most pistol barrels aren't long enough to allow for even one complete revolution of a bullet.

For a discussion on how to calculate the appropriate twist rate, see *Section 10.2.7.*

Throat

The spot where the rifling starts in a barrel is known as the "throat." This is the part of a barrel which starts to degrade first, especially with fast projectiles from magnum cartridges. Degradation

> **Free-bore:** the distance the bullet has to travel before contacting rifling.

of the throat of a barrel is called "throat-erosion." This part degrades because it is exposed to the most heat and abuse from the burning gun powder, where the bullet is initially forced to rotate.

To minimize throat-erosion and to reduce deformities on the bullet, a rifle can have progressive-twist rifling. "Progressive-twist rifling" does not have a consistent twist-rate, instead it gradually increases the rate of twist as it travels down the barrel until it reaches the desired twist-rate for the particular cartridge at the end of the barrel. Progressive-twist rifling avoids the abrupt twist in the throat of a normal barrel and instead allows for a gradual increase of twist. This type of rifling is nice to have but it's more expensive than consistent-twist rifling and not necessary for most cartridges.

The distance between the throat and where the bullet rests when the cartridge is chambered prior to firing is called "free-bore." If

> **Throat-erosion:** the wearing-down of the beginning of the rifling.

there is not enough free-bore, the cartridge may not be able to be properly chambered because the bullet will be stopped by the rifling. Even if the cartridge can be chambered with the bullet touching the rifling, the bullet can stick in the rifling when you attempt to unload an unfired round. This leaves you with a stuck bullet in your barrel and loose gunpowder in your magazine. If there is too much free-bore, you may have accuracy issues because the bullet "jumps" from the cartridge too far before it contacts rifling. This can cause inconsistent alignment of the bullet.

Contour

Remember, consistency is the key to accuracy.   To help ensure consistency, a barrel on a precision rifle should be free-floated. As mentioned above, this is important because the barrel moves during firing due to harmonic vibration, sometimes called barrel

> Consistency is the key to accuracy

whip, that occurs while the bullet is traveling down the barrel. By keeping the barrel from touching anything, the barrel is free to flex/ vibrate/whip consistently without interference.

Another way to help minimize flex is to have a stiffer barrel. The contour of a barrel is the outside shape of the barrel. A thicker barrel, sometimes called a bull barrel, is more rigid and more consistent than a thinner barrel. The downside to thicker barrels is their weight. This is why you'll usually see target barrels with thicker contours or profiles and hunting barrels with thinner contours.

Length

Barrel length does not have the effect that you might expect on accuracy; a longer barrel is not necessarily more accurate than a shorter barrel. In fact, all a longer barrel does is allow more time for the powder to burn, producing a faster bullet.

As mentioned above, a stiffer barrel allows a rifle to be more consistent. And, as you know by now, consistency is the key to accuracy. A barrel can be made stiffer by making it thicker or by making it shorter. Think about it this way: imagine holding a 12 inch long stick that is just barely too thick to break in your hands. Now, if a 48 inch long stick of the same diameter were placed in your hands it would be easier to break. This is because you have more leverage with the longer stick. The same principle applies to barrels.

For years, my go-to rifle has been a 308 Win bolt action rifle with an 18 inch barrel. It is extremely accurate and it usually turns a head or two at the range because of how short the barrel is. Even though it has a short barrel, it can reach out to targets at 800 yards just as well as a 308 rifle with a 24" barrel. Now, my shorter barreled rifle will need more elevation dialed into the scope to hit the same target as the longer barrel, but it will be just as (or more) accurate. To me, the trade off of having to dial up 34 MOA instead of 32 MOA is negligible in exchange for having a handy and portable rifle (*See Chapter 7* for a discussion on MOA). And, if I'm shooting at 1,000 yards or beyond, I'm typically going to use a caliber more suited to the task.

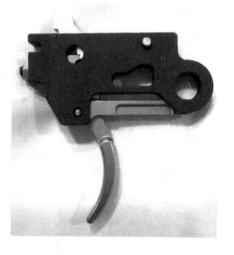

4.2.3 Trigger

The trigger is the part of the rifle which is manipulated to cause the rifle to fire. Although the trigger (or trigger shoe) is really only the part of the firearm which your finger touches, the term trigger can sometimes be used to describe the entire firing mechanism. For example, someone might refer to a rifle as having a good or bad trigger. They usually aren't talking about the quality of the part touching their finger (the trigger shoe) but rather are referring to the pull-weight or crispness of the entire firing mechanism.

Ideally, a trigger's break (the point at which it releases the tension) should be crisp and it should have a consistent pull weight. Appropriate pull weight is largely a personal preference of a shooter. A lighter pull-weight trigger is generally desirable when accuracy is concerned because it is easier to fire the rifle without disturbing the sights.

Single / Double-Stage

Triggers (i.e., the mechanism) can be "single-stage" or "double-stage." A single-stage trigger has one pull-weight and one tactile obstacle to overcome. A single-stage trigger typically has one point of resistance which is overcome when the proper pressure is applied. I have heard people describe a good quality single-stage trigger to be like a candy-cane breaking. Pressure is applied against a steady surface until - "snap" - the mechanism fires (the candy-cane breaks).

A double-stage (or two-stage) trigger has two mechanical obstacles to overcome and two corresponding pull weights. Typically, the first stage is more difficult to overcome than the second stage. For example, it might take three pounds of pressure to move the trigger through the first stage but only one additional pound of pressure to move the trigger through its second stage. Overall, the trigger takes 4 pounds of pressure to fire, but the first three pounds can be pulled and overcome while the shooter is still lining up the sights. Then, the shooter must only add 1 additional pound of pressure to fire the rifle. This mechanism can give the performance of a 1 pound trigger with the safety of a four pound trigger.

Do not confuse single-stage with single-action. A single-action mechanism has one action upon pulling the trigger - the hammer or firing pin is released. A double-action firing mechanism performs two actions when the trigger is pulled - the mechanism is "cocked" or charged and then released. Because a double-action mechanism must overcome the spring tension of the hammer or firing pin and it must perform more mechanical steps, the double-action trigger is typically a heavier and longer pull.

I prefer two-stage triggers. This is partly because I value crispness in a trigger over lightness. For example, I've never had a trigger on any of my rifles that has less than 2.5 pound overall trigger pull. If a trigger is any lighter than that, I may accidentally fire the rifle while I'm trying to get in the final steps of firing.

I like to have a purposeful placement of my finger on the trigger - with too light of a trigger, the rifle can go off while I'm placing my finger in the proper position. In fact, when the trigger is too light, I have more of a tendency to "slap" the trigger because I know that if I place my finger on the trigger to start a gentle increase in pressure, the rifle is liable to fire too soon. Of course, I like "tactical" style shooting and you may prefer a much lighter trigger for bench-rest style shooting.

With a two-stage trigger, I am able to place my finger on the trigger and apply pressure until I feel the second stage. From there, I only have to add a small amount of pressure to fire. This gives me the ability to "pre-stage" my finger in the proper position while still having a small effort to fire the rifle.

Lock-Time

The lock-time of a firing mechanism is the amount of time it takes from the moment the trigger "breaks" until the round is fired. It is ideal to minimize the lock-time. If the lock-time is too slow, the rifle has a chance to move after the trigger has been pulled but before the round has been fired.

4.2.4 Hammer/Striker

The hammer or the striker of the rifle is what is released upon pulling the trigger. It's the part of the rifle that is under tension when the rifle is cocked or charged.

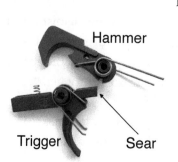

A hammer is released by the firing mechanism and rotates forward under spring tension to strike a firing pin and drive it into the primer of a cartridge. This operation is much like an actual hammer (think tool-box hammer) swinging forward to strike a nail. Semi-automatic rifles are usually fired with a hammer and firing pin.

A striker is essentially a firing pin that is under tension. A normal firing pin generally sits passively within the rifle until it is struck by the hammer. A striker, on the other hand, is pulled rearward under spring tension and then released when the trigger is pulled. This operation is much like a ball launcher of a pin-ball machine. Bolt-action rifles usually have a striker.

The striker of a bolt-action rifle is often called a firing pin. This is not necessarily incorrect - just understand that a true firing pin is usually struck by a hammer whereas a striker is basically a firing pin which is pulled and released.

4.2.5 Sear

The sear is the most misused term I hear associated with firing mechanisms. The sear is the part that holds the hammer or striker back until the rifle is fired. By pulling the trigger, the sear is moved out of the way and the hammer or striker, which was previously "cocked" under spring tension, is released. The sear may be a separate part in the mechanism (like in most bolt-action rifles) or it can be a part of the trigger (like in most hammer-fired rifles).

Fully automatic rifles, or machine guns, which are not the topic of this book, can have a second sear that releases the hammer when it is moved by the bolt closing as it returns to battery.

4.2.6 Stock

The rifle's stock connects the action of the firearm to you. On bolt-action firearms and some semi-automatic firearms, the stock is the piece of wood, synthetic material, or sometimes metal (on newer chassis systems) which has a portion to rest against your shoulder (butt), a place to rest your cheek (comb), a place to grasp with your firing hand (grip), and a place to support the rifle up front with your non-firing hand (fore-end). On some semi-automatic firearms, the butt stock is a separate piece from the fore-end.

In order to free-float a barrel, the channel of the stock where the barrel passes over the fore-end (cleverly called the barrel channel) is opened up so that it's larger than, and doesn't make contact with, the barrel.

Bedding

For consistent contact with the receiver, an action can be "bedded" into a stock. Bedding is the process of making a solid mounting surface, using a compound (generally some form of fiberglass resin) which is molded into the stock. This custom molding process is called "glass-bedding." The stock can also have an aluminum bedding block that is a consistent mounting surface, but isn't as precisely molded to the action.

Although glass-bedding is the most consistent, and therefore most accurate solution, I have always preferred stocks with aluminum bedding blocks instead. Largely, this is from bias of my learning to shoot long range with a U.S. Army M24, which has an HS Precision stock with a full-length aluminum bedding block. The benefit to a bedding block is its strength. Glass-bedding can be more fragile and although rare, it can crack. The M24 needed to withstand being bounced off of the tarmac of an airport's runway when it was being parachuted down with a jumper.

Style

I am a sucker for a standard grip on a rifle stock and I don't like thumbhole stocks (or AR-style pistol grips). This all comes back to not imparting too much control on the rifle. With a thumbhole stock, shooters have a tendency to grip and control the rifle with their firing hand. Also, with this style stock, the shooter must remove their thumb from the hole before they can manipulate the rifle and then place it back in the hole before firing. I'm much faster and more comfortable resting my hand on the top or side of a standard rifle stock.

4.3 Add-ons

The following items could probably have been categorized as accessories in another chapter but I decided to include them here because I treat them like they are a part of my rifle. Once they're added, they tend to stay where they're put.

4.3.1 Bipod

Bipod legs are like kickstands for rifles - they are helpful to keep your rifle from falling over when you set it down. Of course, bipods can be useful to shoot off of, but I think they're over-used in this area.

Watch what happens to your bipods the next time you use them on a hard surface. You should notice that they'll bounce and move while you're shooting. The problem with this movement is that it is inconsistent - they jump different amounts depending on the surface you are shooting from. If you shoot off of a shooting bag instead, you'll have the same platform for the rifle regardless what surface is under the bag. (*See Section 6.1*).

4.3.2 Sling

As a bipod is a rifle's kickstand, I often say that a sling for a long-gun is like a holster for a handgun - it holds the firearm securely when you don't want to hold it in your hands. When it comes to precision rifle shooting, however, a sling is also a functional tool. In the U.S. Military's Special Operations Target Interdiction Course (SOTIC), we had to learn to shoot with a sling, and demonstrate our proficiency with it before we were allowed to use bipod legs.

A discussion on sling use for providing support in shooting positions can be found in *Chapter 16 - Alternate Positions.*

4.3.3 Cheek Bag

As you'll read later in *Chapter 12 - Scope Mounting and Setup,* I think it's crucial to have the rifle and scope set up to fit you. The adjustment most shooters need in order to have their rifles fit properly is to raise the comb (cheek-rest) of the stock. One of the easiest ways to raise the comb of a stock is to add a cheek bag. The cheek bag not only adds height to the stock, it also makes a great platform under which you can add more spacers.

Additionally, the cheek bag provides comfort and some even allow for storage capacity. Most cheek bags have a suede-like finish for your cheek to rest upon and a bit of padding which is much more comfortable than the hard rifle stock. In the zippered compartment of my cheek back, I keep the Allen wrenches I need for my scope and rings and some extra rounds of ammunition.

4.3.4 Bubble Level

Many folks include a bubble level on their rifle or scope. As discussed in *Section 13.2.1,* you can miss the target if your rifle is not perfectly level. I don't have one on any of my rifles. Perhaps I should, I just never learned with them and I never got around to working with them. The idea behind their use is that an angled rifle, even one at an angle that is not readily perceptible to the human eye, is enough to affect your bullet's impact. Therefore, a bubble level is needed to aid in determining whether the rifle is level.

Although this makes sense, I have yet to see a bubble level or a mount for a bubble level that didn't have more of an error in it than folks claim can be solved by using the bubble level. I have tested many of these by purposefully angling a rifle enough that I could tell it was angled with my naked eye and then looked at the bubble level. The room for error was too large in the bubble level to be useful to me. You, however, might like using one. Who knows, you might see one on my rifle someday at the range.

5 AIMING SYSTEMS

Ideally, we'd like to look through the barrel when aiming the rifle so that we can see exactly where it is pointed. Unfortunately, that's not possible. So we must rely on an external device(s) to give us a reference point of where the barrel is pointed. For long range shooting, we use optics with adjustable aiming reference points or we use iron sights which are aligned with each other. We need to adjust these reference marks first to zero the rifle and later to compensate for different distances and environmental effects. In either case, our aiming system must first be properly aligned with itself, and then lined up with the target.

It is important to know how your sights adjust to get a proper zero. The zero is the baseline setting on our sights/scope that allows us to hit where we are aiming at a specific distance. It is the starting point from which all other adjustments to your sights/scope are made. For example, I generally zero my rifles at 100 yards. This means that I will hit where I am aiming at 100 yards when my sights/scope are at their baseline setting. Then, when I want to adjust the elevation or windage settings for targets at other distances or in different environmental conditions, I make adjustments for those specific situations and then return my sights/scope back to their zero when I am finished. "Zeroing" a rifle is discussed in detail in *Chapter 15.*

Once your zero is established, the adjustments you make for distance and environmental conditions are all relative to your zero - they are made from your baseline zero setting. For example, if I need to move up 12 MOA to hit a 500 yard target, the adjustment I make on my scope is up 12 MOA from my 100 yard zero.

5.1 Scopes

Quality optics are crucial to the precision scoped-rifle platform. This is not to say that a scope is necessary for accurate shooting. In fact, many competitors can shoot better with iron sights than most people can with a scope. Also, during my first two weeks in SOTIC we shot only with iron sights. It wasn't until after a benchmark shooting test out to 800 meters that we were given and allowed to use scopes. This forced us to focus on our fundamentals first.

If you are going to use a scope, please have it be a quality scope. A high-quality scope on a standard rifle will allow for better long range performance than a high-quality rifle with a low-end scope. A general rule is that the scope needs to cost at least as much as the rifle. Except for the extreme high-end, you get what you pay for with scopes.

Scopes are often identified by a series of numbers such as "3.5-10x40mm." The "3.5-10x" represents that the scope has variable power magnification from 3.5 power up to 10 power. The "40mm" represents that the scope has an objective lens with a 40mm diameter.

Scopes are a blessing and a curse. Sure, they clearly make long-range shooting easier but they can make it too easy for beginning shooters. How can a scope make things too easy? Well, many new shooters improperly mount their scopes, don't set the scope up properly for them, and don't utilize the scope properly while shooting.

The problem is that these new shooters are often unaware of their improper use of the scope because the scope can be moderately forgiving. What I mean is this - an improperly setup scope is still a good enough tool that it will get a beginning shooter close to where they need to be. Unfortunately, however, they will never be able to shoot to their, or their rifle's, full capability unless it is set up and used properly. Modern scopes are so nice that they often hide the shortcomings of their imperfect use.

By all means, use a scope - but use it properly for best results.

5.2 Scope Components/Features

This is a discussion of the major parts and features of a scope. A discussion on how to use scopes is found later in this book.

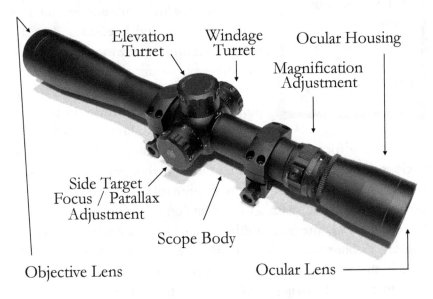

5.2.1 Lenses

Quality glass is an important feature on a scope but I'm not convinced that it's *the* most important feature. Don't get me wrong, a scope with good glass is important. After all, if you can't see your target, it's difficult to hit it. However, too much money can be spent on a scope with astronomically expensive glass which doesn't translate into significantly better performance. A scope that costs $3,000 because of its superb glass won't necessarily perform twice as well as a $1,500 scope with good glass – the law of diminishing returns applies.

> **Protect your lenses! When not in use, your lenses should be covered with scope caps. Scope lenses are difficult to clean without scratching.**

The lens closest to your eye when shooting a rifle is called the "ocular lens." Generally, the ocular lens's focus can be adjusted. In my experience, this is the most over-looked adjustment on a scope. It's also the one adjustment on the scope that is unique to each shooter and is a baseline setting which ensures that the scope is set up properly to your eye. This adjustment is so important that I ensure that each student has the ocular focus properly adjusted for themselves before I start any long range shooting class.

The ocular focus allows your eye to focus where it should - on the reticle inside the scope. When it comes to shooting accurately, you should be focusing your attention primarily on your reticle. I constantly repeat this mantra to students on the firing line, "Focus on the reticle, steady pressure on the trigger."[9] You can't focus on the reticle if it's blurry or if your eye must strain in order to see it clearly. Also, if the reticle isn't clear, you run the risk of focusing on the target instead and looking "beyond" the reticle. That is a sure way to miss what you're aiming at.

---

[9] I have often joked that if I could make one product that would help people shoot better, it would be to make this mantra into an audio file that can be played in head-phones while shooting.

The distance from the ocular lens to your eye when properly positioned behind the scope is called the "eye relief." A longer

> "Focus on the reticle, steady pressure on the trigger."

eye relief means that your eye must be farther away from the scope to see a clear picture. If the eye relief for a particular scope is too long, you may have trouble seeing through your scope if you can't mount it forward enough on the rifle. Conversely, if the eye relief is too short, you run the risk of smacking your eyebrow with the scope when the gun recoils... resulting in a "scope bite", the tell-tale curved cut on the eyebrow.

The lens facing the target is known as the objective lens. The larger the objective lens, the more light is gathered by the scope, which is especially useful in low-light situations. Higher magnification scopes need more light and generally have larger objective lenses.

Just because they gather more light doesn't necessarily make larger objective lenses better. The tradeoff to a large objective lens is that the scope usually needs to be mounted higher on the rifle so that the lens doesn't contact the rifle's barrel. As we'll discuss later, low is stable and stable is accurate. (*See Chapter 16 - Alternate Positions*).

Scope Caps

Please protect your scope with scope caps! There's no need to get fancy here - plastic Butler Creek scope caps work great. Cleaning a lens is difficult to do without scratching the lens or its coating and the best way to clean a lens is to not allow it to get dirty in the first place! If you aren't shooting your rifle and/or looking through your scope, your scope caps should be closed.

5.2.2 Reticle

The reticle's primary function is to be the aiming point within a scope. Reticles can come in many shapes and sizes to perform secondary functions like range estimation and "holds" for windage and elevation.

The standard reticle is a vertical line bisecting a horizontal line within the scope. These are sometimes called "crosshairs" because these reticles used to literally be formed by a vertical and horizontal hair which crossed in middle of the scope. Modern reticles are either wires (lower-end scopes) or they are etched into glass (high-end scopes).

Variations on the standard reticle include "duplex" reticles which make the lines easier to see due to their thicker outer lines, and range-finding variants such as "mil-dot" reticles[10]. For precision rifle work, I suggest using a reticle that allows for range-estimation and holds such as a mil-dot or similar reticle. Use of these reticles is covered later in this book in *Chapters 17* and *18*.

5.2.3 Scope Body

Larger scope bodies allow for more elevation and windage adjustment. Most scope bodies come in 1 inch or 30mm tube diameters but many new high-end scopes are coming in larger 32mm or 34mm tube diameters.

Hunting scopes are generally 1 inch tubes and long-range scopes are typically at least 30mm tubes. When shooting long range, however, it is not uncommon for a scope to run out of elevation adjustment even with a 30mm scope tube. For example, a Remington 700 in 308 Win. with a Leupold MkIV 3.5-10x scope with a 30mm tube (my recommended setup for beginners starting with long-range shooting) will usually run out of elevation adjustment before 1000 yards if teamed with a scope base without some elevation built-in.

---

[10] See the front cover of this book for an example.

5.2.4 Turrets

The elevation and windage turrets are used to adjust the impact of the bullet vertically and horizontally. The elevation turret is on the top of the scope and the windage turret is generally on the scope's right side.

Turrets on hunting scopes are often covered with caps while tactical-style scopes most likely have exposed turrets. Capped turrets can be useful to protect the turrets and prevent accidental adjustments. Exposed turrets are typically on ruggedized scopes that don't need as much protection, and some also have a mechanism to lock the turret in-place to prevent accidental adjustments. For exposed turrets that don't have a locking mechanism, it's important to monitor their position to ensure that

they haven't moved unintentionally. Also, turrets on hunting scopes typically need a tool (screwdriver, coin, or rim of a cartridge) to adjust while exposed turrets can be adjusted quickly without tools.

On exposed turrets, and some capped turrets, the turret itself is typically like a cap that is covering the adjustment mechanism. The turret (turret cap) is attached to the inner mechanism so that when you turn the turret (turret cap), the internal mechanism also turns. I tell people to think of the turret as a wrench that's attached to the inner mechanism like a bolt. When they turn the turret (the wrench), the inner part (bolt) also turns, so long as they're attached.

Typically the outer part of the turret is attached to the inner mechanism by a series of screws around the outside edge. These screws are tightened, and thereby clamped onto the inner portion. If these screws aren't tight enough, the outer turret can come loose and turn freely with no actual adjustments made to the scope. If you don't know exactly where in your adjustment the turret came loose, you might need to re-zero your rifle. That is, of course, unless you followed my instructions in *Section 15.5* and knew your mechanical zero.

If you try to tighten the turret screws too much, they can strip because they're typically small and fragile - those of you with gorilla-sized meat-hooks take note.

Zero-Stops

Some scopes have a feature called a "zero-stop." A zero-stop prevents the scope from being turned below "zero." Typically, zero stops only prevent the outer part of the turret from turning below zero.

This is important to understand for at least two reasons. First, just because the turret won't turn to a lower setting doesn't mean that the scope can't adjust down any further. The zero-stop may just be preventing the outer turret from moving down. Often, if the outer turret is loosened, turned to a higher setting, and then retightened, the inner mechanism can be adjusted further down.

Second, if your turret accidentally comes loose in the field, you can't rely on the zero-stop to get you back to "zero." This is because the zero-stop is often a reference point for the outer turret and not the inner mechanism, which is actually what was likely adjusted away from zero when your turret came loose.

Bullet Drop Compensators

The markings on most elevation turrets correspond to the actual adjustment being made. However, some turrets also have estimated distance marks for the elevation needed for a particular bullet. These type of turrets are sometimes called Bullet Drop Compensators (BDCs).

BDCs can be useful, but do *not* rely on them. Each rifle, round of ammunition, and scope behave differently. It is extremely rare that a BDC is dead-on accurate. It happens, and many are fairly close, but there are too many different variables for them to be exactly right. For example, I've seen five of the same make and model of rifle and scope combinations all shoot the same ammunition on the same day at the same target and they had a variation of impact equal to multiple "clicks" on the scope.

BDCs are a good reference to start with if you have no other information on how your rifle will perform at a certain distance. Please pay special attention to ensure that the correct BDC is being used. For example, BDCs are typically made for a particular bullet, weight, and velocity. A 300 Win. Mag. BDC won't even be close on a 22 LR rifle.

The scope on one of my M24s in the military only had a BDC. I made the adjustment by referencing how far off the BDC number was from where I needed to be for a particular distance. For example, for 500 yards, I needed to turn the turret to "5 minus 1 'click'."

5.2.5 Target Focus/Parallax Adjustment

Parallax is the perceived change in position of objects at different distances from different vantage points. For an example of parallax, close one eye, hold one finger on each hand out in front of your face at different distances, and line them up so that the far finger is hidden behind the closer finger. If you move your head around while keeping your fingers still, you'll notice that they seem to change positions and are no longer in-line with each other. This perceived position shift happens because your fingers are at different distances from your face. If your fingers are moved to the same distance so that they are touching each other, the perceived position change no longer happens.

With iron sights, parallax is good because it is what allows you to know when your front and rear sights are properly aligned. With a scope, however, the effect of parallax between the reticle and the target's image in the scope is bad. If you move your eye slightly to one side while looking through the scope, parallax can make it appear like the reticle is no longer lined up properly on the target. If you didn't realize that your eye position caused the perceived shift, you'd likely move the rifle so that the reticle appeared to line up with the target again. This adjustment will cause the rifle's barrel to be in different positions for each shot even though the reticle was lined up on the target each time.

When the ocular focus on your scope is properly adjusted, your eye is focused on the reticle inside the scope. The target's image, as it passes through your scope's objective lens, is focused at a certain location within your scope. If the target image's focus and the reticle are at two different locations in your scope, you can experience parallax. Also, with the reticle and target image's focus at two different locations, your eye will clearly see one or the other, but not both. This results in the bad practice of changing your eye's focus back and forth from the target's image to the reticle to ensure that they're properly aligned.

In order to remove the effect of parallax, and to have both the target image and the reticle clear, the focus location of the target image inside the scope must be changed so that it is at the same location as the reticle. You can adjust the target image's focus location with your scope's target focus or parallax adjustment. Both names for the adjustment are suitable. No, parallax is not the same as focus, but by adjusting the target's focus, we are removing the effect of parallax.

Adjustable Objectives vs. Side-Focus Knobs

Scopes with adjustable parallax either adjust the target's focus location via turning the objective housing ("adjustable objective" scopes) or a knob on the side of the scope ("side-focus" scopes). I much prefer side-focus scopes because they're easier to use while in a shooting position. Because of this, higher-end scopes will almost always have a side-focus knob instead of an adjustable objective.

Be careful when shopping for a scope. I have heard the term "adjustable objective" misused often by "gun-store experts." Adjustable objective doesn't refer to all scopes with the ability to adjust for parallax / target focus. Instead, it only refers to scopes that adjust by rotating the objective lens housing. Therefore, if you go looking for an "adjustable objective" scope because you want the ability to adjust for parallax (you do), you're going to end up with the less desirable adjustment option. Instead, look for a scope with adjustable parallax / target focus with a side focus knob.

Fixed Parallax

Some scopes do not have the ability to adjust for parallax. These scopes are called "fixed-parallax" scopes and are generally pre-set from the factory to be free from the effects of parallax at a specific distance. These scopes are fine for hunting or plinking, but are generally unsuitable for long-distance shooting. For example, a typical fixed-parallax hunting scope is parallax-free at at 100 yards. And a fixed-parallax scope meant for a 22 LR rifle is parallax-free at 50 yards because it's at a distance more likely for rimfire shooting.

5.2.6 Magnification

Higher magnification does not make you a better shooter. In fact, it can have the opposite effect. Although magnification is often needed in order

> **Magnification is not always your friend.**

to see the target, too much magnification can make it difficult to initially find the target and it can encourage improper trigger control. Magnification is not always your friend.

With a scope's magnification just high enough to properly identify the target and ensure that the reticle is on it, it's comparatively easy to keep the reticle on the target while applying pressure to the trigger. With too much magnification, shooters are often tempted to jerk the trigger when they think that the reticle, shaky from the excess magnification, is perfectly in the center of the target. If you don't believe me, try shooting a group at high magnification and then try it again at lower magnification. You might just be surprised.

Adjustable Magnification

Adjustable magnification scopes zoom in or out (increase or decrease magnification) with their reticle image in either the first or second focal plane. The magnification adjustment on a scope changes the size of the target image. Don't confuse higher magnification with better accuracy. In fact, it's often easier to use lower magnification in practical situations. Higher magnification can reduce your field of view (how big of an area you can see) and it can magnify your errors and cause the target's image to be too shaky.

The greater the magnification range, the more expensive the scope. Most adjustable scopes have about a 3x magnification range. This means that their maximum magnification is 3 times as large as the lowest magnification. For example, common scope magnification ranges are 2.5-8x, 3-9x, 3.5-10x, and 4.5-14x. On the high end, scopes can have as much as an 8x magnification range.

Fixed-Power

Some scopes do not have adjustable magnification settings. These are called fixed-power scopes. Unlike fixed-parallax scopes, fixed-power scopes can be suitable for long-range shooting. In fact, some of the best scopes I've used are fixed-power. For example, the standard issue scope on the U.S. Army's M24 sniper rifle was a fixed-power scope, and bench-rest shooters, who above all are concerned with extreme accuracy, often use fixed-power scopes. These scopes have fewer internal moving parts, making them more rugged and more consistent.

5.3 Scope Adjustments

5.3.1 Elevation and Windage Adjustments

The elevation and windage adjustment turrets are located on the top and side of the scope. When used, the impact of the bullet will be adjusted up, down, left, and right by moving the reticle within a scope via the turret. When the reticle is moved in one direction, the entire rifle must be moved in the opposite direction to bring the reticle back onto the target. For example, rotating an elevation turret in the direction marked "up" will actually lower the reticle in the scope. With a lower reticle in the scope, a shooter must raise the muzzle of a rifle in order to bring the reticle back onto the target. By making the barrel point higher, the shooter will also have raised the impact of the bullet thereby making the impact move up the target.

The repeatability and precision of these adjustments is paramount in a scope. You need to have the confidence that the scope will adjust the same every time. If a scope doesn't adjust for elevation or windage consistently, get rid of it or you'll have an impossible time engaging targets at distance.

Turrets are typically graduated to allow for incremental adjustments in minutes of angle (MOA) or milliradians (mils). Turrets also generally have markings on the outside which correspond to clicks which can be felt and/or heard as the turret is rotated. There is no standard amount of adjustment per click. One scope may adjust 1/4 MOA per click, while another may adjust 1 MOA, or even 1/10th of a Mil, per click.

Because scopes adjust different amounts per click, I encourage you to abandon referring to "clicks" and instead use the actual adjustment being made. For example, imagine that we are both at the range with our 308 Win. rifles. I know that I need to come up 12

MOA from my 100 yard zero in order to hit a target that is 500 yards away. My scope on that rifle happens to adjust 1 MOA of elevation per click which means I am adjusting up 12 clicks. If you asked me what elevation adjustment you should try in order to shoot the 500 yards target and I answered, "12 clicks," you wouldn't be anywhere near the target if you scope adjusted 1/4 MOA per click.   If however, I answered, "12 MOA," then you'd be able to adjust your scope accordingly. By referring to the actual adjustment being made, it is up to each shooter to know how their scope adjusts.

Elevation

If I have the time, I like to adjust my elevation turret for each different target distance. By adjusting the elevation, I know that the horizontal portion of the reticle is in the correct spot. I can then "hold" left and right along that horizontal reticle for windage. See "A" in *Figure 5.3-1*.

Of course, it is possible to just aim higher than the target and "hold-over" for elevation. See "B" in *Figure 5.3-1*. It is much quicker to do so (as long as you don't waste time calculating how much to hold-over) but it doesn't allow you to have a reference point on a standard reticle when you also "hold" left or right for windage. If you "hold" for both elevation and windage, the target will be floating off away from the reticle.   See "C" in *Figure 5.3-1*. This is bad because, as we'll discuss later, the key to accurate shooting is focusing on the reticle instead of the target. If the reticle is no where near the target, you surely can't focus on it properly.

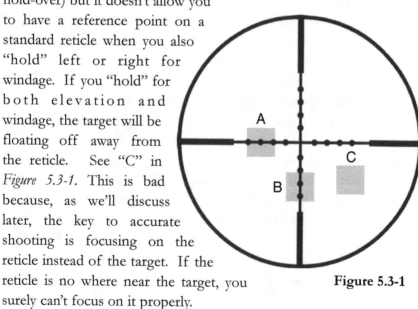

Figure 5.3-1

Newer reticles, such as the Horus reticle, are changing things. Instead of a typical cross-hair setup, they have graduated lines for both elevation and windage holds. See *Figure 5.3-2*. This allows for quick "holds" and allows the use of a scope that doesn't adjust perfectly every time but retains its zero setting. This is because once the scope is zeroed, you should be able to shoot targets at different distances without needing to rely upon the accuracy of the adjustments as you won't be making any.

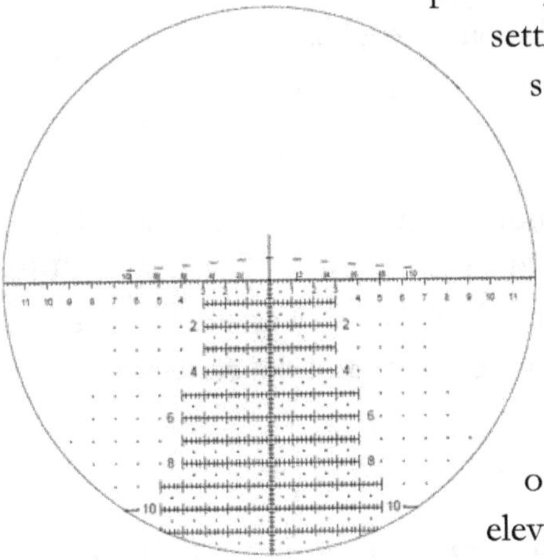

It is common for American-made scopes to raise the impact of the bullet by turning the elevation turret counter-clockwise. The opposite is true for many European-made scopes which often adjust upwards by rotating the elevation turret clockwise.

Figure 5.3-2

Windage

I find that adjusting my windage turret to compensate for wind is mostly futile because the wind can change faster than I can adjust a turret and get ready to shoot again. However, I do use my windage turret when zeroing my rifle and when accounting for spin-drift and the Coriolis effect because these variables don't change while I am shooting at the same target.

For MOA scopes, hunting scopes adjust in 1/4 MOA per click of the windage turret, while many tactical scopes adjust in 1/2 MOA per click of the windage turret. Be sure to know how your scope adjusts.

You should also become familiar with which direction your turret turns to move the impact of the bullet a certain direction. On my scope, rolling the windage turret away from me (clockwise) moves the impact of my bullet to the left. A trick I use to remember which way to turn the turret is this: "I don't want to be *left out*, so I'll be *right back."* This reminds me that I turn my turret away from me (out) to move the impact of the bullet left and I turn my turret towards me (back) to move it right. Your scope may not turn in the same direction - it's up to you to find out and remember. It isn't always ideal, or possible, to move your head to the side while in position to see which way the windage turret should be adjusted.

5.3.2 *Adjustable Magnification*

Scopes with adjustable magnification settings either have the reticle in the scope's first focal plane (FFP) or its second focal plane (SFP). The first focal plane is between the objective lens and the reticle. The second focal plane is between the reticle and the ocular lens.

Second Focal Plane (SFP)

Second Focal Plane adjustable magnification scopes are, by far, the most popular type of adjustable magnification scopes. With magnification in the SFP, only the target's image changes in size with a magnification adjustment. The reticle stays the same size throughout the magnification range. This is important because some reticles have marks which correspond to certain measurements. In these scopes, the reticle measurements are only accurate at one magnification setting - typically the highest setting. Refer to your scope's user manual to determine which magnification setting is correct for your scope.

SFP scopes are common because they are cheaper to manufacture and most scopes don't have reticles with measurement marks. And, for those scopes that do have measurement marks, they are usually used when the scope is at full-power anyway. For example, reticle marks are often used to measure a target's height for range estimation purposes. When estimating range with the reticle, precise measurements are crucial and are usually best done at high magnification.

The downside to these scopes is noticed when a shooter is trying to shoot at a lower power and also use the reticle's markings for wind holds.   This is generally a bad idea because the markings on the reticle are inaccurate at lower power.

First Focal Plane (FFP)

First Focal Plane adjustable magnification scopes are becoming more popular as new reticle designs with measurement marks are being used.   FFP scopes change both the size of the target and reticle together throughout the magnification range.   This means that if marks on a reticle correspond to a target's size at a low magnification setting, then they will also match at a high magnification setting.

FFP scopes are more expensive than SFP scopes because they are more difficult to manufacture. Also, at low power the reticles on FFP can be very difficult to see - they almost disappear into a blur of tiny lines.   With reticles having advanced elevation and windage holds, however, FFP scopes are useful because the holds can be used at all magnifications.   Remember, magnification isn't always your friend and it is often better to shoot at a lower power magnification. With a FFP scope, this can be done while still utilizing the advanced features of the reticle.

5.3.3 Adjustable Parallax / Target Focus

Some scopes have distances marked on the objective housing or the side-focus knob. These markings are largely irrelevant. What matters is what you see through the scope while looking at the target.

There are two methods of adjusting your target focus knob to remove parallax - move your eye around while making the adjustment to confirm the absence of the effect of parallax or making the adjustment until the reticle and target image are clear.   I prefer the second method because it is faster and requires less movement. However, the second method only works if you have first properly set up your eye to your scope with your ocular focus. *See Section 12.4.1.*

If you want to use the first method, move your head around while you are adjusting the target focus and watch for the effects of parallax to increase or decrease. As you find the location in the adjustment range where the parallax decreases, fine tune the adjustment until the reticle and the target move as one.

If you want to use the second method, stare at the crisp and clear reticle while you make the adjustment. Once the target's image is also clear, you know you have the right setting.

5.4 Scope Mounts

5.4.1 Rings

The rings are what hold the scope to the base. Just like with scopes, you get what you pay for with rings. I haven't found a decent set of rings for precision long range shooting for under $100. This is not to say that cheaper rings won't work for you. But, if you want to do it right, buy good rings the first time.

My classic go-to rings have always been Leupold Mk4 rings. They are usually the least expensive of the upper-tier of quality rings. Lately, however, I have really been liking Vortex's high-end line of rings.

When buying rings, ensure that they are the correct height, correct diameter for your scope, and the correct mounting platform for your base. If your rings aren't high enough, then your objective lens will interfere with your barrel and you won't be able to properly mount your scope. If your rings are too high, then you'll have to build up a high platform on your stock's comb or you'll have to strain to hold your head high enough to properly see through the scope, neither of which is a good idea.

Most precision long range scopes require 30mm rings, but the current trend in bigger scope bodies can require rings up to 36mm (or more) in diameter. Most rings will also need to be made for a Picatinny rail, generally the strongest and most common system.

I don't believe that quick release rings belong on a precision rifle. Yes, my Mk12 SPR in the military had quick-release rings, but the military doesn't always make the best decisions. I have seen too many quick release rings fail completely or move while on the rifle - both are bad outcomes for something that is more complicated than it needs to be. With standard bolt-on style rings, you can ensure that the torque setting is exactly where you want it to be.

Also, if you want backup sights on your rifle, please consider angled offset sights (iron sights or optics). They are much faster than removing your scope, you're more likely to zero and practice with them, and they allow your scope to maintain its position on your rifle.

5.4.2 Base

The base is the mounting surface on top of the receiver for the scope rings to attach. As mentioned above, ensure that your base is the proper mounting platform for your rings. Also, ensure that it is the correct base for your rifle!

Bases can be one or two pieces. One-piece bases are preferred for precision rifle work because of their rigidity. If you spend a lot of money on a consistent and repeatable scope but you mount it on a base that flexes or moves, then you just wasted your money. The base is truly the foundation for the rings and scope.

For long range work, bases can also come with built-in elevation. For example, my 308 Win rifle has a 20 MOA base on it. This means that the base is angled - it's higher in the back and lower in the front. This allows for scopes with limited elevation to get a "running head-start" and be able to reach out further without hitting the limits of their turrets. Often, with cartridges like my 308 Win, a typical scope will run out of elevation adjustment before it can adjust to 1000 yards. By adding an elevated base with 20 MOA, for example, the scope has 20 more MOA of adjustment available.

I used to always recommend the Leupold Mk4 20 MOA base for short action Remington 700s and it was the most common base I saw for that platform. As of the time of publishing however, Leupold has discontinued them. Instead, the next best option is the Nightforce 20 MOA base.[11]

---

[11] A link to this base, and more, is available on this book's page at RyanCleckner.com

5.5 Iron Sights

I'm a big fan of shooting with iron sights. There's a sense of satisfaction shooting with iron-sights and they're great for helping you work on your fundamentals of marksmanship.

Iron sights are a combination of a rear and front sight which are aligned by the shooter in order to aim at a target. The front sight is usually mounted as close to the forward end of the barrel as possible/reasonable and the rear sight is mounted as far back on the receiver as possible. The reason the sights are typically mounted as far away from each other is because it is easier to see slight variations in alignment when they are farther away from each other.

The distance between the sights is called the "sight radius." The longer the radius, the more precise the shooter can be. The shorter the radius, the faster the shooter can be.

There are two basic types of iron sights, namely open and aperture. As the name suggests, open sights have a rear sight that is open at the top. The front sight should be centered between the opening in the rear sight and the top of the front sight should be flush with the top of the rear sight. Aperture sights have a rear sight that is closed at the top. The shooter looks though the hole in the rear sight (the aperture) to align the front sight within the hole. Open sights are generally quicker to use, but aperture sights generally allow the shooter to be more precise.

5.6 Adjusting Iron Sights

Most iron sights that you'll encounter on rifles suitable for long range precision shooting are adjustable. They are usually adjustable either by being "drifted" with a hammer and punch or by turning a knob (on the sight itself).

If your iron sights have marks indicating the direction of adjustment, then move the sight or the sight's adjustment knob in the noted direction to move the impact of the bullet in that particular direction. For example, if your sights have a knob with a "U" and an arrow pointing in a clockwise rotating direction, then the impacts of the bullets will move up the target as you turn that knob clockwise in the direction of the arrow. Also, turning the opposite direction will move the impacts down. There is no standard direction for a particular adjustment. Each style and brand of iron sights might be different. It is up to you to know how your sights adjust.

Some sights, however, do not have direction indicating marks. In these cases, it is important to know which direction a sight should be physically moved in order to have a certain effect. For example, turning a sight adjustment knob clockwise might move the rear sight to the left or a front sight might get taller as you unscrew it out of its base. It is often necessary to move an unmarked adjustment in a certain direction to see what effect it has on the movement of the sight.

When adjusting iron sights, the front sight is physically moved in the *opposite* direction you want the impact of the bullet to move and the rear sight is moved in the *same* direction. For example, if you want to move the impact of the bullets down, you can either move the front sight up (opposite) or move the rear sight down (same direction).

After raising the front sight and attempting to reacquire your target, you will then need to lower the front of the rifle in order to get the sights to line up properly again. By lowering the front of the rifle, you'll lower where the bullets impact. Likewise, if you lower the rear sight you need to raise the rear of the rifle in order to have proper sight alignment. This also will move the impacts down the target. Both solutions result in the barrel pointing lower on the target.

If you ever forget which direction the sights must move to have a particular effect on the target, you can use your fingers as mock sights. I've been seen on the range more than once holding my hands out using this trick to remind myself. Hold your left hand out with your index finger raised mimicking a front sight and hold your right hand in front of your face with two fingers raised mimicking a rear sight. Line up your finger sights and then experiment by folding your left hand's finger (your mock front sight) to lower the height of the front sight. Notice that you will have to raise your left arm (the barrel) to realign your pretend sights. This reminds you that if you lower the front sight, you must raise the barrel to realign the sights, which raises your bullets. Likewise, you can move your rear hand to the right. You'll notice that you'll also have to move your left arm to the right in order to realign the sights. This reminds you that if you move the rear sight to the right, the barrel and the bullet's impact also moves right.

If a front sight has the ability to adjust left and right, I like to first adjust the rear sight so that it's aligned side to side where I can most comfortably see through the sight with my head rested properly on the stock. Once the rear sight is where I want it, I adjust the front sight left and right to zero the rifle. After all, it makes no sense to have the front sight in the center of its adjustment range and have the rear sight so far to one side that it is difficult to see through and use. I also do the same thing for elevation, if possible. I'd rather have a comfortable

> If possible, adjust the rear sight to your eye and then the front sight to the target.

view through the rear sight and have the adjustment in the front sight. This, of course, is only a suggestion - a lot depends on your setup as to whether this is even possible without misaligning the front sight so much that it'll cause a problem with its integrity.

5.7 Laser Sights

We used laser sights on some of our rifles in the military. Although they were handy in certain situations, they didn't make any of us better shooters.

The biggest benefit to using laser sights is experienced when using nightvision. They allowed us to point-out and engage targets without needing to see through a scope.

The down-side to laser sights is that they aren't easily adjusted and shouldn't be relied upon for precision shooting at different distances. Also, get more than one shooter with laser sights pointing at the same target and you'll see how difficult they are to use as you spend half of the time figuring out which dot is yours.   I recommend zeroing a laser sight at medium/close distance (whatever that is for you). Personally, I like zeroing a laser sight at 200 yards so that it gets me "close-enough" from 0 yards out to 400 yards.

Be aware of the offset of the laser from your barrel when zeroing. If the laser is 2 inches to the right of your barrel, I recommend zeroing it so that your bullets impact 2 inches to the left of the laser's dot. If you don't do this, you will have to worry about where the laser crosses for windage in addition to worrying about it for elevation. For example, the bullets would impact to the left closer than your zero distance and to the right further than your zero distance.

One last thing to know about lasers - they work both ways. This means that it allows you to see a clear line to the target and the target can see a clear line back to you.

6 ACCESSORIES

If you're not careful, you can easily get carried away with accessories. I love gadgets and gear as much as the next guy but please make sure that both your rifle and optic are of enough quality that allow you to shoot long range effectively before you purchase the latest top-of-the-line laser rangefinder.

For example, if your laser rangefinder costs more than your scope, you might be doing it wrong. Sure, you'll know exactly how far away that 912.3 yard target is, but you're not going to be able to hit it. Remember that quote from the beginning of this section, "It's the Indian, not the arrow." Some of the best shooters I know can use a rifle with a sling and iron sights to out-shoot most others with a rifle with bipod legs and a scope.

6.1 Shooting Bag

I firmly believe that a shooting bag is a crucial part of the precision rifle system. Where my rifle goes, my pack follows. My shooting bag serves as a platform for my rifle and it carries things for both the rifle and me.

A shooting bag is the best all-around platform for shooting your rifle. The beauty of a shooting bag as a platform is its consistency. As discussed above, bipods can react inconsistently depending on the surface they are on. A rifle rested on a shooting bag, however, reacts the same whether the shooting bag is on grass or concrete.

In addition to serving as an accurate and stable platform for shooting, a shooting bag does something else - it carries things. If I am going to carry around equipment with me, it must be for a purpose. For example, I carry extra ammunition in case I need more than I have on my person or in my rifle, I carry my 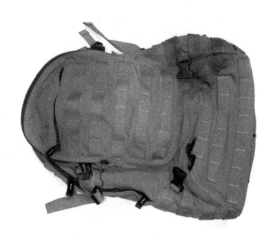 DOPE book so that I can add and reference information, I carry a calculator and rangefinder to help with range estimation, and I carry water and food in case I am thirsty or hungry.

By using my shooting bag as a shooting platform, I'm able to access each of these things directly in front of me. Instead of breaking my position to go searching for a bag laying on the ground behind me, I can reach in my bag for a snack while staying on my rifle and looking at the target. If I need to get up and move quickly, I can simply grab my rifle in one hand, my bag in the other, and go.

I encourage you to employ a practice we used in the military - only have one thing out of your bag at a time. If you do this, you won't have gear strewn about you on the ground making it hard to pack up in a hurry and easy to lose. Having your gear scattered everywhere is often called a "gypsy camp" or a "yard sale." Don't do it.

Here is a list of things, at a minimum, that I keep in my shooting bag:

- ☐ Water
- ☐ Food
- ☐ Ammunition
- ☐ DOPE Book
- ☐ Sand Sock
- ☐ Calculator
- ☐ Range-finder
- ☐ Tools
- ☐ Mil-dot Master
- ☐ Binoculars
- ☐ Flashlight
- ☐ Rain Jacket
- ☐ Jacket for warmth

6.2 Sand Sock

A "sand sock" is my favorite shooting crutch. I can shoot without one, but it sure makes it easier to shoot with one - especially while in the prone position. Just as a shooting bag is a consistent platform for the front of your rifle, the sand sock is a platform for the back.

I've been accused more than once of being a smart-ass. Probably because of how I answer questions like, "How do you make a sand sock?" I typically reply, "Take some sand and put it in a sock." Although that clearly is one method, and how the rear bag got its name, sand is heavy, and not exactly fun to carry around.

In the military, we used rice in a sock and we convinced ourselves that in an emergency, we could eat the rice. Now I know better, and would rather just carry an extra granola bar in my bag. Currently, my favorite material for making a sand sock is airsoft ammunition beads. They're light, cheap, and conform well to the shape I need. I've found that opaque (not transparent) airsoft beads work best. In my experience, transparent airsoft beads tend to be noisier and slicker. The opaque beads seem to stick together better under pressure which helps me hold the sand sock at a particular height with the proper tension.

If you are looking to purchase a sand sock, there are finally some great options in the marketplace. My favorites are made out of Cordua nylon for toughness and are filled with what feels like a light polyfill insulation material for lightness. Check out PrecisionRifleBlog.com for a great comparison of these bags and many other things. If you like gear, and researching it, you'll love this website.

According to the most recent survey of pro shooters, Wiebad, Str8 Laced Gun Gear, and TAB Gear make the top three most popular sand-socks or rear-bags. Personally, I like the Wiebad bags best and have included links to my recommendations in this chapter's section on this book's website.

6.2.1 Sand Sock Use

The sand sock is used as a rest under the buttstock of your rifle while it is gripped in your non-firing hand. By squeezing tighter or by relaxing your grip on the sand sock, you can change its height. By squeezing tighter, I can raise the sand sock which in turn raises the rear of my rifle thereby lowering the reticle on the target, because the angle of my rifle has changed and it's now pointing lower.

I recommend tying your sand sock to your shooting pack with a cord long enough to use the sand sock while it's still tied to your pack. If your gear is tied to your pack, it's an exception to the anti-gypsy camp/yard sale rule of having only one item out of your pack at a time. My pack has a small strap and buckle on the side that I use to secure my sand sock. This way, it's easy to get to my sand sock with one hand.

6.3 DOPE Book

"DOPE" stands for Data On Previous Engagements. I have always struggled to find a pre-printed DOPE book that works for my needs. Every DOPE book I've seen so far includes pages of useless information and is hard to use. I'm constantly on the search for one, however, and if I find one, I'll update this chapter's web page with a link.

My best solution for a DOPE book has always been to make my own. 3x5 index cards, a binder clip and a pencil have always served me well. Note that I mentioned a pencil and not a pen. I know some folks who want a fancy "write at any angle" pen for their field book. Leave it to NASA to spend money and time to design and develop a "space pen" that can write at any angle and on most surfaces because of a special pressurized ink cartridge. The Russians, on the other hand, just used a pencil.

Another reason I like a pencil is that if I break it, I now have two pencils. And in an extreme scenario (as in, not ever going to happen but it's fun to mention and pretend that it'll be useful), you could whittle your pencil with your knife for some dry kindling.

I am often asked what information you should keep in your DOPE book. Here's my controversial answer: "Only keep as much as you are going to reference and use later." Shooters who take themselves very seriously tend to record everything they can. Now, if they can use the information, then they're doing exactly what they should be doing, but if your DOPE book looks like a Manhattan phone directory, you should ask yourself just how much info do you really use before committing to writing it all down. Wouldn't you rather be making your way to the next target?

As an example, I often see a place on pre-printed DOPE books to record the angle of the sun while shooting. Knowing this information can be useful in some rare circumstances. However, if you're never going to use it, why overwhelm yourself with the extra info?

Your adjustments needed to hit targets at certain distances in certain conditions is the core purpose for a DOPE book. However, if all you end up with is a diary of your shooting experiences, and you never convert the information into something useful for reference later, then all you are doing is keeping a diary. . .

> "Dear diary, I shot a bunch and missed a bunch today. Today was the Autumnal Equinox, the sun was kinda bright, the soil had high mineral content, and there were exactly three clouds in the sky. Also, Ryan Cleckner yelled at me for capturing air samples in Ziplock baggies and for closing my eyes before I smack the trigger. He's a jerk."

Another problem I have with pre-printed dope books is that they often dedicate an entire page for a particular distance. This is great for bullseye-style shooters, but I get bored with a target after I have hit it a couple of times and I want to move on to something else (or at least use a different shooting position). If I used a new page for every shooting position and distance, I'd not only be recording the environmental data over and over, I'd also leave the range with 20 or so pages filled up.

Instead of using the standard approach of "I'm recording this information because this really cool looking 'sniper' book says I should," try focusing on what you'll need instead. Take a stack of index cards and take notes. These notes should include variables that matter to you. If you're going to ignore humidity when you shoot, then you might not need to figure it out and write it down. Then, when you get back home and after you've cleaned your rifle, pull out a small notebook for that rifle and consolidate your information into something meaningful that can be referenced later. I like to keep all of the info for a particular rifle condensed to just a few index cards that I keep in my rifle's stock pack.

Of course, I'm not saying not to use a DOPE book. If you can make use of the info and you are at the level of shooting that you want to know the humidity, then by all means record it and use it.

6.4 Calculators

Ballistic calculators have come a LONG way since I was working as a sniper. Now, when you go to the range you're likely to see most long range shooters looking at their phones in between shots. They're not updating Facebook or taking a selfie (well, they might be), they are referencing their shooting data.

There are three types of "calculators" we are going to explore for long range shooting: mechanical calculators, standard electronic calculators, and modern ballistic calculators.

6.4.1 Mechanical Calculators

In this category I'm including a seriously handy tool to have in your shooting bag: a Mil-dot master. I hardly use mine anymore, but it was very handy while I was learning.

The Mil-dot master is a plastic slide rule that allows you to calculate a target's distance by lining up the size of the target with the size of the target in Mils as measured through your scope.

It also helps with angle calculations. By tying a string through one of the holes, you can use the angle guide to measure the angle to a target and then you can see the corrected distance for that angle in the information on the slide rule.

It's a great tool and I wish I'd thought of it first.

6.4.2 Standard Electronic Calculators

I also keep a cheap solar and battery powered calculator in my shooting bag. A simple/no-frills calculator works best. I suggest, however, getting one with a cover to help protect the buttons and screen. Also, a lighted screen can be handy at dusk – but it can also light up your face more than you want at night.

This calculator is handy for more things than you know. Well, that's not true, its only handy for mathematical calculations, but you'll find yourself using this thing a lot – especially in situations where you don't feel like getting your phone out to make a calculation.

6.4.3 Ballistic Calculators

I'm going to warn you up front – it will seem as if I don't like these. That isn't true. Ballistic calculators can be extremely useful. In fact, modern equipment, including ballistic calculators, is the reason why shooters are so much better now than they were even 20 years ago. However, the problem with ballistic calculators is that they can be a dangerous crutch.

Most people use ballistic calculators on their phones but some ballistic calculators are built into other devices like wind meters, for example.

If I need to shoot any target quickly within the capability of any of my rifles, I'm confident that I'd be able to grab my rifle, make the appropriate adjustments and at least get close. This is because I am comfortable with my rifles and their abilities. If there was a race to see who could hit a 500 yard target the fastest, I would grab my 308 Win rifle, dial the scope to 12 MOA of elevation and shoot the target. If the particular environment made it so the 12 MOA adjustment was not accurate, I'd be able to adjust and re-engage the target by the time the other shooter was still opening their ballistic calculator software.

I have seen, on countless occasions, shooters take a long (very long) time messing with their ballistic calculators instead of shooting. Then, after they think they have made the necessary adjustments, they get on their rifle and take a shot. Often, they don't get the results they want so they scratch their head and go back to their ballistic calculator to figure out why the information is wrong. Then, after they think they figured it out, they try again with the new information.

If ballistic calculators are so amazing (and they are) then why are these shooters missing? Well, there are many possible reasons. One reason is that they may have put too much of their focus on their equipment instead of their technique; they've traded hours of practice for technology. They get a precise adjustment from the ballistic calculator but they didn't have proper fundamentals on the rifle and simply made a bad shot.

Another reason is that they are using bad information to input into the calculator - garbage in, garbage out. Bad information can come from incorrect settings in the calculator, incorrect information about the environment or target distance, incorrect information about their rifle or scope, or incorrect information about their ammo. Each of these are common mistakes I see – especially with new shooters.

The standard is that there is no standard. Every rifle, scope, and ammo combination is unique.   If you enter the manufacturer's information into the software and you don't tune it for your specific system, then you're in for a bad day. At the very least, you'd better have a chronograph out to see how fast your bullet is actually flying. You also should consider confirming the Ballistic Coefficient of the bullets – manufacturers might have motivation to advertise better than actual BCs. These distinct tweaks are better covered in another book.

For now, know that ballistic calculators are amazingly useful. However, please learn to shoot without one so that you get the fundamentals down first and have a strong understanding of how things work. This is directly relational to my recommendation to learn to use a map and compass before relying on a GPS.

6.5 Wind Meter

Knowing the wind speed and direction is extremely important when shooting long range. However, in order to provide accurate wind information, you'd need to have a wind meter set up every few yards all the way to the target, they'd have to be able to measure the wind speed and direction at the height the bullet would be traveling, and you'd have them tied in to a computer that can normalize all of the different data into something you could use for an adjustment. I'm not saying that a wind meter is useless unless used in this way, but I am encouraging you to not completely rely on one - especially while you are learning to shoot.

If I haven't upset any readers yet and caused them to exclaim that I have no idea what I'm talking about, then this section surely will. I don't carry a wind-meter in my shooting bag. For reasons I'll discuss later in *Chapter 18*. I don't like using a hand-held wind meter. My problem with hand held wind meters is that they are one extra thing to carry, and they only tell me what the wind speed and direction was at my location before I set it down to get on my rifle and shoot. I am also a tactical-style shooter and, as such, I simply don't like taking the time to make tons of calculations with a lot of equipment before I shoot. I understand my style of compensating for wind is not as precise as some shooters. That's ok – these are just different techniques.

Because most wind meters give you just wind speed and direction and, unfortunately, these values still need to be converted into a meaningful adjustment on your scope. You may learn how to adjust for a 7 mph 90 degree wind, but will you be able to recognize that the wind is 7 mph at 90 degrees when it is only happening halfway downrange the next time you are shooting?

Even though I don't keep one in my shooting bag, a wind meter can still be a handy tool to have and use. This is especially true when you are first learning to compensate for wind. Get one if you like and use it. There are many better shooters than me and a lot of them use wind meters religiously. I think that they'd agree with me, however, that they need to pay attention to the wind all the way to the target and take that into consideration when they are shooting. They can't use a wind meter for that down-range information, they have to learn how to read wind with their eyes and make a judgment call from experience.

Some fancier wind meters also have ballistic calculators in them. If someone gave me one to use, I'd probably keep it with me to try it out but I'm more comfortable spotting with my eyes because of the same issue I see with ballistic calculators – many shooters use them, trust them, miss, then go back to them to try again.

6.6 Chronograph

A chronograph is another tool that I don't carry with me in my shooting bag but it is absolutely crucial when you start to develop your own ammunition loads while reloading and also for working with ballistics calculators.

Chances are, your bullet isn't flying the speed that the manufacturer said it would. This is because the temperature and variations in barrel internal dimensions and length can change the velocity of bullets. The only way to know your bullet's speed – which is probably the most important data to know about your rifle system - is to measure it with a chronograph. Links to suggestions of both styles of chronographs are included in this chapter's webpage.

6.6.1 Optical Chronographs

Standard chronographs measure the bullet's speed through optical sensors. These chronographs "see" when the bullet passes over a closer and farther sensor and calculate the bullet's speed. If you're just starting out, a basic shooting chronograph will work. Fancier models can store and display more information but at the beginning, just knowing each bullet's speed is most useful. You can use a calculator or computer spreadsheet to calculate the data you're interested in, for example the extreme spread and standard deviation.[12]

Here are two considerations for working with optical chronographs. Don't shoot your chronograph and make sure the ambient light is appropriate. You might laugh at the first one but it can be easier to do than you think. As I mention in *Chapter 10*, what you see through the scope isn't exactly where the bullet is going. Your scope may be high enough to see through the chronograph, but the barrel may not be. If you're ever in doubt, pull the bolt out of your rifle, aim at the target through your scope, and without moving the rifle, look through the barrel to ensure that you have a clear view

---

12 These topics will be explored in the next book in this series, *Advanced Long Range Shooting*

to the target.

Optical chronographs are handy because they are relatively inexpensive and you can measure your bullet's accuracy on a target as you shoot through it. However, they can be finicky if the ambient light is too bright or too dark. They can also be difficult to set up. In order to use one at a public range, you'll have to wait for a cease fire to get in front of the firing line to set it up and you'll have to rig some solution to hold the chronograph at the right height.

6.6.2 Electromagnetic Chronographs

Electromagnetic chronographs are fairly new. They are extremely handy and they are quickly gaining in popularity. This style of chronograph generally attaches a device to the barrel that senses the bullet passing over a section of the device via electromagnetic sensors.

The benefit to this style of chronograph is that it's easier to setup and isn't finicky due to its environment. The downside to these is that they are more expensive and the attachment of the device to your barrel affects accuracy. I won't say it has a negative effect because I know of at least one rifle that shoots better with it attached. This means that if you're gathering data for reloads, you'll have to shoot some of each recipe for speed and then shoot more for accuracy with the device removed.

6.6.3 Doppler Radar

The true new kid on the block is portable Doppler radar. While you're starting out, you probably shouldn't be worrying about your own personal Doppler radar system. However, know that it exists because it is just going to get cheaper and better.

6.7 Tools

Let's talk about tools that are useful to have back where you store your gear and tools that you should carry with you in your shooting bag. These tools are just the basics for long range precision shooting - these are not every tool you'll need to build your own rifle.

6.7.1 At-home

At a minimum, you should have a good set of equipment for cleaning your rifle. A quality cleaning rod (buy a good one the first time) and a set of brushes, jags, and patches for each caliber are a must. Extras, like chamber guides, special solvent containers, and other items discussed in *Chapter 20 - Cleaning*, are nice to have but not necessary if you are just starting out.

Your basic tool kit can be fairly...well...basic. In fact, most of these tools may already be in your tool kit for household or automotive applications. Personally, I have a duplicate set of tools for guns and for the garage. This is because I don't like having to go back and forth between each area to find the tool I need and the tools for my guns are usually more precise and/or fragile than the tools in my garage. Also, it's nice to just grab my gun tool box and put it in the truck if I think I will need them at the range or a friend's house.

I recommend starting with the following from the list below. Of course, there are many more tools that you can use (like vise blocks for AR-15 receivers, specialized wrenches, etc.) but this is not a discussion on home-gunsmithing. Instead, this is a quick list of items you should have at home as you start to get into long range shooting.

- ☐ Full set of Allen (hex-key) wrenches (metric and standard)
- ☐ Torx wrenches in sizes for your rifle and scope
- ☐ Small tack-hammer (preferably brass or nylon)
- ☐ Set of brass punches (buy quality)
- ☐ Set of screwdrivers
- ☐ Torque wrench
- ☐ Wrench socket-heads for your torque wrench in sizes appropriate for your rifle and scope.
    - ☐ Often 1/2" socket for scope rings
    - ☐ Often Torx size T-10 and T-15 for rings and base
    - ☐ Action screws differ - check your rifle

Make sure to start with brass punches and a brass hammer because steel tools can easily scratch and damage your rifle. Steel punches can be appropriate in certain circumstances, however. For example, I have a set of roll-pin starter punches that are steel, but those are specialty tools. Also, if you have a job that is so tough that it will deform your brass punch, only then is it time to upgrade to stronger steel punches.

If your rifle has roll-pins that need to be driven in and out, it is worth considering using specialized roll-pin punches. Not only will the specialized punches help you start a roll-pin into the hole, they can save your pins from becoming distorted and damaged.

Using regular screwdrivers can also potentially damage parts of your rifle. Regular screwdrivers have a slight taper towards the point. This makes them easy to use for general application. However, the taper allows all of the force to be applied to the top edge of the screw head where it is at its weakest instead of at the base of the slot where it's strongest. Hollow-ground tip screwdrivers are a nice (but not necessary) upgrade and will save you from marred screw heads. Hollow-ground tip screwdrivers have parallel surfaces. They may not slide into a screw as easy as a regular screwdriver, but they can keep from ruining your screws by applying torque where the screw head is strongest, at its base.

6.7.2 In Your Range Bag

If you're not careful, you can quickly get out of control with the number of tools that you carry in your shooting bag. At a minimum, I recommend carrying Allen (hex-key) wrenches and standard wrenches for your scope rings, base and action screws. This way, you can tighten up anything that comes loose in the field. Also, a simple cleaning kit and something to clean off your scope's lenses is also nice to carry.

In the military, we kept a spare part of most small/replaceable parts on our rifles, wrenches for everything (including a torque wrench), and even backup iron sights and a bolt-disassembly tools all in a small Pelican case. This kit was called our Deployment Kit (D-Kit) for short. It was very handy because there was only one location for every tool you needed. The down-side to the kit, of course, was the size and weight.

Now it's not likely that my life or somebody else's life will depend on my rifle so I don't carry the extra weight of a full D-Kit. But I still carry the bare minimum tools as I mentioned above.

6.8 Spotting Scope / Binoculars

Some of the same advice I gave regarding your rifle scope also applies to your spotting scope and/or binoculars. Don't skimp on quality and higher magnification isn't necessarily better.

It may be painful to purchase a high-end spotting scope or pair of binoculars but you will be happier in the long run. Also, too high of magnification will make it too difficult to find your target, spot your rounds, and keep the optic steady enough for a clear view. Quality lower power glass is much better than cheap high powered glass.

> Quality lower power glass is much better than cheap high powered glass.

6.8.1 Spotting Scope

A spotting scope is an extremely handy tool for spotting the impacts of bullets on or around a target. Also, it is handy when observing long distances. It is not, however, necessarily the best option for an afternoon of "glassing" (looking for game while hunting). Spotting scopes can cause fatigue from straining to see through only one eye and it can be difficult to find and identify targets/animals at distance.

Be careful to not get too large of a spotting scope. At some point, you're going to need to carry it around! I highly recommend the Leupold Mark 4 spotting scopes, their non-tactical counterpart Golden Ring spotting scopes, and the medium powered higher-end

Vortex spotting scopes.

I warn against too much magnification because it can make the spotting scope difficult to use. Not only is it difficult to find a target on high power, the image might end up being so shaky that it is difficult to see. Also, on too high of power, the mirage caused by heat waves can really cause a problem. When it comes to spotting rounds, I generally don't like to use anything over 15x. This is because higher magnification doesn't allow me to see the full picture.

You're going to need a tripod and some sort of mount that allows you to pan and tilt. My absolute favorite system is the Manfrotto "pistol grip" style head. Lightweight tripods are nice to carry but heavy tripods tend to be more stable.

I really like range-finding reticles in spotting scopes. These reticles allow you to range-estimate better than you can with a rifle scope and they make spotting much easier because they allow for precise incremental corrections that match the shooter's scope.

6.8.2 Binoculars

When it comes to observing an area to find something, nothing beats a good pair of binoculars. When using binoculars, your eyes are able to better see depth and contrast and a quality set of binoculars allows your eyes to just ... relax. When I would sit for hours and look for sniper students, I would use my 10x binoculars to find them and then only switch to a spotting scope if I needed to see more detail. My favorite pair of binoculars are my Cabela's 10x42 Euro binoculars. These are made by Meopta and are an incredible value for the money. The higher-end Vortex binos are also impressive.

If you've never felt your eyes relax while looking through an optic, ask to look through somebody's pair of quality binoculars the next time you're around them. This is a difficult concept to experience while looking through optics in a store - it is easiest to see while looking at distance.

Also, in order to get the maximum benefit of binoculars, they must be set up properly. Once you learn how to do this, you will be showing this technique to other people - the difference it makes is impressive and it's surprising how many people don't have their binoculars set up properly.

Internally, there are moving parts/lenses within each side of the binocular that are controlled by the external focus adjustment. When the focus adjustment is moved, the lenses in each side of the binocular move in tandem.

Unfortunately for most of us, our eyes aren't identical. Therefore, it is often desirable to have these lenses at slightly different positions (distances from your eyes) in each side of the binocular. The diopter adjustment on your binoculars allows you to move the position of one of the lenses independent of the other. For example, in a middle focus position, the internal lenses might both be 2 inches from your eyes. By adjusting the diopter, you are able to get one lens 1.5 inches from one eye while the other lens is still 2 inches from the other eye. Then, when you move the focus adjustment, the lenses will move back and forth together but they'll always be 0.5 inches apart.

Changing this setting will solve the common "double-vision" issue or the focus problem when neither eye seems to be perfectly in focus. This setting is unique to each person. If I hand my binos to you, you will need to adjust this setting for you. When you return them (don't steal my binoculars), I will have to put the setting back for my eyes. Therefore, you should mark the setting for your eyes on your binos so that it is easy to return to your setting.

Setting up Binoculars

Note on your binoculars which side has the diopter adjustment. Usually, this adjustment is on one of the eyepieces but sometimes, as with my Meopta binos, the adjustment dial is in the center even though it only changes one side. The diopter adjustment is usually a dial that has a center mark and a plus and minus direction either side of the center mark. Once you have figured out which side has the adjustable diopter, focus on the other side first.

While looking through the non-diopter adjusting side only (close your other eye or block the diopter adjusting side), adjust the focus on your binoculars until the eye for that side can see the target image clearly. I find that it is best to do this while looking at something close. This is because the focus settings on binoculars are usually unforgiving up close and it is therefore easier to find the exact right spot. For example, at long range, I can move the focus adjustment slightly and the binoculars will still seem like they are in focus. Up close (10 ft away), however, the focus adjustment must be in the exact correct position in order to see clearly.

Once you have the main focus adjusted for the non-diopter adjusting side, switch sides and eyes. You should now be closing the first eye or blocking the non-diopter adjusting side. Then, use only the diopter adjustment to make the image clear for the eye on that side. Now, each lens on each side is exactly where they need to be for the difference in your eyes. When you adjust the main focus for different distances, the lenses will move in tandem but they will be offset by however much you made the change.

Once you have done this, note/mark the setting and start enjoying looking through binoculars. If you've never done this before, get ready for a notably better experience!

6.9 Laser Rangefinder

Laser rangefinders are extremely useful tools. They are the most precise method you'll likely have to determine a target's distance. They are so precise, in fact, you should use them even when you're at a range with targets of a "known distance." You might be surprised to find that the "known distance" isn't correct. As we'll discuss later, however, you should learn to estimate range without your laser rangefinder just like you should learn how to use a map and compass before relying on a GPS.

Laser rangefinders are getting better and cheaper. I encourage you to purchase a rangefinder with an advertised range well beyond the distance you intend to use it. This is because the laser rangefinder relies on receiving the reflection of a laser beam it shoots at a target and many surfaces, especially the farther out you go, don't reflect the laser well. For example, a laser rangefinder advertised as a 1000 yard rangefinder usually won't work too well on a deer past 600 yards because the deer's body won't reflect the laser well.

As discussed later, some laser rangefinders also have the ability to determine and account for targets at different angles (up or downhill).

7 SELECTING THE RIGHT RIFLE, SCOPE, AND AMMUNITION

If you're prone to running out and purchasing the next new piece of gear to make you a better shooter, I suggest that you skip this chapter and come back to it later. I warned you at the beginning of this book to read through the entire book before you rush out to purchase equipment. This is because I think your decision on what to purchase should be informed by what you've learned so far. Also, I don't want you to think that you need to run out and purchase anything if you already have suitable equipment.

There is no perfect rifle or cartridge. The decision on what is "right" for you is largely subjective. It depends on what you will be using it for, what your skill level is, and what you can afford.

For example, if your intended use is hunting, you will likely look for a light rifle to carry that is chambered for a cartridge with enough energy. A light rifle will be easier to carry in the field but it will also kick more - especially with a powerful hunting load. The increased kick is probably a welcome trade-off to having a light rifle to carry especially because you probably won't be shooting it much. If your intended use is target shooting out to 1000 yards, however, a heavier rifle in 6.5 Creedmoor might be best. The heavier rifle will have less felt-recoil and it will be more stable. And, a smaller and more efficient target cartridge like 6.5 Creedmoor will kick less and fly to the target better. The trade off of having a heavy rifle and less bullet energy is not a bad thing when you're only carrying the rifle from your truck to the firing line on the range and you're only shooting at targets that don't require lots of bullet energy.

7.1 Bolt Action Rifles

If you are just starting out, many off-the-shelf bolt action rifles will work for you. Generally, I used to recommend starting with either a Remington 700 SPS Tactical and upgrading the stock or a 700 Police. They are simple, reliable, usually accurate enough, and there's plenty of available upgrade parts. Personally, I still have a Remington 700 Police rifle in .308 Win with the barrel cut down to 18 inches that has served me well for many thousands of rounds over many years. There's something nostalgic about that 700 action and it's been in service for a long time.

I am also really impressed with Tikka T3 rifles. For the money, I don't think you are going to find a more accurate or better quality rifle. I now recommend a Tikka T3 Varmint or CTR in 308 as a starting platform. With the fit, finish, function, and accuracy, I don't think you'll regret starting here. There aren't near as many upgrade parts available but I don't think they are needed.

If you want to upgrade to something nicer, look at some purpose-built offerings like the Ruger Precision Rifle. It may not be more accurate than the Tikka T3s, but it may have the chassis system and features you desire. Ruger really jumped head-first into the precision rifle market with this rifle and I've heard and seen nothing but great things. If money is no object, purchase an Accuracy International, a Nesika, or my personal favorite factory-built rifle, a Sako TRG.

Although a Remington 700 is a fine starting point, in order to get them to shoot truly accurately, a lot of work must be done. There has been an entire sub-industry built on accurizing Remington 700s so that they'll shoot really well.   For example, many custom precision rifle makers use 700 actions, but a lot of the dimensions on the rifle are re-cut.   This is called "blue-printing" an action and it involves getting the angles and surfaces the way they should be in the first place. You can shop around to see the many great shops out there or I can just let you in on the guy I use - Zach Benge from Benge Machine Works.   He's been a well-kept secret (until now), he does great work and he's a great guy.

7.1.1 Trigger

If you are looking to upgrade your current entry-level rifle, start with a nicer trigger. If you already have an entry-level "tactical" model rifle, chances are that the barrel should be good enough to shoot close to a 1 inch group at 100 yards with the right ammunition. A better trigger will give you the best improvement for your money.

Unless you are adjusting a trigger that the manufacturer specifically intends to be adjustable by the end-user, I do not recommend adjusting your trigger without proper training. For safety and performance concerns, it is usually best to just upgrade triggers that aren't supposed to be adjusted (even though they technically can be).

As I mentioned above, I'm a big fan of two-stage triggers. If I have a choice, I'll install a two-stage trigger on my rifle over a single-stage trigger. My favorite Remington 700 style two-stage trigger is made by X-treme Triggers.

Your trigger should always be crisp and repeatable - not necessarily light.

7.1.2 Stock

The next upgrade you should consider is a rifle stock. A decent barrel and a good trigger will perform up to their potential in a proper stock. If you purchase a purpose built rifle like the Tikka T3 CTR or the Ruger Precision Rifle, you'll already have a great stock. Most bolt action rifles that you can find at your local sporting goods store, however, do not have stocks suitable for precision work.

There are many options for upgrading your stock. I like to break down the stock into two main categories - those that require custom molding of the action into the stock (bedding) and those that don't. Especially if you are just starting out, I recommend upgrading to a stock that doesn't require bedding. You can get standard-looking stocks that have "bedding blocks" embedded in them. These bedding blocks are usually large pieces of aluminum in the stock that provide a solid and consistent mating surface for the action of the rifle. My personal favorite stock of this style is the H-S Precision stock with a full-length aluminum bedding block. There are plenty of people selling these online because they don't know how great their stock is and they wanted to "upgrade" to something else. If you use a H-S Precision stock and you want detachable magazines, you'll need to upgrade that with an additional part.

Magpul has really impressed me with their new Remington 700 stock. It seems to provide all the features a shooter like me would desire (standard stock profile, detachable and affordable magazines, aluminum bedding block, adjustable cheekpiece, and it's relatively cheap). However, as of this book's publishing, I haven't had the chance to test one out.

Another option for a stock that doesn't require bedding is the relatively new chassis systems. These chassis are generally all one solid piece of machined aluminum. They provide the same mounting surface for your rifle's action but they also provide a homogenous platform (no mating of aluminum bedding block to the stock's material) and they often provide "tactical" features like rail sections, the ability to accept detachable magazines, and pistol grips.

The market is flooded with aftermarket aluminum chassis that will help the performance of a poorly stocked rifle. Be careful when choosing to go with a chassis, however, and be sure that you want a pistol-grip style platform. The cost of the chassis can be quite high.

You can look for a used stock that will fit your action to save some money and still have a quality platform.

7.1.3 Barrel

Only upgrade your barrel if you know that your current barrel doesn't shoot well or you are sure it's getting to the end of its life cycle. I often hear of folks buying a rifle and having it immediately re-barreled. Don't do this. Always try the factory barrel first - you might be surprised at how well it shoots. I'll admit that I've replaced a perfectly good barrel and regretted it later.

A barrel has a limited life. For 308 Win., you can get well over 5,000 rounds out of a barrel and still have good results. With 300 Win. Mag., however, don't plan on getting over 1,000 rounds out of a barrel before it needs replacing. If you're new to this, consider practicing and learning on your "good enough" barrel and upgrade to the premium barrel when you're good enough to make the most of its limited life-span.

7.2 Semi-auto Rifles

A good semi-auto rifle is all about the barrel and the trigger. You can take an entry-level AR-15, put on a good barrel and install a nice trigger and have a tack-driving accurate system. This is one of the appeals to semi-auto platforms - they may seem more complicated but there's less professional gunsmithing work required to get them to shoot. I'll replace my own AR-15 barrel myself but I'll leave it to a professional to change my bolt-action barrel.

7.2.1 Trigger

If you are looking for a solid precision rifle trigger for an AR-15, I suggest you try the Geissele (pronounced 'guys'-'lee') SSA-E trigger. It is my favorite trigger for precision AR-15 rifles. It isn't the lightest, but it is crisp and consistent.

7.2.2 Stock/Exterior

There's a lot you can change on the exterior of an AR-platform rifle. Two upgrades I recommend which will make a difference in your accuracy are a free-floated fore-end and a suitable butt-stock.

Free-float Fore-end

If your rifle doesn't already have one, you should upgrade to a free-floated fore-end so that your barrel can be free-floated. There are many options for you to choose from. Personally, I really like the low-profile Midwest Industries G3-series hand-guards.

Also, I find a benefit to having a long rail on my precision rifles. With a longer rail, I can place the front support farther forward on the rifle and have a more stable platform.

Buttstock

Collapsible stocks are cool, but you might find that they aren't ideal for precision rifle shooting. Full-length fixed stocks offer more stability and more consistency. My personal favorites are the inexpensive and dead-simple Magpul rifle stock and the fancier and adjustable Luth-AR adjustable stock or the TACMOD stock.

7.2.3 Barrel

A good barrel is everything on a precision AR-15. Any of the higher-end offerings will work fine. Just ensure that you get the appropriate length and twist-rate you need. For example, I like an 18" 1:7 twist barrel for shooting 223 Rem long range which generally requires heavier 75 or 77 grain bullets.

Ensure your gas block is the appropriate size. If you're not careful, the gas-block can be too big and interfere with your fore-end and scope.

Adjustable gas blocks are a nice feature. By adjusting the amount of gas flow, a shooter can minimize the felt recoil of an AR-15 platform. This is because AR-15s typically redirect more gas than is needed to ensure that the firearm will operate in less than ideal conditions. An adjustable gas block can restrict the gas until the rifle barely functions with a particular load of ammunition. Please be careful here - if the firearm will be for official/duty use, this can be a bad thing. I recommend an adjustable gas block only on sporting rifles.

7.3 Scopes

You get what you pay for with scopes (to a point). Moderately priced scopes will be better than cheap scopes, but you may not notice much of a difference between a really high-end scope and your moderately priced one. As mentioned earlier, your scope should cost at least as much as your rifle and if you are trying to budget, purchase a cheaper rifle and a nicer scope. The cheaper rifle will probably be enough for you for a while and you can always sell it and upgrade it later. The cheaper scope, however, will end up in the trash later.

My go-to entry level scopes for students are Leupold's Mk4 series of scopes - specifically, their 3.5-10x offering. For higher-end performance scopes, I'm a huge fan of the Vortex Razor HD Gen II scopes. In my opinion, scopes just don't get any better than these.

7.3.1 FFP/SFP

Unless you specifically want a first focal plane scope, a second focal plane scope will usually be just fine. This is especially true while you're starting out.

7.3.2 Reticle

If you can afford it, I highly recommend a reticle with marked measurements. At a minimum, a standard mil-dot reticle is fine (and it's what I have on some rifles). Newer reticles, however, that have markings for holding both elevation and windage are extremely handy and desirable. These newer/style/type of reticles solve the problem of not being able to focus on the reticle while trying to hold for both elevation and windage. See *Section 5.3.1.*

Word of advice: Make sure that the reticle is in the same unit of measurement as your turrets, if possible. You can use a MOA turret scope with a Mil reticle (heck, I do), but it sure is nice to have them match.

7.3.3 Turrets

It will be up to you to determine if you want fine or coarse adjustments on your turrets. On some rifles, I prefer coarse adjustments (1 MOA per click) because they allow me to quickly change my elevation and shoot out to the distance capability of the rifle while staying under one full revolution of the turret.

With a coarse adjustment, you'll never be further than half of the adjustment away from your intended point of impact. For example, with my scope that adjusts 1 MOA per click, I'll never be more than 1/2 MOA away from where I want to be. If I am 3/4 MOA too high, I will come down 1 MOA and I'll end up being 1/4 MOA too low. For a tactical style rifle, this is as precise as I need the adjustment to be.

Some scopes have turrets which lock into place - this can be handy to prevent accidental movement. If you aren't used to unlocking them before adjustment, however, they can be frustrating.

7.4 Ammunition

Quality ammunition is important. Great ammo in an entry-level rifle will perform well. Poor ammo in the best rifle won't. Also, caliber selection is important - 22 LR is unsuitable for 1000 yards and 50 BMG is unsuitable for 25 yards.

7.4.1 Match-grade Ammo

The only difference between match-grade (high quality/precision) ammo and bulk/cheap ammo is the consistency of the components and the care with which they are manufactured.

I often encounter people that think match-grade ammo is inherently more powerful. As discussed earlier, it is more accurate because it is more consistent. In fact, it might have the worst performance specifications on paper, but it performs consistently and therefore accurately.

Match-grade ammo is usually unsuitable for hunting and vice versa. This is because match grade ammo is made for consistency and is intended only to punch holes in paper. Hunting ammo, on the other hand, is designed to transfer as much energy to the target and for its bullet to mostly hold-together upon impact with an animal. Consistent match-grade ammo generally doesn't transfer energy well and energy-transferring hunting ammo isn't generally as consistent. If you want the best of both worlds, go buy some Hornady ammunition. There may be more accurate ammunition (e.g. Federal Gold Medal Match) and there may be better ammunition for hunting (I'm partial to Barnes bullets), but I've recommended and used Hornady ammunition countless times and I've never been disappointed.

7.4.2 Caliber Selection

Having the appropriate caliber is important, but there is more latitude here than you might think.

For strictly target shooting purposes, 223 Rem and 308 Win can both be great out to 800 yards and maybe even 1000 yards with the right rifle and quality ammo. Heck, I've had hits at 1,200 yards but I wouldn't exactly call them consistent or reliable. If you want more predictable results at 1,000 yards I suggest something such as 300 Win Mag, 6.5 Creedmoor, or 260 Rem. If you want to reach-out past 1,200 yards, pick up a 338 Lapua Mag or one of its relatives (338 Norma Mag).

Be careful about over estimating your access to long-range targets. If you are just starting out, I highly suggest you get a 308 Win and learn how to shoot well before you step up to something else. The

308 Win will force you to learn how to make wind calls. It is also abundant in supply, has a long barrel life, and is fairly mild on recoil. If you rush out and get a 338 Lapua Mag, you'll be spending a significant amount of money every time you pull the trigger, you'll beat yourself up with the recoil, and you won't make any friends at the range due to the blast and target damage.

Don't fall for the trap of chasing the latest new cartridge fad. Start simple and master that first. Whatever you currently have will likely be good enough to learn on.

You can scour the Internet for ballistic charts to find the "best performing" cartridge but for now you should find a good/suitable cartridge that you can find and afford in enough quantity to practice. I'm currently converting a rifle to 260 Rem but I'm thankful for the years of practice I had with it as a 308 Win first. The ammo was cheap and available and there's a ton of data and information for it.

Fundamentals

Up until this point in this book, we've covered what the gear is and how it works. I may have covered a few pointers here and there when I explained my preferences but we haven't really covered how to shoot long range. You might know that you want a scope that adjusts in 1/4 MOA per click, but you might not be quite sure what an MOA is or when or how much you need to adjust your scope. You know that some bullet shapes are more efficient than others but you might not know how that affects a bullet's trajectory to a target.

This section will cover what you'd expect to learn in the classroom portion of a long range precision shooting school. This is the chalkboard stuff.

I expect you to come back and reference this section of the book more than the other two sections.

In *Chapter 8,* we're going to cover things like the fundamentals of marksmanship including how to aim, how and why to call your shots, and proper trigger control.

In *Chapter 9,* we're going to cover the building blocks of our more advanced discussions - units of measurement like MOAs, mils, and ballistic coefficients. These may sound simple, but this is often a challenge for new shooters. Also, even if you already know what these are, I hope to improve your understanding.

In *Chapter 10,* we're going to dip our toe into the topic of ballistics. At a level appropriate to an introductory book on long range shooting, we will cover what happens in the rifle (internal ballistics), on the way to the target (external ballistics), and at the target (terminal ballistics).

We'll finish this section with *Chapter 11,* as we explore what effect different environmental/external variables have. You'll learn how elevation, temperature, the Coriolis effect, and more affect bullets and how to account for the changes.

8 FUNDAMENTALS OF MARKSMANSHIP

Shooting accurately comes down to having a steady position, proper sight picture, and proper trigger control. Of course, this over simplifies the issue, but I'm trying to make a point.

- Position
- Sight Picture
- Trigger Control

By simply repeating my super special sniper mantra, I've helped many students hit their target. We are often too wrapped up in the minutia of long range shooting that it is easy to forget the fundamentals. I see students get frustrated as they can't hit the target and I walk over and say (ok, sometimes, I just yell), "Focus on the reticle, steady pressure on the trigger." And it's amazing how well the mantra works. The majority of the time, they go from worrying about everything *but* the fundamentals, to focusing only on what they can control,

"Focus on the reticle, steady pressure on the trigger"

namely what they're focusing on and how they're pulling their trigger. Frustrated misses turn into confident hits because they "focus on the reticle" and apply "steady pressure on the trigger."

I do not subscribe to the "eye-dominance" theory. Yes, I believe that shooting with a dominant eye may make it easier to see the target and the sights. However, I do not think it is necessary and too often it is blamed for poor fundamentals. I have witnessed numerous right-handed students shoot better while using their left hand and left eye. This is not because of a dominance issue but rather their need to focus on the fundamentals to make a non-typical arrangement work. If I can see bad habits built into a shooter, I'll make them switch sides so that they can no longer rely on the bad habits and instead focus on the basics. Also, every test I have seen for determining eye dominance says that I am left eye dominant but I shoot right handed and usually with both eyes open.

In this chapter, we're going to discuss how to aim and how to have proper trigger control.

8.1 Aiming with Iron Sights

I'm a big fan of iron sights on a rifle. I'm not sure why - the nostalgia of the old way of doing things, the trust and discipline required to focus on the fundamentals, or the idea that I can still effectively employ the firearm if the scope fails. As you'll read later, I strongly believe that the magnification provided by a scope is not always your friend when it comes to shooting accurately. Of course, you can't hit the target if you can't see it. But, if you can see the target and your eyesight allows, I encourage you to try shooting with iron sights. You will become a better shooter for it.

There are three things which must be aligned with iron sights: the rear sight, the front sight, and the target. Of the three, the front sight is the most important and it is where your eye should be focused.

Fight the temptation to focus on the target. If you focus on the target, you risk having bad sight alignment. When you are properly focusing on the front sight, the rear sight and the target should both be blurry and out of focus.

Both proper sight alignment and sight picture are required to shoot accurately.

8.1.1 Sight Alignment

"Sight alignment" is how the front and the rear sights are lined up with each other. For open sights, the front sight should be centered left and right between the opening in the rear sight and the top of the front sight should be flush with the top of the rear sight. For aperture sights, the tip of the front sight should be centered within the rear aperture. Aperture sights are sometimes called "peep" sights because your eye peeps through a tiny hole in the rear sight.

Some front sights have a circular hood around the front sight or "ears" on either side. These features can serve two different purposes. First, they can help to protect the front sight. Second, especially in the case of a hood on a target-style aperture sight (also called a "globe"), they can help with centering the front sight in the rear aperture. *See Figure 8.1-1* for an example of proper alignment of open and aperture sights.

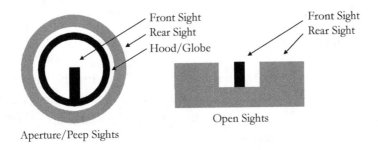

Front Sight
Rear Sight
Hood/Globe

Front Sight
Rear Sight

Open Sights

Aperture/Peep Sights

Figure 8.1-1

8.1.2 Sight Picture

"Sight picture" is the alignment of your front sight with the target. Perfect sight alignment is more important than perfect sight picture. For example, if your sights are perfectly aligned but they are aimed at the edge of the target, you may still hit the target. However, if your front sight is perfectly aligned with the target but it is not properly aligned with the rear sight, it's probable that you'll miss.

In *Figure 8.1-2*, the example with improper sight picture should still hit the edge of the target. The example with improper sight alignment, however, will likely miss the target high and left even though the front sight is on the target.

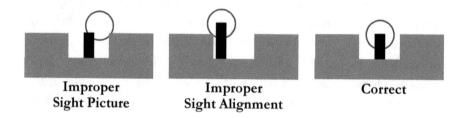

| **Improper Sight Picture** | **Improper Sight Alignment** | **Correct** |

Figure 8.1-2

Center Hold

Generally, the front sight should be centered on the target. This means that if the sights are adjusted properly for the target's distance, the bullet should impact the target right where the tip of the front sight lines up with the target.

When shooting targets with a known shape and at a known distance, however, it is sometimes desirable to have the front sight align with the target somewhere other than the center. This is because it can be difficult to determine the exact center of a target, but less difficult to determine another reference point related to the center of the target. In these cases, shooters will zero their sights so that the bullets will impact in the center of the target even though their front sight is not in the center of the target.

Again, it's important to note that these alternate holds are only recommended when you will be shooting at targets of predictable size. This is because you will be purposefully adjusting the sights so that the bullet impacts a measured amount higher than the sights at a particular distance. If you try to shoot at another size target, the bullets may not impact in the center of the target. This is why I use a center hold on my rifles - my bullets impact where the tip of the front sight lines up on the target for a particular distance. I can shoot at targets of any size and know where the bullets will hit.

6 o'clock Hold

A 6 o'clock hold is where the front sight lines up with the bottom edge of the target. This allows for a more precise placement of the sight instead of trying to determine the middle of a target.

Line of White/Sub-6 Hold

Of all the non-center holds, this one is my favorite. This hold is where the front sight post is just below the target (below the 6 o'clock hold) so that a "line of white" appears between the tip of the front sight post and the bottom edge of the target.

I like this hold because it allows me to better focus on the front sight when I'm shooting. When using the 6 o'clock hold, I often catch myself focusing back and forth between the   front sight and the target to ensure the front sight is exactly on the bottom of the target. With this hold, however, I can quickly see the line of white under a blurry target while I stay focused on my front sight.

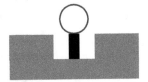

8.2 Aiming with a Scope

Aiming with a scope isn't that much different than aiming with iron sights. Proper sight alignment and sight picture are still required. Often, shooters will shoot better groups with iron sight because they are focusing on the fundamentals. When they are using a scope, it's easy for them to look past the reticle and focus instead on that nice, big, and pretty target. This is one of the reasons I'm fond of saying that magnification is not your friend.

Scopes can also cause shooters to unnecessarily strain their eyes. Although you may not be ready to try this yet, I shoot through a scope with both eyes open. This is because it allows me to relax my eyes and in a tactical situation, it lets me better see the world around me.

8.2.1 Sight Alignment

If you don't have proper sight alignment in a scope, you'll see a black fuzzy ring around the edge of your view called "scope shadow." Although scope shadow is often cursed, it is a good thing. Without it, you wouldn't know that you weren't looking directly through the scope.

Fundamentally, set up the scope according to the previous chapter and focus on the reticle and you will have a much easier time hitting the target.

8.2.2 Sight Picture

As with iron sights, I believe that sight alignment is more important than sight picture. I can't prove it with a scope, but I believe it, so I'm going to write it in this book like it's a fact - so maybe you'll believe it too.

Get your head behind a scope that is set up properly for you, ensure that you have good scope alignment, and focus on the reticle and you'll do fine. Focus too much on the target, specifically over-analyzing where the center is, and you won't even notice that you've allowed your sight alignment to slip and you won't get the results you want.

8.2.3 Magnification

Too shaky? Turn that magnification down! Try it sometime and you'll be surprised. As long as there is enough magnification to see the target, you'll probably shoot better on lower magnification. This happens for two reasons: First, by getting the target image smaller, you're less likely to look past your reticle and focus on the big, pretty target. Second, you won't see all of the errors or movement in your scope, so you'll be less likely to overcorrect and yank on the trigger when you think the reticle is finally lined up in the center. As one of my SOTIC instructors said, "Scopes don't make you shoot better, they just magnify your errors."

8.3 Aiming Generally

8.3.1 Focus on What you Can Control

Perhaps this is also a life lesson – focus on what you can control. Whether the front sight with iron sights or the reticle in a scope, fight the temptation to focus on the target.

It's a known trick amongst firearm instructors (especially with iron sights on handguns) to turn the target around so that you can't see the target image and instead only see a blank sheet of paper when the shooter is having trouble putting up a good group. After doing this, a surprising number of students shoot better groups without something to aim at. This is because they no longer have a pretty target to look at and instead can focus on their front sight like they are supposed to. I learned this lesson when it was used on me while visiting the Army Marksmanship Unit (AMU) when trying out some of the Olympic-style air pistols.

8.3.2 *Aim Small / Miss Small*

Wait a minute, didn't I just tell you to not focus too much on the target and now I'm telling you to "aim small?" Yes, that's true, but they're different things entirely. To me, the theory of aim small / miss small is a product of the target you define.

For example, when hunting, if you aim at the whole deer and you miss (even by just an inch), then you just missed the whole deer. Instead, if you "aim small" and choose only the center of the "kill-zone" and miss by an inch, you'll still be in the kill-zone. It is all about defining what your target is – the whole deer vs the center of the kill-zone. Once you have defined your target, all of my prior advice still applies.

I remember an old television episode of Kung Fu where the students were learning to shoot archery. The master walked behind each student and one by one they shot an arrow at a stuffed bird for a target. Prior to each shot, the master would ask the student to describe the bird and each student, before shooting their arrow and missing the target, would describe the color and size of the bird. By the time the master made it to the character played by David Carradine, the master asked the younger character the same question. The student responded, "I can not describe the bird, Master, for I can only see its eye." Of course, the arrow is released and it goes through the stuffed bird's eye.

Although this is a great example of aim small / miss small, I would change it slightly if I were teaching sniper students. I would rather ask you the color of the bird's eye and have you respond, "I do not know, for I can only see my reticle." [cue Kung Fu music]

8.3.3 *Calling Your Shots*

This is one of the few sections that I considered making its own chapter because of its importance. LEARN TO CALL YOUR SHOTS. It isn't impressive for you to hit a target and not know why. On the other hand, I'm happy to hear a student miss a target and know exactly why they missed. If you don't know what you are doing right, you can't repeat it.   If you know what you are doing wrong, you can fix it.

Calling your shots involves determining exactly where you were aiming right as the gun went off.   Once you are able to do this, your shooting will automatically improve.   First, it will keep you from stopping and peeking where you hit or missed – you'll already know where the bullet impacted because you know where you were aiming. Second, it will allow you to communicate better with a spotter because you can tell the spotter to ignore that shot to the left – it wasn't the wind, it was you.   Third, it will make you more aware of your affect on the rifle, and your trigger control.   You can't fix what you aren't aware of.

Either out-loud (if you are shooting with a spotter), or to yourself, you should be calling every shot by saying whether the shot was where you intended it to be or whether you pulled the shot one way or another.   I prefer to say "center" when the shot happened when the reticle was exactly where I wanted it to be.   It is important to note that "center" means you made a good shot, it does not necessarily mean that it was lined up with the center of the target.   For example, your spotter may have you hold on the left edge of the target to compensate for wind.   If your reticle was properly lined up on the left edge of the target as you shot, then you say "center."   In effect, the spotter has defined your new target as the left edge.

If your shot was not perfect, you should call where your reticle was.   You can do this with a clock-direction and distance or by just using the general direction (high, low, left, or right).   For example, I could say, "7 o'clock 5 inches," or I could just say "low."

It is important to call the shot based off of where the reticle was and not where the bullet impacted.   For example, if the shooter was aiming at the center of the target, and they called their shot "center" but the bullet impacted to the right of the target, the spotter knows to adjust the shooter's aim to the left.   If the shooter sees the impact to the right and instead calls, "right," then the spotter doesn't know whether the wind or the shooter is to blame for the miss.

8.4 Trigger Control

One would think that this would be one of the longest sections, but it'll be one of the shortest.   Although trigger control is supremely important, it is easy to describe.   Perfect trigger control is simple, poor trigger control is everything else.

Proper trigger control is making the gun fire without disturbing the alignment of the sights. That's it.

I explain how I do this by making an analogy to drawing a line in the sand with your finger. A proper trigger pull is a process and not a specific thing. (Note: Some people prefer the term "trigger press" as proper trigger control involves steady building pressure on the trigger.) As you imagine drawing a line in the sand with your finger, continuously add steady pressure to the trigger.   As you continue to add pressure (or draw the line), the trigger fires the gun and you continue drawing the line and holding pressure as follow through.

8.4.1 Follow Through

Proper follow through is important; maintain pressure on the trigger for a brief moment after the rifle has fired.   Some believe that without it, you'd somehow disturb the rifle ever so slightly, changing the bullet's path as it went down the barrel. I do not buy into this reasoning.   Notice next time what is happening while you are following through, the rifle is violently kicking back into your shoulder – which is surely more movement than your finger could impart.

Follow through is important to me because it shows that I was adding steady pressure and allowing the gun to fire.   If I see a student's finger jump off the trigger immediately, I assume that they made a choice to take a jab at the trigger with their finger.

Remember it's a process. "Draw a line" with your finger and add steady pressure up to and after firing.   Focus on the reticle, steady pressure on the trigger.

8.4.2 Dry-Fire

Now, how does one have proper trigger control every time? You might not like this answer, but . . . practice. Dry-fire your rifle all the time, especially as a beginner. Dry fire your rifle more than you fire it with ammunition in it.

Dry-firing means pulling the trigger and letting the hammer fall or releasing the firing pin on an empty chamber. No, it's not going to hurt your rifle as long as it is a modern centerfire rifle (made since 1950). If you are one of the guys that believe it does, even though I, and every other professional sniper or shooter I know, has neither seen nor heard it cause a problem, then use snap caps in your rifle to make yourself feel better.

Dry-firing makes you a better shooter – even more so than with live ammunition. This is because when you practice dry firing properly, you'll be focusing on the reticle, pulling the trigger, and watching to see if the reticle moved when the gun "fired." With live ammunition, the recoil hides any deviations of the reticle that you can see while dry-firing. You'll also get better at calling your shots when dry firing.

If you ever doubt how much I like dry firing for practice, just ask my wife about the constant clicking she hears. I'm pretty sure she can tell the difference between certain firearms now just based on the noise they make while being dry-fired.

When you get to the range, dry-fire a few times before you fire your first group. You might just find that your previously normal poor first group had nothing to do with a cold barrel, and instead was more a result of a cold shooter who hadn't warmed up yet.

When dry firing at the range remember the first chapter of this book and the discussion on treating all firearms as if they are loaded. At a range, you should only dry fire while on the firing line, with the rifle pointed down range, and never while the range is "cold" when you aren't supposed to be shooting nor handling your rifle. This is because other shooters won't know that you are only trying to dry fire and if you do accidentally fire a round of ammunition, it will go safely down-range.

8.5 Stable Position

Having a stable position is the third side of the fundamentals of marksmanship triangle. It is important to at least mention here that a stable position is important. See *Chapter 13* for more.

8.5.1 Breathing/Pulse

I honestly believe that far too many new shooters are worried about their breathing and pulse. I'm not sure if this is because there have been too many Discovery Channel specials that focus on breathing and pulse or whether it's because it just sounds cool to imagine a super cool sniper controlling his pulse. I get it, it sounds sexy and it introduces a bit of Zen to shooting. The fact of the matter is, though, you may be worrying about it too much.

Whatever works best for you is what you should do. If I have a choice, I like to shoot after I have exhaled and I'm relaxed for a moment before I take another breath. I have heard just about every theory on how I "should" breathe when shooting, but this works best for me. But remember, consistency is the key to accuracy. If you are breathing and therefore unstable or inconsistent from shot to shot, you're going to have problems.

If breathing can affect your shots, then why did I just write that new shooters are worried about it too much? Simply, because the shooter doesn't always get to choose when it is time to shoot and because there are many other things to worry about first.

In military or hunting applications, the target often decides when it's time to shoot. And, even with tactical style target shooting, there often isn't enough time to get your breathing back to normal after you've just sprinted across a field to the next target.

The keys I suggest are these: don't hold your breath, try to be consistent, and try to relax. The key to controlling your pulse is: don't worry about it. If you are at the point in your shooting ability where you've mastered everything else and are trying to find ways to control your pulse, then you are reading the wrong book.

9 UNITS OF MEASUREMENT

There are many measurements that we must take into consideration when shooting long range: distance to the target, size of the target, elevation compensation, windage compensation, barometric pressure, temperature, and others. You need to get familiar with all of them, as we need to speak the same language.

9.1 Linear Measurements

Linear measurements are generally used to describe the distance to a target. However, they are also sometimes used to describe a target's size for range estimation purposes.

9.1.1 Yards (yds)

A yard is an English/Standard unit of measurement and it equals exactly 3 feet (36 inches).

9.1.2 Meters (m)

A meter is a metric unit of measurement and it is the basic linear unit in the metric system. From this unit of measurement, prefixes are added to describe different lengths. For example, since the metric prefix for 1000 is "Kilo," 1000 meters is 1 Kilometer. Likewise, "Centi" is the metric prefix for 1/100th and therefore 100 Centimeters make up 1 meter.

9.1.3 Converting Between Yards and Meters

Yds x 0.9 = M
M x 1.1 = Yds

There is about a 10% difference in size between yards and meters. To be accurate, 1 meter equals 1.09 yards and 1 yard equals 0.91 meters. This means that there is actually closer to a 9% difference, but for simplicity's sake, I prefer to just use 10% since I can easily calculate 10% of a number by moving the decimal place one position to the left. For example, to find 10% of 450.0, move the decimal point one spot to the left for an answer of 45.0. The ability to calculate percentage in your head is better than relying on a calculator in the field.

If I want to convert meters to yards, I add 10% and if I want to convert yards to meters, I subtract 10%. For example,

When converting between yards and meters, the number for meters will always be smaller than the number for yards. Here's a trick for remembering when to add and when to subtract 10% for your conversion estimation.

The letter 'm' for meters is lower in the alphabet than the letter 'y' for yards. Therefore, a change from 'm' to 'y' is going up the alphabet and 10% should be added. Likewise, a change from 'y' to 'm' is going back down the alphabet and 10% should be subtracted.

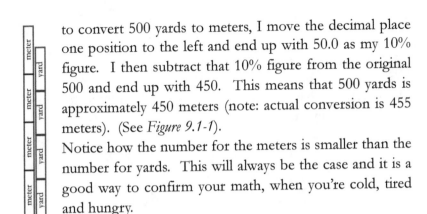

to convert 500 yards to meters, I move the decimal place one position to the left and end up with 50.0 as my 10% figure. I then subtract that 10% figure from the original 500 and end up with 450. This means that 500 yards is approximately 450 meters (note: actual conversion is 455 meters). (See *Figure 9.1-1*).

Notice how the number for the meters is smaller than the number for yards. This will always be the case and it is a good way to confirm your math, when you're cold, tired and hungry.

Figure 9.1-1

SECTION QUIZ
(answers at end of chapter)

1. Which unit of measurement is longer, a yard or a meter?
2. When converting from yards to meters, will the number for meters be larger or smaller than the number for yards?
3. 900 yards equals approximately how many meters?
4. 420 meters equals approximately how many yards?

9.1.4 Linear Conversion Charts

The following charts (*Figures 9.1-2 and 9.1-3*) are used for converting linear measurements.

Conversions from Metric		
Convert From:	**Convert To:**	**Calculate:**
Centimeters	Inches	Centimeters / 2.54
Centimeters	Feet	Centimeters / 30.48
Centimeters	Yards	Centimeters / 91.44
Centimeters	Meters	Centimeters / 100
Meters	Centimeters	Meters x 100
Meters	Inches	Meters x 39.37
Meters	Feet	Meters x 3.28
Meters	Yards	Meters x 1.09

Figure 9.1-2

Conversions from Standard		
Convert From:	Convert To:	Calculate:
Inches	Feet	Inches / 12
Inches	Yards	Inches / 36
Inches	Centimeters	Inches x 2.54
Inches	Meters	Inches x 0.0254
Feet	Inches	Feet x 12
Feet	Yards	Feet /3
Feet	Centimeters	Feet x 30.48
Feet	Meters	Feet x 0.3048
Yards	Inches	Yards x 36
Yards	Feet	Yards x 3
Yards	Centimeters	Yards x 91.44
Yards	Meters	Yards x 0.91

Figure 9.1-3

9.2 Angular Measurements

Angular measurements are used to describe linear size relative to distance. The most common uses are incremental adjustments to the bullet's impact, estimating the distance of a known-size target, holding for windage or elevation, and measuring accuracy by shot-group size.

The most important thing to understand about these measurements is that they are *angular!* For example, when we adjust our scopes, we move the reticle inside the scope which then forces us to move the barrel of the rifle up, down, left, or right in order to get the reticle back on to the target. This difference between where the rifle's barrel was pointed prior to an adjustment in windage or elevation and where the barrel is pointed after the adjustment is a change in angle. This same angular adjustment translates into smaller changes in the bullet's impact at closer distances and larger changes at further distances.

To help you understand how an angular measurement translates into different sizes at different distances, imagine holding two laser pointers next to each other and pointing them down range. If you spread the two laser pointers apart at a certain angle, the lasers would gradually get further and further apart from each other as they went down range. For a certain angle, however, the rate at which the dots spread apart is consistent. The dots will be twice as far apart at 200 yds - and ten times as far apart at 1000 yds - as they were at 100 yds. See *Figure 9.2-1*.

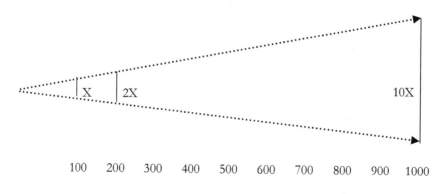

Figure 9.2-1

9.2.1 Minute of Angle (MOA)

In the term Minute of Angle, the word "minute" means 1/60th (for example, there are 60 minutes in 1 hour so 1 minute of time is 1/60th of 1 hour) and the word "angle" refers to one of the 360 degrees in a circle. So, 1 Minute of Angle is 1/60th of a degree. See *Figure 9.2-2.*

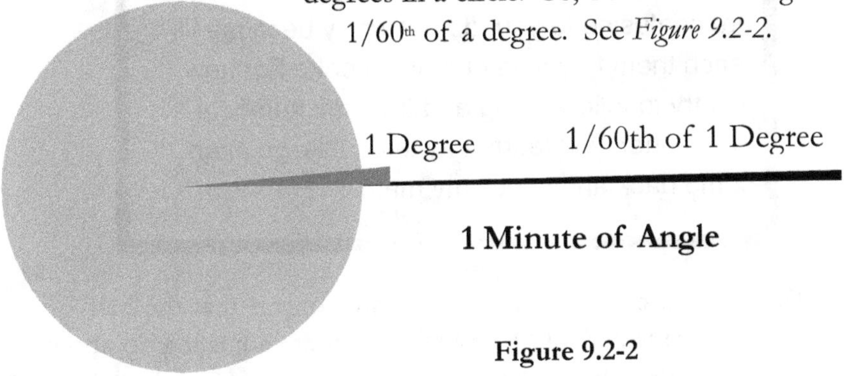

1 Degree   1/60th of 1 Degree

1 Minute of Angle

Figure 9.2-2

If we spread two laser pointers apart 1 MOA (1/60th of a degree), the dots would be about 1 inch apart at 100 yards, about 2 inches apart at 200 yards, about 3 inches apart at the 300 yards and so on. Simply stated, this means that 1 Minute of Angle is about 1 inch per 100 yards. I say "about" 1 inch since 1 MOA is truly 1.047 inches per 100 yards, but using 1 inch per 100 yards is close enough for our purposes.

Now, this is a point of contention among shooters. Many will argue that it is crucial to use 1.047 inches per 100 yards. I agree that it's more accurate, I just don't notice enough of an impact to use the more accurate number. Let me qualify that. At 1000 yards, when I use 1 inch per 100 yards, 1 MOA equals 10 inches. When 1.047 inches

> **ADVANCED NOTE**
> It is impossible to know the linear size on the target of an angular measurement without knowing the distance to the target. For example, the question, "how many inches is 1 MOA?" can not be answered without a corresponding distance. 1 MOA is about 1 inch at 100 yds but it is about 9 inches at 900 yds.

per 100 yards is used, 1 MOA equals 10.47 inches. The difference is less than one half of an inch and barely wider than the width of my bullet.

> NOTE: In order to make a point, I am going to jump ahead a bit with some calculations. If they are confusing to you, do not worry because I'll teach them to you later in this book. For now, just try to follow along and trust my numbers. Later when you learn how to do this, you can come back and check my math.

To be fair, a counter argument to my point is that the half of an inch difference is per MOA and when you are adjusting up about 42 MOA to shoot a .308 at 1000 yards, that half of an inch is realized 42 times over. The extra 0.47 inches per MOA at 1000 yards times 42 MOA equals a 19.74 inch difference. Although this seems like a significant number, with how I'll teach you to shoot a scoped rifle, it is hard to imagine a chance for this number to affect you.

I believe strongly in gathering your own data for your own rifle. This means going out to a range, shooting at 1000 yards and recording how many MOA *you* needed to come up with *your* rifle and *your* scope to hit at 1000 yards. Regardless of how you calculate a MOA per 100 yards (1" or 1.047"), if you need to come up 42 MOA on your scope to hit at 1000 yards, then you come up 42 MOA. If you use someone else's data (such as a store-bought "ballistic card") or you use ballistic software, you are likely to get an estimated elevation adjustment of somewhere between 40 and 44 MOA. Again, regardless of how you calculate a MOA per 100 yards (1" or 1.047"), you are going to simply dial the estimated MOA adjustment into your scope and shoot. Only then, when you are a few inches high or low are you going to need to calculate how many MOA to come up or down.

ADVANCED NOTE
The circumference of a circle is calculated by multiplying the diameter of the circle by π (which is roughly 3.14...) or the circumference can be calculated by multiplying the radius of a circle by π (3.14159...) times 2. Therefore, there are approximately 6.283 radians in a circle. And because there are 1000 Milliradians in every radian, there are approximately 6,283 Milliradians in a circle.

If you tried 40 MOA for your first time shooting at 1000 yards and ended up being 15 inches low, you will need to come up about 1.5 MOA. By using 1 MOA per 100 yards, I can quickly see that 10 (the rough number of inches 1 MOA equals at that distance) goes into 15 (the number of inches I need to correct) 1.5 times and therefore I need to come up 1.5 MOA. However, by using the more accurate 1.047 inches per 100 yards, I would need to find out how many times 10.47 (the precise number of inches 1 MOA equals at that distance) goes into the needed 15 inch adjustment. Since 15 divided by 10.47 equals 1.43 (hardly a calculation I can do in my head), I would need to come up 1.43 MOA.

Because most scopes don't adjust more precisely than 0.25 MOA per click, I'd be forced to choose between 1.25 MOA or 1.5 MOA. I would end up choosing the closer 1.5 MOA adjustment *which is precisely what the rough 1 MOA per 100 yards got me.*

I understand that I hand-picked this example to prove my point. However, the only time I could see the difference affecting your shooting is if you were trying to calculate how to adjust up 420 inches in order to hit a 1000 yard target instead of just adjusting in MOA as I'll teach you later on. Only if you read some data from a pre-filled ballistic card or from some ballistic software which told you to adjust up 420 inches (instead of the much more likely 42 MOA which directly dials into your scope) would you notice a 19" difference at 1000 yds. Bottom line – use 1 inch per MOA. It's way easier and in the field it gets you hits just as precisely.

SECTION QUIZ
(answers at end of chapter)

1. A MOA is how many degrees?
2. Approximately how many inches on the target is 1 MOA at 300 yards?
3. Approximately how many MOA are in 18 inches on a target at 600 yards?

9.2.2 Milliradian (Mil)

Just as the meter is the metric equivalent of the yard for distance, the Milliradian is the metric equivalent of the MOA for angular measurement.

In the term Milliradian, the prefix "Milli-" means 1/1000th and the root "radian" is the metric unit of angular measurement. So, 1 Milliradian is 1/1000th of a radian.

A radian is an angle based on a circle's radius, or half of its diameter.

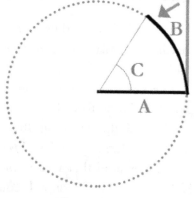

Figure 9.2-3

When the length of a section of a circle equals the radius of that circle, the resulting angle is a radian. In simpler terms, if you placed a string, which is the same length as the radius ("A" in Figure 9.2-3), around the outer edge of the circle ("B"), the angle formed from the center of the circle to each end of the string would be one radian ("C"). Now, if you divided that angle into 1000 equal smaller angles, one of those smaller angles would be one Milliradian.

This is where the simplicity of using Milliradians comes in. If you imagine yourself standing at the center of the circle in *Figure 9.2-3* and you spread two laser pointers 1 Milliradian apart and shine them along the radius to the edge of the circle ("A" distance), then the dots will spread exactly 1/1000th of the length of the radius ("A" distance) apart.

I have heard many people argue over whether 1 Milliradian equals 1 meter at 1000 meters or whether it equals 1 yard at 1000 yards. They are both right! 1 Milliradian equals 1/1000th of any distance. It is 1 inch at 1000 inches and 1 mile at 1000 miles. It doesn't matter what unit of measurement you are using *as long as you keep using that unit of measurement.*

This means that 1 Mil is *exactly* 10 centimeters (cm) at 100 meters (m), 20 cm at 200 m, 30 cm at 300 m, and so on. Let's do the math: Because we are dealing with the metric system, we can simply move the decimal place from 100.0 meters to the left 3 places to find 1/1000th. The result is 0.1 meters (0.1000) or 1/10th of a meter. Because there are 100 cm in a meter, 1/10th equals 10 cm.

Most Mil scopes adjust in 0.1 (1/10th) Mil increments.   1/10th of 10 cm is 1 cm therefore a single 0.1 Mil adjustment on a Mil scope will move the bullet impact 1 cm per 100 meters.

SECTION QUIZ
(answers at end of chapter)

1. How big is a Mil at any given distance?
2. How many centimeters on the target is 1 Mil at 300 meters?
3. How many Mils are in 30 cm on a target at 600 meters?

9.2.3 Using MOA and Mils

When learning how to use MOA or Mils, always think in whole increments for a particular distance. What I mean is this, start with the target's distance and ask yourself how big 1 MOA or 0.1 Mil is at that distance. Then, determine how many of those "chunks" you need to adjust.

For example, with MOA, if your target is 600 yards away, you should first calculate that 1 MOA is about 6 inches and then ask yourself how many 6 inch "chunks" you need to adjust your bullet's impact. If you need to move 3 inches at 600 yards, that is ½ of a 6-inch "chunk" so you need to move ½ MOA. Likewise, if you need to move 12 inches at 600 yards, that is two 6-inch "chunks" so you need to move 2 MOA.

With Mils, if your target is 500 meters away, you should first calculate that 0.1 Mil is 5 centimeters (or 1 Mil is 0.5 meters) and then ask yourself how many 5 cm "chunks" you need to adjust the bullet's impact.

9.2.4 Converting Between MOA and Mils

Approximately 3.5 MOA equal one Mil. To be accurate, there are two different precise conversions because there is a difference between a true Milliradian and a NATO Milliradian. The number of true Milliradians in a circle is not an even number (it's actually 6,283.18...) and therefore it is not easily divided into equal parts. Because of this, many militaries have rounded the number up to 6,400. Therefore, there are 6,283 true Milliradians and 6,400 NATO Milliradians in a circle. One true Mil equals 3.438 MOA and one NATO Mil equals 3.375 MOA.

For practical purposes, when converting from Mils to MOA, multiply the Mils by 3.5. To convert from MOA to Mils, divide the MOA by 3.5. As with my use of 1 inch per 100 yds for MOA, I don't

Mils x 3.5 = MOA
MOA/3.5 = Mils

think it's necessary to use the precise conversion from MOA to Mils. First off, when I'm converting between the two, precision is generally not required. For example, when I was first learning to read wind, I would calculate the wind hold in MOA and then convert to Mils so that I could use the reticle in my scope. Generally, a wind call is not precise enough to have the difference between 3.375 or 3.5 matter. Also, using the precise figure for MOA and Mil doesn't make much of a difference.

For an example, with my rounding of 1 inch per 100 yds for MOA and 3.5 MOA to 1 Mil, I calculate that 1 Mil equals about 3.5 inches at 100 yds. Now, if I use the precise numbers of 1.047 inches per 100 yds for MOA and 3.375 MOA to 1 Mil, I calculate that 1 Mil equals precisely 3.53 inches at 100 yds. By rounding, I was able to calculate approximately 3.5 inches in my head quickly instead of a precise 3.53 inches slowly. The difference at 100 yds is only 0.03 inches. Even at 1000 yds, the difference is only 0.3 inches.

SECTION QUIZ
(answers at end of chapter)

1. Approximately how many MOA are in 1 Mil?
2. How many Mils are in 7 MOA?

9.2.5 MOA vs. Mil

The decision to have a scope which adjusts in MOA or Mil is a personal choice.

My simplest advice is to use whatever you are most comfortable with. If you normally think in inches and yards and have experience with MOA then you might want to stick with MOA. If, however, you are comfortable with the metric system or are starting fresh and don't already have MOA experience, you might want to go with Mils.

Mils are not more precise than MOA. Because most Mil scopes adjust in increments of 0.1 Mil, you can actually adjust in smaller increments when using a 1/4 MOA scope. No matter which number you use for mils (rounded, NATO, or true), 0.25 MOA equals 0.07 Mil. This is not a meaningful difference. In fact, I have some rifles with scopes that adjust in 1 MOA per click because I often want faster, instead of finer, adjustments and I want to be able to adjust out to 1000 yards without using more than one complete revolution of my turret.

Regardless of which unit of measurement you choose, I recommend using a scope which uses the same unit for its turrets and reticle. Newer scopes are available in Mil/Mil and MOA/MOA combinations which are much easier to use than a scope which has turret adjustments in MOA and a reticle with marks in Mil.

Something else to consider is what unit your peers will be using. Regardless of my personal preference, I'd rather use whatever my shooting buddies use so that we can speak the same language while at the range.

9.3 Other Measurements

9.3.1 Mass / Weight

The terms mass and weight are often used interchangeably even though they are different things. Simply, mass is an inherent property of an object and the weight is the result of gravity's effect on that mass.

In long range shooting we are concerned about the weight of our bullets and, if you reload your own ammunition, the weight of your powder charge. Both of these things are measured in "grains."

A "grain" is an old-fashioned unit of measurement. A "grain" equals 64.79891 milligrams (mass) or 1/7000th of a pound (weight). This means it takes 7000 grains to equal a pound.

9.3.2 "Speed"

You will encounter three classifications of speed measurements: speed, velocity, and acceleration. Although each of these refer to how fast an object is moving, they are each unique measurements.

Speed

In long range shooting, we are concerned about the speed of our bullets. The faster our bullet gets to the target, the less wind and gravity can change it off of its original path. Also, if we keep the bullet traveling faster than the speed of sound (about 1,100 fps), we won't have to deal with the effects of the transonic zone (discussed in *Chapter 10 - Ballistics*).

The speed of an object is the amount of distance the object will cover in an amount of time. In America, we measure the speed of our bullet in feet per second (fps). This measurement tells us how many feet our bullet will travel in one second.

Velocity

Velocity is speed with direction. Velocity is a "vector," which is a scientific/mathematical term for a value with both magnitude (speed) and direction (towards the target). Although it could be argued that we are concerned with the velocity of our bullets and not just the speed, it is usually important to know only the speed of the bullet regardless of which direction you are shooting.

On the other hand, the velocity of the wind, and possibly of our target, does matter. This is because wind of a certain speed has drastically different effects based on the direction it is blowing. Likewise, a target's speed is only half the story, you need to know which direction it is moving too.

Velocity is described with the object's speed and direction. Typically, we use miles per hour (mph) for the speed of both the wind and targets and it is up to the shooter to determine what they use to describe direction. Personally, I like to use clock positions to describe direction because they are simple. For example, "the wind is blowing 10 mph from 3 o'clock (the right)." I like clock directions because it is easy to remember that 12 o'clock is always the direction you are facing.

Some people like to use degrees to determine direction. Although this may be more precise (it certainly seems like it would be), it can quickly confuse people. For example, if you are facing due East and someone tells you that "the target is moving 3 mph towards 90 degrees," are they trying to say the target is moving to your right (90 degrees from where you are facing) or straight away from you (because you are facing 90 degrees 'East' on a compass)?

Acceleration

Gravity is an acceleration. Acceleration is the measurement of the rate of change of a velocity (speeding up or slowing down). Objects that are falling due to gravity are falling faster and faster the longer they fall until they reach their "terminal velocity." The terminal velocity of an object is the downward speed at which the force of gravity on that object is equal to the wind resistance of the object.

Gravity causes an object to fall at an acceleration of 9.8 meters per second per second (9.8 m/s^2). This means that after the first second of free fall, an object will be falling at a velocity of 9.8 m/s. It will continue at that 9.8 m/s velocity and accelerate an additional 9.8 m/s for every additional second it falls.

Why does this matter? It is helpful for you to understand that your bullet falls faster and faster the longer it takes to get to the target. It is one of the reasons you need to adjust more elevation the further away you shoot.

9.3.3 Energy

In shooting, we are usually concerned with the energy of our bullet. The energy of the bullet matters both for when the bullet strikes the target and also when you fire the rifle. Too much energy and you're not going to enjoy shooting that rifle.

Energy in shooting in the U.S. is usually measured in foot pounds (ft-lbs). A foot pound is the energy transferred by applying one pound of force over a one foot distance. Elsewhere, energy is measured in Joules.

9.3.4 Bullet Efficiency

The efficiency of a bullet to travel through the air is measured by the bullet's ballistic coefficient (BC). At its simplest level, the BC of a bullet is calculated by a mathematical model based off of a bullet's density, which is a ratio of a bullet's mass and its cross-sectional area, and its particular shape. The higher the BC, the less drag on the bullet. The less drag on a bullet, the faster it gets to the target and the less it is affected by wind and gravity.

BC is a relative measurement and can change depending on the bullet's speed and atmospheric conditions. Do not make the mistake of laying all of your bullet selection judgment at the "BC altar." More than just a bullet's BC matters and I, for one, don't necessarily trust all published BCs. Some manufacturers have been know to get creative with their marketing materials.

There are two main drag models for BCs of bullets - G1 and G7. G1 is the older/standard drag model and G7 is gaining popularity as a drag model for bullet BCs. Each of these models compare the bullet being measured to a standard bullet shape.

G1 Drag Model

The standard shape for the G1 drag model is based on a stereotypical bullet shape with a flat base. The criticism of the G1 is that it does not accurately represent modern long range bullets and that it is too speed sensitive.

A good BC based on a G1 drag model is in the 0.5-0.6 range.

G1 Standard Bullet

G7 Drag Model

The standard shape for the G7 drag model is a more modern and aerodynamic profiled bullet with a boat-tail base. Because this more closely matches modern long range bullets, the number for the G7 BC will not be as high as the number for a G1 BC for the same bullet. This is because the efficient bullet is closer in shape to the G7 model than it is to the G1 model.

G7 Standard Bullet

A good BC based on a G7 drag model is in the 0.2-0.3 range.

Section Quiz Answers

Section 9.1.3
1. **Meters.**
2. **Smaller.**
3. **810 meters.** (estimated) / 819 meters (calculated).   10% of 900 is 90. 90 subtracted from 900 is 810.
4. **462 yards.** (estimated) / 457.8 yards (calculated). 10% of 420 is 42. 42 added to 420 is 462.

Section 9.2.1
1. **1/60th of a degree.**
2. **3 inches.** 1 MOA at 100 yds is about 1 inch. 1 inch times 3 is 3 inches.
3. **3 MOA.** 1 MOA at 600 yards is about 6 inches. 18 inches divided by 6 inches is 3.

Section 9.2.2
1. **1/1000th of the distance.**
2. **30 centimeters.** 1 Mil at 100 meters is 10 cm. 10 cm times 3 is 30 cm. Or another way to solve this answer: 1/1000th of 300 meters is 0.3 meters. 0.3 meters is 30 cm.
3. **0.5 Mils.** 1 Mil at 600 meters is 60 cm. 30 cm divided by 60 cm is 0.5.

Section 9.2.4
1. **3.5 MOA.**
2. **2 Mils.** 3.5 MOA equals 1 Mil. 7 MOA divided by 3.5 MOA per Mil is 2.

10 BALLISTICS

Ballistics, for our purposes, refers the science behind (and the study of) a bullet's path from the rifle to the target. Ballistics can be broken down into three categories: internal, external, and terminal.

Again, this is a handbook for beginners so we will explore the main concepts of ballistics. An entire book can be written, and many have been, on this topic alone.

10.1 Internal

Internal ballistics covers what happens inside the gun. Unless you are designing the firearm or the components of the cartridge, the specifics shouldn't matter that much to you. This is not to say that internal ballistics is not an important area, but rather if you can't change the value of the variables, then it doesn't matter precisely what the variables are.

Of course, if you are reloading your own ammunition, you need to be aware of what is going on so that you stay within the pressure limits for your particular cartridge and rifle. Also, it's helpful to have a general understanding of what's going on when you fire your rifle.

10.1.1 Ignition

As the primer is struck, the base of the primer is deformed and smashed against an internal anvil. The chemical composition, usually made from lead styphnate, undergoes a chemical reaction from being smashed and it ignites. Flame from the primer passes through the flash hole (a small hole in the base of the case) and produces enough heat to ignite the gunpowder in the case.

When the powder in a case is ignited, the powder rapidly burns and gives off gas as a result. The rapidly expanding gas quickly builds pressure. It is crucial that the firearm is designed to withstand the intense pressure from the ignition of the gun powder.

The amount of pressure is a function of the type of powder, the amount of powder, the resistance of the bullet in the barrel, and the volume (internal size) of the combustion area.

Types of Powder

The biggest difference between different types of powder is their burn-rate. Handgun/shotgun powders burn quickly and rifle powders burn slowly. Except in rare cases (300 BLK, for example), NEVER put handgun/shotgun powder in a rifle. Handgun/shotgun powder is meant to burn by the time the projectile is about 5 or 6 inches down the barrel. Having all of the energy of a rifle charge expended in the first 6 inches can make for a bad day at the

Powder	Relative Burn Rate (lower=faster)	Density (gr/cc)
Alliant Bullseye	1	9.398
Hodgdon Clays	2	6.840
Hodgdon H110	3	15.256
Ramshot TAC	4	15.198
Hodgdon H4895	5	13.736
IMR 7828	6	13.793
Vhita Vouri N170	7	14.019

Figure 10.1-1

range and a trip to the E.R.

The biggest difference between different types of powder are their burn rates (speed at which they burn) and their density (ratio of weight and size). Ideally, the powder should fill the internal volume of the case, completely burn just as the bullet leaves the barrel, and not cause too much pressure for a particular cartridge. *See Figure 10.1-1* for an example of some powders and their relative burn rates and densities.

Powder Quantity

Too little gunpowder in a cartridge can be just as dangerous as too much. Obviously, too much gunpowder can lead to too much pressure.

Too little gunpowder, however, can still cause a firearm to have a catastrophic malfunction and blow itself to bits. There are two potential causes for this. The first can happen when the primer gives off enough energy to push the bullet out of the case and lodge it into the rifling. This happens if the powder level is so low that it rests below the flash hole in the cartridge case. In effect, the primer blows the flame across the top of, and over, the powder charge. Then, the powder charge ignites (often more rapidly than it should, because more surface area of the powder was exposed to the primer flash) and builds pressure against a stuck bullet. This can cause the rifle to explode like a cute little grenade.

Another way too little powder (and especially no powder) can cause a rifle to explode is by the primer lodging the bullet in the barrel. Then, an unaware shooter extracts the empty case and chambers a live round of ammunition. As you can imagine, when the live round is fired into the lodged bullet, the rifle can explode.

The lesson here is to pay attention to what you are doing when reloading and when shooting. Even factory ammo can have mistakes. If the rifle doesn't feel or sound right after you pull the trigger, then stop what you are doing, remove the bolt and look down the barrel. Alternatively, you can stick a rod down the barrel and ensure it comes through and out into the chamber.

Resistance

The resistance in the system is produced by the inertia of the bullet and its friction in the case mouth and barrel. The heavier the bullet, the more resistance. Also, some bullets fit tighter in barrels than others – a tighter bullet results in more resistance, which makes for higher pressure. For example, Moly-B coated bullets are lubricated so they have less resistance as they travel down the barrel. Therefore, they usually need more gunpowder than their naked copper equivalent because the lower resistance results in lower pressure behind the bullet.

Volume

The volume (internal space, not noise) of the combustion area plays a big role. For example, if you dump the gunpowder out of a cartridge onto the ground, the volume of the combustion area is as big as the atmosphere. If that gunpowder were lit, all you would get is a big and fast flame (no "boom"). The same powder in a smaller area can create more pressure. This can unintentionally occur when a heavier/longer bullet is used. Because the outside dimension of the cartridge shouldn't change much, a longer bullet needs to be seated deeper into the case which decreases the internal volume.

Handgun powder is designed to burn quickly, because of the relatively short distance (resultant volume) from the chamber to the end of the barrel. Shotgun powder burns quickly because once the projectile(s) get moving, there is way too much volume behind the projectiles for gunpowder to continue to build pressure. In other words, once the projectile is halfway down a shotgun barrel, there would need to be lot of powder to create enough gasses to still build pressure and push the projectile(s).

Also, in shotguns, the barrel is usually very thin once you get past the first third of the barrel, in order to allow a proper balance and swing to the gun. The barrels simply aren't strong enough to withstand high pressure down towards the ends.

10.1.2 Projectile Acceleration

As long as the receiver is strong enough, the easiest way to release the pressure is by the bullet being pushed down the barrel and out of the firearm.

Firearm and ammunition engineers carefully design systems that balance the right amount of pressure in total and over time. They are interested not only in the maximum pressure but also how the pressure might spike or change as the bullet travels down the barrel.

In some cases, the powder is still burning as the bullet leaves the barrel and you may see a "flash" of the still-burning powder. In some rifles, this pressure behind the bullet as it travels down the barrel is diverted and used to operate a mechanism in the rifle.

Recoil

The recoil you feel when firing the rifle is from the acceleration of the bullet. To think of it simplistically, imagine the rearward energy pushing on the bolt-face if the bullet had little legs, and it jumped to create enough velocity to leave the barrel at the proper speed. If you can picture the force you'd feel in your shoulder if something were jumping with that much energy, then you can picture the force you feel from the recoil. The energy transferred into the gun and back into your shoulder is the same or more than the amount of energy that is delivered to the target. This is because of one of the fundamental rules of mechanics in physics – energy can not be created or destroyed - it can only be transferred. The energy the bullet has to transfer into the target had to come from somewhere (the rifle and your shoulder) and the bullet loses energy from wind resistance during its flight.

Gunpowder burns and builds pressure. For as hard as the pressure needs to push on the bullet to get it up to speed, the pressure also has an opposite and equal reaction back into your shoulder. This is why bigger bullets generally kick more – it takes more to get them moving and up to speed. If you want less recoil, shoot a lighter bullet, a slower bullet, or get a heavier firearm.

Technically, the recoil you feel is from the momentum of the projectile being launched and not its energy. Momentum is discussed in more detail below in the section on terminal ballistics.

Heavier rifles have less recoil than lighter rifles of the same chambering. This makes them nice to shoot but difficult to carry. Conversely, a lightweight 300 Win Mag might sound like a good idea for hunting, but you'll be miserable at the range.

10.2 External

External ballistics covers what happens to the bullet as it travels between the gun and the target. This area of ballistics is the most important for our purposes. Simply put, precision long-range shooting is all about ensuring that the bullet makes it to the target. After all, once the bullet is at the target, your job is over.

Each of these variables will affect a bullet in flight regardless of the particular environment or weather. The environmental conditions can, however, allow some of these variables to have more or less of an effect by changing the amount of time the bullet is exposed to these variables.

10.2.1 Gravity

The bullet travels from the rifle to the target in a parabolic arc. *See Figure 10.2-1.* It is not a perfect arc, where the highest point is in the center, because the bullet drops more as it travels down range. The bullet drops more between the 900 and 1000 yard mark than it does between the 200 and 300 yard mark for two reasons, the bullet is falling down faster and traveling horizontally slower.

Rifle   Target

Figure 10.2–1

The first reason the bullet drops more as it travels down range is that the bullet is falling faster, because gravity is an accelerative force. This means that the speed at which an object falls due to gravity increases the longer the object falls.

Time	Speed
1 s	9.8 m/s
2 s	19.6 m/s
3 s	29.4 m/s

Figure 10.2–2

Gravity accelerates objects towards the ground at a rate of 9.8 meters per second every second (9.8 m/s^2). This means that an object falls an additional 9.8 meters per second faster every additional second. For example, after one second of free-fall, an object is traveling at a speed of 9.8 m/s. After the next second of free-fall, an object's speed will have increased an additional 9.8 m/s for a total speed of 19.6 m/s. *See Figure 10.2-2.*

An object's falling speed will continue to increase until the force of drag from wind resistance equals the force of gravity. This maximum speed, which varies for different objects, is known as an object's terminal velocity.

The second reason a bullet drops more per 100 yards as it travels downrange is that it takes longer to cover each 100 yards. Not only is the bullet falling faster and further per second, it also takes more seconds for the bullet to cover the distance from 900 to 1000 yards than it does to cover the distance between 100 and 200 yards. This is because the bullet is slowing down due to air resistance.

Therefore, the faster a bullet reaches a target, the less it will fall. This is not because faster bullets aren't somehow affected by gravity, rather, they are just exposed to gravity for a shorter amount of time. As an example, a bullet from my 308 Win. rifle falls only 4 inches as it travels quickly from 100 yards to 200 yards but it falls 67 inches as it travels slower and falls faster between 700 and 800 yards.

Even though the bullet travels in a parabolic arc to the target, it starts falling due to gravity the moment it leaves the barrel of a firearm. The bullet only rises relative to the ground; it is actually falling from its original path. This happens because the barrel of a firearm must be pointed up at an angle in order for the bullet to hit a target on level ground. As an analogy, imagine throwing a football to a friend across your yard. The football must be thrown up at an angle so that it can travel on an arc to your friend. If gravity turned off the moment you released the football, it would travel along that original upward angle. This concept is more confusing without *Figure 10.2-3*.

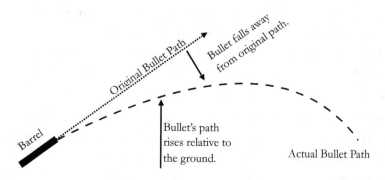

Figure 10.2–3

10.2.2 *Ballistic Line-of-Sight*

If your scope is adjusted for a target's distance, then the reticle is only aiming where the bullet will be when it is at the target. The reticle does not show where the bullet will be before and after the target.

When looking through your scope, the line of sight is the straight line you are looking along from your scope to the target. *See Figure 10.2-4.* When the bullet leaves the barrel, it starts off below the line of sight and "rises" up to meet the line of sight. If the intended target is past the rifle's zero distance, then the bullet passes through the line of sight (A), travels above the line of sight (B), and then drops back down to meet the line of sight at the target (C).

The bullet only meets the line of sight for close targets and crosses through the line of sight and then drops back down to meet the line of sight for far targets. This means that the bullet is at some point below, and often times also above, the line of sight.

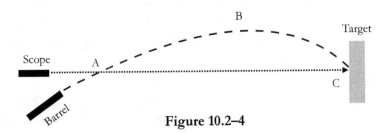

Figure 10.2–4

Ballistic Loophole

This is important because there can be obstacles above or below the line of sight which may deflect the bullet and cause it to miss the intended target. Just because you can see a clear path to the target through your scope, it does not mean that the bullet has a clear path to the target. A term I use to refer to an open path for the bullet's flight is "ballistic loophole."

There have been real-world instances where a sniper has missed a target, and endangered lives, because they did not confirm that their ballistic loophole was clear. An example is that they may have clearly seen the target but they accidentally shot a window ledge a few feet in front of them.

10.2.3 *Calculating Bullet Path*

As I mentioned above, gravity affects a bullet in flight predictably. Once you know what elevation adjustment is need on your scope at a certain distance, you can calculate where the bullet will be on its path at that distance when you are engaging a further target.

With my rifle, I know that a bullet will meet my line of sight (the reticle) at 500 yards when I have adjusted my elevation up 12 MOA from my 100 yard zero. Knowing this, I can determine where the bullet will be on its path when it travels past the 500 yard mark when

I'm shooting at a further target.

For example, if I'm shooting at a target that's 800 yards away, I adjust for the appropriate amount of elevation and then aim at the target. Without moving the rifle, I adjust the scope down to 12 MOA above my 100 yard zero and the reticle will show me exactly where the bullet will be at 500 yards. If the reticle is lined up with a branch at 500 yards, then the bullet will strike that branch on its way to the 800 yard target.

Think about it this way. If you were trying to shoot that branch, you would adjust for 500 yards and line the reticle up with the branch. Your barrel would be angled up from the ground at just the right amount to compensate for gravity and allow the bullet to strike the branch. It so happens that this is the exact angle of the barrel needed to shoot the target at 800 yards.

10.2.4 Uphill/Downhill Effect

When shooting at an angle, either up or down, the bullet doesn't fall as far from the line of sight as it does when shooting across flat ground, which means that the bullet will impact higher when shooting up or down. Therefore, to compensate for shooting up or down, you must treat a target at a certain distance as if it were closer than it really is.

This is discussed more in *Chapter 19*.

10.2.5 Bullet Efficiency

In addition to external environmental factors discussed in *Chapter 11*, features of the bullet can also affect a bullet's path. There are two ways to get a bullet to a particular target faster and therefore reduce the amount of deviation off of its path due to gravity and wind. One is to start with a higher initial velocity and the other is to reduce the drag on a bullet.

Just as a bullet starts to fall once it leaves the barrel, it also starts to slow down because of its aerodynamic drag. The drag on a bullet is directly related to the bullet's efficiency and the density of the air.

Changes in the density of air are discussed in the next chapter.

As explored in greater detail in Chapter 7, a bullet's ability to efficiently move through the air is measured by its Ballistic Coefficient (BC). At its simplest level, the BC of a bullet is calculated by a mathematical model based off of a bullet's density, which is a ratio of a bullet's mass and its cross-sectional area, and it's particular shape. The higher the BC, the less drag on the bullet. The less drag on a bullet, the faster it gets to the target and the less it is affected by wind and gravity.

For example, a Sierra 175-grain HPBT bullet has a listed B.C. of 0.505. If we changed the bullet to a lighter Sierra 168-grain HPBT with a listed B.C. of 0.462, then it will drop 65 inches more at 1,000 yards because it is less efficient and therefore it slows down quicker and takes longer to reach the target. Even if both bullets leave the rifle at 2,600 feet per second, the more efficient bullet will be traveling over 100 feet per second faster at 1,000 yards.

Remember, speed doesn't equal accuracy. A faster bullet will just be exposed to gravity and wind for a shorter amount of time.

10.2.6 Supersonic / Subsonic Flight

Most rifle bullets leave the barrel traveling faster than the speed of sound. This means that they are traveling at a supersonic speed (super meaning "above" and sonic referring to the speed of sound). There are some exceptions to this generalization, of course, but they don't normally belong in a book on long range shooting.

Because the bullet is supersonic, it is making its very own tiny sonic boom as it travels through the air. This is one of the two sounds of a rifle firing. One sound is the expanding gasses out of the barrel and the other is the supersonic crack. If you put a silencer[13] on the end of a rifle and the bullet is supersonic, you'll still hear the supersonic crack and it will be about as loud as an un-silenced 22 LR. To have the firearm truly quiet with a silencer, the

---

[13] Before you feel the urge to rush out and correct me and tell me that it's a "suppressor," I use the term silencer because I am a firearms attorney in my day job and the law (and Hiram Maxim, the inventor of the products), refers to them as silencers.

Yards	Velocity (fps)	Change
0	2606	
100	2428	-178
200	2256	-172
300	2091	-165
400	1934	-157
500	1784	-150
600	1643	-141
700	1511	-132
800	1391	-120
900	1284	-107
1000	1192	-92
1100	1116	-76
1200	1056	-60
1300	1008	-48
1400	968	-40
1500	934	-34
1600	904	-30
1700	876	-28
1800	851	-25
1900	827	-24
2000	806	-21

Figure 10.2–5

bullet also needs to be subsonic so that there's no supersonic crack.

As a bullet travels through the air at supersonic speeds, it is horribly inefficient. The complex pressures and drag exerted on the bullet make it decelerate rapidly. Once the bullet crosses the sound barrier back down into subsonic flight, it coasts through the air much more efficiently. For example, see *Figure 10.2-5* with the velocity calculated for a typical 175 gr Sierra HPBT fired from a 308 Win. from 0 to 2000 yards. When the bullet is supersonic, it loses much more velocity each 100 yards than it does when it is subsonic. In fact, the bullet loses more velocity from 0 to 100 yards (-178 fps) than it does for the last 600 yards from 1400 to 2000 yards (-162 fps).

With that information, it might seem like you could easily shoot 2000 yards accurately with a 308 Win. Unfortunately, this isn't the case.

Trans-sonic Zone

Something unpredictably bad happens when the bullet crosses from supersonic flight to subsonic flight. The transition period is called the trans-sonic zone. As the bullet passes through the trans-sonic zone, it can become unstable. Sometimes, the bullet will keep flying as it should, while other times it can yaw and tumble terribly. This means that although it can be done, it is best to avoid shooting past a bullet's trans-sonic zone when predictable accuracy is required.

This is not to say that it can't be done. In fact, 308 Win can do quite well (even slower flavors of it) at 1000 yards. In SOTIC, for example, we traded turns sitting in the "pits" which is where the targets were when we were shooting on a specific range. After the shooter would shoot, we would pull the targets down to score them and then put them back up.

When the shooter was 800 yards from the target or closer, it was easy to tell when they had finished shooting their allotted rounds because each round sounded like someone taking a bull whip to cardboard as it passed over our heads underneath the targets. Anyone who has had a supersonic bullet fly by them knows that distinct "snap" sound.

When we were past 900 yards, however, we wouldn't even know when they shot. They were too far away for us to hear the bullets pass over our heads. This is because the bullets were subsonic by the time they reached us. I share this as an example to show that subsonic shooting is done – and with favorable results.

However, with the unpredictability that the trans-sonic zone can introduce, you should try to limit the target's distance to within the supersonic range of your particular projectile.

Magnus Effect

This stability change from the trans-sonic portion of the flight is due to something called the Magnus Effect. Simply, there is a "center of pressure" located behind the center of gravity of a bullet when it is traveling at supersonic speeds. As the bullet passes through the trans-sonic zone, the center of pressure shifts to a location forward of the center of gravity of the bullet.

The Magnus effect is a force that is created on a spinning object due to air pressure. With sideways wind, the Magnus effect has a slight upward or downward force depending on the wind's direction. When the center of pressure is in the rear (supersonic), the Magnus effect can actually help stabilize a bullet. When the center of pressure moves forward, however, the Magnus effect can destabilize a bullet.

Ironically, the currently popular very high BC bullets used for long range shooting are affected the most by this effect because their longer and sleeker bullet bodies have more surface area and are easier to destabilize.

10.2.7 Spin Stabilization

A bullet is stabilized in air by being spun – much like a football is stabilized when it is thrown in a spiral. If a bullet is spun too quickly or too slowly, it won't be stable as it travels to the target.

I am going to share a formula (there's more than one) for determining the proper spin rate for a bullet. And then I'm going to tell you not to use it. It's the Miller Twist Rule. This formula was created by Don Miller as an enhancement over the standard Greenhill formula. Don Miller has created and published a simple and surprisingly accurate formula for twist rate in precision shooting.

The Miller Twist Rule formula is:

$$(30*M)/(T^2*D^3*L*(1+L^2)) = S$$

M = bullet mass in grains
T = twist rate in calibers per turn
D = bullet diameter in inches
L = bullet length in calibers per inch
S = stability factor

To determine calibers per turn (T), you take the number of inches required for a full revolution of a bullet and divide it by the nominal bullet diameter. For example, on a .308 barrel with a 1:12 twist, you would divide 12 by .308 to find that there are 38.9 calibers per turn.

To determine calibers per inch (L), you take the length of the bullet in inches divided by the nominal bullet diameter. For example, on a 1.18" long .308 bullet, you divide 1.18" by .308 to find that there are 3.83 calibers per inch.

The stability factor (S) is a number calculated by the formula that doesn't apply to any actual measurement. Instead, it lets you know how stable the entered combination of factors will be. 1.4 is the ideal stability factor.

Now, I'm going to tell you why you shouldn't use this formula. In this day and age, a simple Google search to determine the optimal twist rate for a particular projectile is much easier and more accurate than the formula above. In fact, I've never used the formula myself. This is because there are many additional factors that can affect the perfect twist rate. If you are at the point of determining the ideal twist rate for your projectile, and you are reading this book to learn, then look up what the pros use and you'll be fine.

To ignore what so many have done before us would be foolish. Stand on the shoulders of giants. I've ordered a few barrels and each time, when I call up the barrel company, I have a discussion with them about their recommendations. They will know better what will work for your needs than your calculator will.

So, why did I include the formula? One, because it's nice to know that it exists and to have it as a reference if you ever want to use it. It's also interesting (for me at least) to note that muzzle velocity is not a consideration. And because if I didn't mention it, some reader would cry that I left it out.

10.2.8 Spin Drift

Spin drift is the changing of a bullet's path due to the rotation of the bullet. On a rifle with a right-hand twist barrel (the vast majority of rifles), a bullet can drift up to 4 inches right at 800 yards, and up to 10 inches right at 1000 yards. This is not a variable that changes with the weather, your location, or the direction you are shooting - it happens every time.

I have heard this theory explained by analogizing it to a spinning quarter on a table. This is a bad example and I am only going to explore it here to disprove it. I've been told by many people that a bullet spinning to the right drifts to the right for the same reason that quarter spinning to the right on a table drifts to the right on the table. Without even getting in to the mechanics of what is going on here, picture somebody sitting to your right along the right edge of the table. To them, the quarter is also spinning to the right but it is moving towards them. I'm convinced that a right-spinning quarter travels to the right because you flicked it on it's left side to get it to spin to the right.

In actuality, spin drift is happening because the bullet isn't pointing exactly straight downrange. The rotation of the bullet causes the bullet to "yaw" and the bullet points slightly up and to the right. This equilibrium yaw, or "yaw of repose" as some call it, is very slight. It is enough however to cause a right-spinning bullet to track to the right because its nose is slightly right.

For a 308 Win., I don't start worrying about spin-drift until I get to about 750 yards. Spin-drift can actually start affecting the bullet sooner than that, but in my experience (remember, I'm a tactical shooter and not a bullseye shooter), the wind or something else will cause a bigger problem at 500 yards than spin-drift ever will. I see about a 1 MOA shift right at 1000 yards and about ½ MOA shift right at 750. At 500 yards, the shift is barely over an inch (1/5th of an MOA).

Every bullet behaves differently due to spin-drift depending on the length and the spin rate of the bullet.

Poisson Effect

Some people say that the Poisson effect also plays a role in spin-drift. The Poisson effect has to do with the bullet "rolling" off of an air bubble of higher pressure under the bullet. They may be right.

However, I've already dedicated more words to spin-drift than needed for this book's purpose.

Spin-drift happens, you know the general reason why it happens, now don't forget to account for it when you're shooting.

10.2.9 Coriolis Effect

Contrary to popular belief, the Coriolis effect is not about the target moving with the surface of the Earth as it rotates below a bullet in flight. Although the rotation of the Earth does cause the Coriolis effect and thereby causes the impact of the bullet to change, the deflection of a bullet from its original path is a consequence of inertia and centrifugal forces and not of the target moving out of the way.

The Coriolis effect can be broken down into two components, the horizontal and the vertical effects.

Horizontal Component

Horizontal changes due to Coriolis depend on your location on the Earth and not on the direction you are shooting.   Specifically, your latitude is all that matters for this component.   Bullets will always drift to the right in the Northern hemisphere of the earth and to the left in the Southern hemisphere. The horizontal effect is greater the further you are from the equator and closer you are to the poles.

For example, if you were shooting in Mexico at 20 degrees North latitude (closer to the equator), a 175 gr. 308 Win. bullet will only drift about 1.5 inches to the right at 1,000 yards.   If you were shooting in Alaska at 65 degrees North latitude (closer to the pole), your bullet will drift about 4 inches to the right at 1,000 yards. Remember, these shifts will happen regardless of the direction you are shooting.

Vertical Component / Eotvos Effect

The vertical component to Coriolis isn't really the Coriolis effect at all but rather the Eotvos effect. Unlike the horizontal changes from the Coriolis effect described above, the Eotvos effect is greatest at the equator and it changes depending on which direction you are shooting. Because most people refer to it as the Coriolis effect, for simplicity, I will just call it the vertical component of Coriolis.

Shooting directly North or South results in no vertical change. The closer you shoot to directly East or West, however, the more vertical change you will see.

When shooting East with the rotation of the Earth your bullet will impact high and when shooting West, your bullet will impact low. I've seen this effect described as result of the target to the East moving away and down beyond the curve of the Earth. If the target was moving that far away while the bullet was in the air, wouldn't the bullet strike low because it had so much farther to travel and therefore have more time to fall?

What is really happening has to do with the bullet's angular velocity and centrifugal force. Simply, when a bullet is traveling with the spin of the Earth to the East, its angular velocity and centrifugal force are increased which make it seem like less gravity is pulling down on the bullet. This results in less drop on the way to the target and therefore, a higher impact. The opposite is true when shooting West.

For example, shooting East in Mexico at 20 degrees north latitude will cause the bullet to impact the target about 4 inches high at 1,000 yards. If you were shooting the same direction (East) in Alaska at 65 degrees north latitude, the bullet will only impact about 2 inches high.

10.2.10 Additive Shift

The effects of spin drift and the horizontal components of Coriolis will add to each other in the Northern hemisphere because they will both cause the bullet to shift to the right.   In the Southern hemisphere, however, the effects will counteract each other because spin drift will move the bullet right and Coriolis will move the bullet left.   Likewise, the effects of the uphill/downhill effect and the vertical component of Coriolis can add to, or subtract from, each other.

For example, in the examples above, a bullet will drift 10 inches right because of spin drift and about 4 inches right in Alaska because of the Coriolis effect for a total shift of 14 inches to the right. This is, of course, without even considering the wind, which can be *by far* the biggest horizontal influence on a bullet.

If you are new to this and your eyes are starting to cross, don't worry. Spend time worrying about the fundamentals first. Yes, these effects will make a difference, but the difference is so slight, that improper trigger control or a bad wind call will move the bullet further off the target than the Coriolis effect will. Additionally, this minutia is just one more thing to worry about and keep track of while you are just starting out. Please worry about the basics first.

When I am making an adjustment for these effects, I dial the adjustments into the turrets of my scope because I don't have to worry about these values changing while I am shooting at a particular target.   As I'll discuss with wind in *Chapter 18*, I don't dial wind adjustments into my scope because the wind can quickly change while shooting.

10.3 Terminal

Terminal ballistics covers what happens at the target. And simply, the purpose of hitting a target with a bullet is to transfer energy to the target.

10.3.1 Energy

The energy that a bullet can transfer to a target is calculated by multiplying half of the mass of the projectile by its speed squared. This means that a fast heavy bullet can transfer more energy than a slow light bullet. It also means that speed is more important than mass when calculating energy. This is because the mass is taken at half value in the equation while the velocity is squared.

For example, let's start with a 150 grain (gr.) bullet traveling at 2600 feet per second (fps). This bullet has 2252 ft/lbs of kinetic energy. If we increase the mass by 50% (make it 1.5 times heavier) and keep it at the same speed, then the energy increases to 3378 ft/lbs. If we keep the mass the same and increase the velocity by 50% instead, then the energy increases to 5067 ft/lbs. Increasing the mass gave us 1,126 ft/lbs more energy and increasing the speed gave us 2,815 ft/lbs more energy. As you can see in *Figure 10.3-1*, the increase in velocity had more than twice the effect on energy that the increase in mass had!

	Mass	Velocity	Energy
Standard	150 gr	2600 fps	2252 ft/lbs
150% Mass	225 gr	2600 fps	3378 ft/ lbs
150% Velocity	150 gr	3900 fps	5067 ft/lbs

Figure 10.3-1

For hunters and some tactical applications, having enough energy at the target is a concern. Even if there's enough energy at the muzzle to accomplish the task, once the bullet has traveled a long way, it has lost significant energy because it has slowed down due to drag. If a bullet's energy is important to you, then you need to know how much energy the bullet will have at different distances.

Maximizing the energy at the target is not always ideal. More energy at the target also translates into more energy at your shoulder. I don't care how tough you are, you will be able to shoot more rounds of, and more accurately with, lighter recoiling ammunition. With light enough recoiling ammunition, some shooters are able to stay on target to watch their own impacts. Also, less recoil equals faster follow-up shots, and surely helps reduce flinching.

When target shooting, only a small amount of energy may be

required. For example, the only energy required in target shooting is whatever is enough to score a "hit" on the target. With paper targets, only enough energy to poke a hole in the paper is needed. With steel targets, only enough energy to register a hit, or perhaps knock the steel down, is required.

10.3.2 Momentum

Momentum, as mentioned above, is the true measure of the recoil impulse felt by the shooter. It is also controversial in some circles when discussing whether energy or momentum is more important with respect to stopping power of a particular bullet.

Some formulas for determining knock-down power for hunting focus on momentum over energy. Instead of getting into a debate of the merits of either, just remember this: a heavier and/or faster bullet will hit the target and your shoulder harder.

Momentum is calculated by multiplying the mass of an object by its velocity. Unlike with the calculation for energy, mass and velocity are of equal importance in the equation for momentum. This means that a certain percentage increase or decrease in the mass of a projectile will have the same effect on its momentum as the same percentage increase or decrease in velocity.

11 ENVIRONMENTAL EFFECTS

There are really only two major variables[14] that change a bullet's path on the way to the target, namely gravity and wind. Other variables, such as air pressure, temperature, and humidity, the target's distance, and even the bullet's speed and shape, don't actually change the bullet's path by themselves. Instead, these variables only change how much gravity and wind affect the bullet's path due to changing the bullet's speed.

Don't mistake a bullet's speed with a bullet's accuracy. Just because a bullet gets to the target faster does not mean it's necessarily more accurate - it only means that it's exposed to gravity and wind for less time. For example, I have a .308 Winchester rifle with an 18-inch barrel that is very accurate. Because of the short barrel, however, bullets leave the rifle at a slower speed than they would leave a 24-inch barrel. This means that gravity has a longer time span to affect its bullets and I have to adjust up more for a particular distance target. Even though my bullets drop more, they are still very accurate.

---

[14] Except for spin drift, the Coriolis Effect, and the Eotvos Effect

Gravity is discussed above in Chapter 10, and wind is so important and difficult to master, it gets its own chapter, Chapter 18.

This chapter is a discussion of the effects of environmental variables that can change even when you are only shooting at the same range. It's important to note that any particular value for these variables doesn't change the path. Instead, a change from one value to another is what has an effect. Other effects, like gravity, shooting at angles, and the Coriolis effect will stay the same throughout the year while shooting at the same target from the same position on a range. The effects discussed in this chapter, however, can change from one range trip to the next.

For now, you'll need to rely on ballistic calculators for your data. In the sequel to this book, we'll discuss the figures and formulas in detail.

For each of the examples discussed below, I'll give estimated changes for a 175 grain Sierra HPBT bullet fired from a 308 Win.

11.1 Air Density

Bullets start to slow down the moment they leave the barrel, because of aerodynamic drag. Increased drag, or wind-resistance, means that it will take longer for a bullet to reach a target and therefore it can be affected more by gravity and wind. Air pressure, temperature, and humidity all change the air's density.

11.1.1 Air Pressure

Air pressure can change the air's density. It's important to note that it's not necessarily altitude that causes the change. It is true that higher altitudes generally have less dense air, however, weather conditions can change the air pressure at the same altitude and can cause the same air pressure at different altitudes. Therefore, a measure of the actual air pressure is more important than how high you are up a hill. After all, air pressure is really what changes the air's density.

Station Pressure

"Station pressure" is the actual air pressure at a particular location. Air pressure is measured by the height of a column of mercury in a barometer. Simply put,the mercury is in a glass column which is closed at the top and the open bottom is resting in a pool of mercury. The vacuum from the closed top keeps the mercury from falling down and out of the tube. As more air pressure pushes down on the surface of the pool of mercury, more mercury is pushed up the column. Air pressure readings can be measured in inches of mercury (inHg) or millimeters of mercury (mmHg).

Station pressure is useful when you are trying to determine the air's density for shooting, because it's a true measure of the air pressure at that location.

Barometric Pressure

Barometric pressure is a measurement of the air pressure that has been corrected as if the measurement location were at sea level. Barometric pressure was created to make it easy to compare weather conditions in weather reports from different areas. It effectively negates the effect altitude has on the air's pressure so that you can compare the air pressure in Denver and San Fransisco. To convert from barometric to station pressure, subtract about 1 inch of mercury for every 1,000 feet of elevation.

I don't like using barometric pressure when calculating effects on my bullet because it gives me a normalized pressure instead of the actual pressure on my bullet. In order for barometric pressure to be useful, either I or my ballistic software, must convert it to station pressure. Check your settings in your ballistic calculator, whichever one you decide to use.

Effect on a Bullet

Of the three environmental factors affecting air density, air pressure has the greatest effect. For example, the change from a higher station pressure of 30 inches of mercury to a lower station pressure of 24 inches of mercury will cause our 175 grain 308 Win bullet to impact over 50 inches higher at 1,000 yards because it's getting to the target faster in the thinner (less dense) air.

If we had used barometric pressure in the example above, the air pressure readings may have been the same and we would have needed to determine the altitude of each location in order to convert the barometric pressure to meaningful data.

11.1.2 Temperature

Both the ambient air temperature and the ammunition's temperature can affect a bullet's velocity. The ambient air temperature has an effect on the air's density while the ammunition's temperature has an effect on the burn-rate of the gunpowder.

Ambient Temperature

Ambient air temperature can change the air's density because warmer air is less dense than cooler air. Therefore, higher temperatures result in shorter bullet flight times because of reduced drag.

A change from 110 degrees Fahrenheit to 30 degrees can cause the bullet to drop 35 more inches at 1,000 yards because it travels slower through the denser air.

Ammunition Temperature

Higher temperatures may also create faster bullets because gunpowder in a hotter cartridge generally burns faster and produces higher initial bullet velocities.

Despite how some powders are marketed, all powders are affected by temperature. Some are just affected more than others.

For example, leaving ammunition out in the sun or in a hot chamber can increase the temperature of the cartridge, even if the ambient air temperature hasn't changed.

A discussion on the temperature sensitivities of every gunpowder used in precision rifle loads is not suitable for this book.

11.1.3 Humidity

Despite what you may think, as humidity increases air density decreases. As crazy as it sounds, the more moisture there is in the air, the less dense the air is. Therefore, an increase in humidity will result in a faster bullet and therefore less time for it to drop due to gravity.

Of the environmental factors, a change in humidity has the least effect on air density. For example, a change in humidity from 100 percent to zero percent would cause a bullet to impact only about 3 inches lower at 1,000 yards, so there's really no need to obsess over it.

3 inches may sound like a lot, but unless you can notice the 3 inch shift in your group at 1000 yards, don't worry about it yet. There's plenty of time to sweat the small stuff after you've mastered the fundamentals. And, for your purposes, it may not matter at all. For example, in the military, I'd be more likely to take the shot before someone can even ask what the current humidity is.

I'm a big believer that 1 MOA of accuracy now is better than ¼ MOA accuracy too late. From my background, and in a hunting context, it is often the target that decides when it is time to shoot. You may not have time to calculate everything you'd like before the target is gone. If the error won't bring you outside 1 MOA of error, I suggest that you at least consider ignoring it for that particular shot.

11.1.4 Additive Effect

The effects from temperature and air pressure can partially cancel each other out. At higher altitudes, both the air pressure and the temperature are often lower than at lower altitudes. In the examples above, the lower air pressure causes the bullet to strike about 50 inches high, while the lower temperature causes the bullet to strike about 35 inches low. If both the lower air pressure and the lower temperature happened at the same time, then the net effect to the bullet would only be about 15 inches high (the difference between 50 inches up and 35 inches down).

Application

This is the section where the rubber meets the road (bullet meets the target?). By this point in the book, you have a basic understanding of what the equipment is and how it works. This book has also given you an introductory understanding of the principles of long range shooting. You've got the "what it is" and the "how it works." Now, let's get to the "how to use it."

You've likely tried some variation of many of these topics on your own. I encourage you to start fresh with what you've learned in the book so far. For example, if you've already mounted your scope but you're not 100% sure that you have it set up properly for your rifle, take it off of your rifle and re-mount it the way I'm teaching you here.

If you are not confident in your understanding of the previous sections of this book, this is a good time to go back and reread them to try to understand the concepts better. You'll have a tough time zeroing your rifle and making adjustments if you don't know what the adjustments will do.

12 SCOPE MOUNTING AND SETUP

Despite the title, this chapter is about setting up the entire rifle system - rifle, scope, cheekrest, sling, etc. - to fit you. If the rifle doesn't "fit" you, you are going to have a hard time using it effectively – especially to its full performance capability. I equate this to buying a performance sports car and then attempting to drive it without having the seat, steering wheel, and mirrors adjusted for you. Sure, you might be able to physically drive it, but you won't be able to enjoy the full benefit of the car's abilities. The same is true with your rifle system – you'll be frustrated and have a sore neck when it doesn't work as well as you thought.

When it comes to setting up your rifle system to fit you, the scope's position is the single most important variable. For example, if the trigger is a half inch lower than the ideal position, it isn't going to affect your shooting (or at least not by much). If the scope, however is half an inch lower than it should be, you aren't going to be able to get your head low enough to see through and use it.

There's a good chance that you'll need to adjust the height of your cheekrest. If you have a fixed cheekrest, you'll likely need to add material to raise the height of your head. You can use anything from pieces of dense foam, to pieces of leather, to my infamous approach: a block of wood. I whittled a piece of scrap wood to be the exact right height for my head, because I was tired of using the duct tape and foam method. There are now products on the market that are made just for adjusting the height of the comb (cheekrest) under a stock pack.

If you have an adjustable stock, congratulations. You're in luck. You can avoid the trial and error method of building a proper cheekrest. Be careful, however, to ensure that your adjustable cheek rest is properly tightened - many are known to spontaneously re-adjust in the middle of shooting.

I recommend using a witness mark somewhere on the adjustable mechanism that will let you know when it has accidentally moved and also let you know where it needs to be reset. This is handy not only for after it is accidentally adjusted, but also when you may have to move the adjustable comb while cleaning your rifle.

12.1 Mounting the Base

The base is, well, the base of your optical system. It's the part which mounts to the top of your rifle's receiver and to which the scope rings mount.

12.1.1 Integral Bases

It is possible that your rifle doesn't need a base. If you have a rifle with an integrated rail on the top of the receiver, like AR-platform rifles and some bolt action rifles like the Barrett MRAD, then you can skip this section.

12.1.2 Ring and Base Combos

If your rings and base are combined into one unit, you'll still follow these instructions but you'll skip the section on how to mount the rings to the base because they're already one piece.   These are sometimes found in hunting rifle setups.

Ring and base combos must be screwed into the receiver and mounted as if they were a base. Don't confuse these with rings that are joined by a common section and mounting platform which still must attach to a base.

12.1.3 Bedding Your Base

Bedding the base involves using bedding compound to fill any gaps and to ensure that the contact is uniform. I have never chosen to bed any of my bases because I've never found it to be necessary. You may choose to do so. If you choose to have your base bedded, I suggest that you have an experienced person do it for you (this is a beginner's book, after all).

12.1.3 Mounting Instructions

1. Ensure that the top of the receiver and the bottom of the base are both clean and free of debris.
2. If either the base or the receiver has bare metal, place a light coat of oil on the exposed sections, or the base may rust in place.
3. Align the base on the receiver – ensure you have the proper end forward. On bases with elevation built in, the thinner end is the front.
4. Screw in the screws to the appropriate torque (this can change per manufacturer). If you are just starting out and don't have a torque wrench, I suggest that you use the short-end of an allen wrench for leverage to tighten the screws (long end attached to screw). This way, it is difficult to apply too much torque.
5. Ensure that the base is properly aligned and securely mounted to the receiver. If you're not careful, a base can be misaligned and

you'll think it's on tight because the screws are binding against an edge or a lip.

6. Remove one screw, apply a small drop of blue Loctite. Red Loctite is "permanent" and inappropriate here.

7. Reinsert the screw with the Loctite on it.

8. Repeat steps 6 and 7 until all screws are inserted with Loctite.

12.2 Mounting the Rings

I mount the rings on the scope and the rifle as one project. You can't mount the rings only on your scope and then later attach the scope to your rifle with good results.

Make sure your rings are the proper diameter and height for your rifle and scope. Ideally, you want the lowest rings you can get that both allow you to have a proper sight picture, and that allow the objective lens of the scope to clear the barrel. This is always a trade-off – bigger objective lens scopes allow more light to be gathered but they require that the scope is mounted high enough to provide clearance for the larger objective. A high scope means that you need to raise your cheekrest to see through it properly. Also, the higher everything is, the less stable you will be.

12.2.1 One-piece Rings

It is becoming popular to have rings which are joined by a common section so that they operate as one piece. If this is how your rings are, follow the instructions below but ignore the "spacing" instructions below.

12.2.2 Quick-Detach Rings

As a general rule, please avoid quick-detach rings. I don't believe that quick release rings belong on a precision rifle. I have seen too many quick release rings fail completely or move while on the rifle - both are bad outcomes for something that is more complicated than it needs to be. With standard bolt-on style rings, you can ensure that the torque setting is exactly where you want it to be.

I understand the desire to be able to get the optic off of your rifle quickly if it ever fails and you want to use alternate sights. However, in reality, I have never needed to quickly remove my scope, nor have I ever seen or heard of anybody needing to do so.

By using quick-detach rings, you are introducing more complexity to a system where stability is crucial. After all, if your rings aren't stable, then it doesn't matter how nice your scope or rifle are or how well you can shoot – you still won't hit your target. In addition, quick-detach rings can sometimes be heavier than normal rings because of the extra parts.

I have seen plenty different styles of quick-detach rings fail. I have seen some that utilize a dove-tail mount and roll-pin begin to wobble and come loose. I have seen others slide back and forth on a rail even when they are "locked" into position. But, to be fair, I have a mount from Vortex that uses a Bobro quick detach mechanism – I love and highly recommend this mount especially for AR platforms. Also, I have heard of good results from Larue's quick-detach mounts.

Also, if you want backup sights on your rifle, please consider angled offset sights (iron sights or optics). They are much faster than removing your scope, you're more likely to zero and practice with them, and they allow your scope to maintain its position on your rifle.

12.2.3 Vertically Split Rings

Most rings are split in half horizontally, which means there is a clear top and bottom half. Some rings, however, are split vertically into right and left sides. With these rings, you'll have to modify the instructions below slightly but the overall process should be the same.

12.2.4 *Mounting Instructions*

1. Estimate the appropriate distance the rings should be from each other.

2. Attach the bottom half of the rings to the base so that they are only finger-tight. During scope mounting, you may need to readjust the position of the rings on the base. Ideally, you want the rings as far apart from each other as you can get. The rings' position will be limited by the length of the rail and the position of the scope.

    a. There will likely be some "slack" in the movement of the rings in the rail before they are tightened – ensure the rings are pushed all the way forward in their respective slot on the rail before tightening. This is because the rings will have a tendency to slide forward under recoil due to inertia. They'll want to stay in the same spot while the rifle recoils back.

    b. I prefer to have the adjustment mechanism on the opposite side of the rifle as the ejection port. This way, the rings' knobs or nuts don't interfere with my operation of the rifle.

3. Stop here and skip to the scope mounting section. After the scope has been mounted, you can come back and continue with Step 4.

4. While being extra careful not to disturb the alignment of the scope, insert the screws for the top half of the rings until they are finger tight while ensuring that the gap on each side of where the top and bottom halves join is equal.

    a. It is not necessary to be perfectly equal, you are just looking for a fairly consistent gap on each side.

5. Tighten the screws to the appropriate torque (this can change per manufacturer). If you are just starting out and don't have a torque wrench, I suggest that you use the short-end of an allen wrench for leverage to tighten the screws (long end attached to screw). This way, it is difficult to apply too much torque.

6. Confirm that the scope's position has not changed.

7. Remove one screw, apply a small drop of blue Loctite. Red Loctite is "permanent" and inappropriate here.

8. Reinsert the screw with the Loctite on it.
9. Repeat steps 7 and 8 until all screws are inserted with Loctite.

Once my rings are mounted, I like to put a small witness mark on each of the screws so that I can easily see if they have loosened. White nail polish works perfectly for this. I make the tiniest dot I can make that covers both the edge of the screw and the edge of the material next to the screw. By simply looking at my scope, I can see if any of the dots are misaligned.

12.3 Mounting the Scope

While mounting the scope into the rings, you will likely need to re-adjust the position of the rings as you determine the proper position for the scope.

12.3.1 Mounting Instructions

1. Set the scope into the rings and loosely mount the top half of the rings onto the lower half. Ensure that the scope can easily move back and forth in the rings. It is not necessary to attach the top half of the rings but I recommend it because they can act as "seat-belts" which will keep you from knocking what is most likely the most expensive (and most fragile) part of your equipment on the ground.
2. Lay down behind the rifle in the position you will mostly be shooting in and put your head in the most comfortable position. Do not alter the position of your head to see through the scope.
3. Move your cheekrest up or down and the scope forward or back until you have a perfect sight picture through the scope. Perfect sight picture is a completely clear view through the scope. If you see any black fuzzy ring around the edge, then you are not properly aligned – this ring is called "scope shadow." Scope shadow is a good thing, it lets you know when your head is not properly aligned. You can start by checking this on the lowest power setting for your scope (most generous setting) but you

must finish by confirming the scope's position on its highest power setting.

a. If the scope shadow is only on the top or the bottom, then your eye is too high or low. You need to adjust the stock so that your head can rest naturally and see through the scope.

b. If the scope shadow is equal around the edge, then your eye is either too close or too far away from the scope. Move the scope back or forth until the image is perfectly clear.

c. If the scope shadow is only on the left or the right, you won't be able to solve this through scope mounting. Reassess your position and get your head directly behind the scope.

4. Without disturbing the front to back position, level the scope. There are numerous methods to leveling a scope.

a. Use bubble levels – You can use bubble levels to level the rifle via the top of the base and then the scope via the top of the turret. Although quick, this method leaves room for error from both the accuracy of the level to the position of the turret.

b. Use your eye/line-leveling mechanism – There are devices that you can strap onto your rifle which provide lines to either side of the scope to help you match with the reticle. I've never had luck with these. Although I wouldn't trust my eyeball alone to level a scope, I can usually see with my eye when someone's scope is crooked.

c. Use the base of the scope – If your scope has a flat base, there's a neat trick I like to use. You can ensure that the flat bottom of the scope and the flat top of your rail are parallel to each other by inserting something in between the two. You can use a set of feeler gauges, or any flat object if you tilt it so that one side of the material is lined up with both the top and the bottom.

d. Use a plumb bob – You can use a hanging plumb bob as a vertical line to align with the vertical part of the reticle. The problem with this method is that you can end up with a scope that is perfectly level to the ground but not necessarily to the rifle. If the rifle is not perfectly level under the scope, you'll have problems. I often hear this method touted as the most precise because bubble levels can't be trusted. If that is so, then how do they intend to ensure the rifle is level, if not for relying on a bubble level?

e. Whichever method you use, confirm and confirm again.

5. Without moving the scope, go back to Step 4 of the ring mounting section.

12.4 Adjusting the Scope

After the scope is mounted to the rifle and your cheekrest is properly adjusted or built up to support your head, you still need to adjust the scope for your eye. As I mentioned in Chapter 8, this is the most over-looked part of setting up and mounting a scope. This is also usually an "Aha!" moment in most classes I teach.

When adjusting the target focus, or the parallax adjustment, on a scope, you are changing the focal point of the target image within the scope. The purpose of this adjustment is to get the focal point of the target image on the same plane as the reticle – which is where your eye should be focused. This is discussed further in Chapter 12.

In order to be able to properly focus on the reticle, and the target image once the target focus is adjusted for each target, the scope first needs to be set up so that your eye can focus on the reticle.

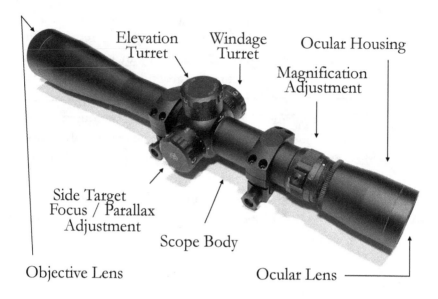

Elevation Turret

Windage Turret

Ocular Housing

Magnification Adjustment

Side Target Focus / Parallax Adjustment

Scope Body

Objective Lens

Ocular Lens

12.4.1 Ocular Focus

The ocular focus allows the scope to be adjusted to your unique vision. Do not expect someone else's scope to work for you any more than you'd expect their eyeglasses to work for you. You know that your ocular focus is not properly set when one (or both) of two things happen while you are shooting: your eye begins to strain and gets easily fatigued and/or you have to choose to focus back and forth between the reticle and the target while you are trying to aim. Once the ocular focus is set properly, your eye will be able to relax and focus naturally on the reticle. Then, when you adjust the target focus for each target, you bring the target image into the perfect spot where your eye is already focused without straining.

On most scopes, the ocular focus is adjusted by turning the rearmost portion of the ocular housing. On some scopes, such as Nightforce, the ocular focus is adjusted by turning the entire housing. Reference your scope's manual to see how to properly make this adjustment on your scope.

To adjust the ocular focus, you should look through the scope at a blank white image. This ensures that you are not mistakenly focusing on the image through the scope.

It is very useful to have a friend help you with this. The friend, or hired person if you don't have friends, can hold a blank sheet of paper about one foot in front of the scope for you. Your job as the shooter is to lay behind the rifle with your eyes closed. Once in position, open your shooting eye for a couple of seconds and then close it again. Take a mental snapshot of what the reticle looked like. Next, have your friend make bold adjustment to the ocular focus (a complete turn in one direction or the other). Then, open your eye again for a couple of seconds and note whether the reticle looked better (clearer) or worse (fuzzier) than the last time you saw it.

Keep repeating this until a "sweet-spot" is found that can be fine tuned. When I'm adjusting for someone else and I don't think that they are giving accurate better/worse directions, I'll sometimes pretend like I made an adjustment without moving the focus at all. It's usually amusing to hear the shooter still claim that the image looks better or worse.

It's important to note that if the shooter keeps their eye open for longer than a couple of seconds, the process won't work. Their eye will naturally change the shape of its lens to bring the reticle into focus. For this exercise, it is important to adjust the ocular focus so that their eye sees a clear reticle without straining. To help prevent your eye from correcting itself, focus only on the "better" or "worse" technique – don't try to make a value judgment on the level of clarity of any particular setting.

Once the ocular focus is set, consider putting a piece of 100 mph tape around the ocular housing to prevent the setting from accidentally changing. If you've never adjusted this before, you'll be amazed at how much easier, and more relaxing, it is to look through your scope.

12.4.1 Target Focus

The target focus, or parallax adjustment, is adjusted for each target.

Don't worry about the markings on the turret – they are often wrong. Instead, look through the scope and turn the knob until the target is clear. If you adjust the ocular focus correctly, this will be an easy adjustment for each target and you won't have to play that game of moving your head around to be sure that there's no parallax.

13 SHOOTING

One might think that the entire book should have been this chapter alone. As I hope you've learned thus far, however, there's a lot to know and do before engaging (shooting at) targets effectively. If you are a beginner and you're reading this book to learn how to shoot long range, then you've likely skipped much of what has been covered so far in this book on your own and jumped right to this task on the range. But I would recommend beginners read this entire book, front to back.

This chapter covers what it takes to engage targets as a baseline. The rest of this book, however, explores how to vary what's covered in this chapter. Targets will be at different distances, you'll be in different shooting positions, the environment will change, and so on. As a baseline, we are going to cover how to shoot your rifle at targets directly in front of you from the prone position. For alternate positions, see *Chapter 16.*

13.1 Shooter Position

I believe that the shooter is the least accurate piece of a quality precision rifle system. The more the shooter introduces their body and muscle control into the system, the less accurate they can be. Remember, a rifle bolted into a vise will shoot better than the same rifle in the best shooter's hands.

Also, when muscle control is used, the shooter will become fatigued and may either be unable to stay in the position or they will start shaking in their effort to hold themselves a certain way.

Therefore, I believe that the shooter should be as relaxed as possible behind the rifle - so relaxed that they could take a nap. By being just as relaxed and stable on the first shot as the 100th shot, the shooter will be more consistent. And remember, consistency is the key to accuracy.

13.1.1 Body

With your rifle pointing downrange, either rested on its bipod legs or your shooting bag, lay directly behind and in-line with your rifle.

In SOTIC, we were taught to lay slightly at an angle behind our rifles with our body angled toward our non-shooting hand side. Then, we would raise our shooting-hand side knee up in a frog-leg like position. This position allowed us to slightly raise our stomachs off the ground so that we could breathe easier. For many years I used this position. It may work great for you but I encourage you to try a different technique that I've found works better for me.

My current technique is to lay straight behind the rifle with both legs straight, toes pointed outward, and heels laying relaxed. The frog-leg knee to the side position looks like it would work better (well, it surely looks cooler), but it doesn't allow me to practice what I preach - let your body completely relax.

When demonstrating this position to a new shooter, I have them lay on their stomach with their legs extended with their heels naturally laying inward. I then have them put their elbows out to the side and lay one hand on top of the other so that their forearms make a straight line. I then have them lay their head down on their hands like they were a pillow while facing away from their shooting side.

Shoulder

Once the shooter is in this position, I take the rifle and bring it back into their shoulder. This is an important step - the shooter gets into a neutral position and then the rifle is introduced. This is similar in concept to how I recommend setting up your scope and rifle to fit you. If you must force yourself into an awkward position in order to use the rifle, you won't be nearly as effective, or comfortable, as you can be.

It is often easier to coach a student by watching them instead of their holes in the target. If they have poor trigger control, or if they are not manipulating the rifle properly or in an improper position, I can see it by watching them only. A bad group on the target only tells me that there is a problem, it doesn't tell me what the problem is.

Head

Once the rifle is in the shooter's shoulder, the shooter raises their head and rests the full weight of their head on their cheek on the stock. At this point, I will touch the shooter's neck and shoulders to confirm that they aren't supporting their head with muscle and are, in fact, resting it completely on the rifle's stock.

13.1.2 Natural Point of Aim

When you have the option, having a natural point of aim is important. Sometimes, you'll have no choice but to shoot in an awkward position. But, when you have the choice, choose a natural point of aim.

A natural point of aim is where the rifle points when you relax your body and let it rest naturally. Notice a trend here? Less control by you equals better results. Ironically, the best shooter may be the one that does the least to the rifle.

To find your natural point of aim, close your eyes and let the rifle slightly sway back and forth and settle into a natural position. Open your eyes and look where the rifle is pointing. If it is not pointing at the target, move your entire body so that your natural point of aim is right at the target. By doing this, you'll be ensuring that you aren't forcing yourself onto target and coming off of the target when you relax.

13.1.3 Shooting Hand

The shooter's firing hand is then pulled out from under the stock and will rest upon the grip of the stock. I do not like to "grip" the rifle with my firing hand and instead merely lay the weight of my hand on the stock without wrapping my thumb around the stock. This is where a stock with a "palm-swell" is beneficial. A palm-swell is a part of the grip that bulges out to provide a shelf on which you can rest your hand.

This all goes back to not imparting too much control on the rifle.

If I wrap my thumb around and grip the rifle, I may end up unnecessarily torquing the stock. On bolt-action rifles, keeping your thumb on the same side as your fingers generally puts it in a good position to manipulate the safety. Also, it makes it much faster to grab and manipulate the bolt handle.

If your rifle has a pistol grip which protrudes beneath the action of the rifle (e.g. AR-15-style), you can still implement my theory of not gripping the rifle by keeping your thumb on the same side as your fingers. If available, an ambidextrous safety is handy here so that you can manipulate it with your thumb without reaching back around the grip.

When watching a student shoot, I can diagnose a hard grip by watching their fingernails. If part of the skin under the shooter's nail turns white, especially right before firing, then the shooter is gripping too hard on the rifle.

13.1.4 Support Hand

The shooter's support hand is generally placed under the rear of the buttstock. Ideally, the support hand is also holding a sand-sock. The sand-sock at the rear of the rifle can be manipulated, folded, squeezed, etc. into the proper height for the rifle. The support hand and the sand-sock should be a stable platform for the weight of the shooter's head and the rifle.

In some situations, the shooter's support hand may be on the front of the stock. This position can help hold the rifle on an uneven surface or provide a good pivot point while shooting at moving targets.

13.2 Rifle Position

The rifle will be most stable, and be able to better handle recoil, when it is resting on bags. If you must make the choice between whether the front or the rear of the rifle should get more support, it is better to have the front of the rifle stabilized by something (bag, bipod legs, ledge, etc.) and the rear of the rifle held with your support hand.

The position of the front support has an effect on the rifle's stability and mobility. The further forward the front rest is, the more stable the rifle will be. The closer towards the middle of the rifle the front support is, the easier the rifle is to maneuver.

13.2.1 Cant

If the rifle is leaning and angled to the side, or canted, then the impact of your bullet will be low and towards the direction of the lean. This is because the barrel is not pointing directly at the target in the first place. Instead, the barrel has a slight upward angle to compensate for the bullet's drop due to gravity. As the rifle is canted, the barrel no longer points straight up, it starts to point slightly in the direction of the lean. The rifle needs to be perfectly vertical if you want good results. A cant of as small as 1 degree can change the impact of a typical bullet about 5 inches at 1,000 yards.

As the barrel moves to one side or the other, the barrel also isn't angled as high as it originally was. Think about it this way, if the rifle was rotated all the way to one side or another, the barrel would have no vertical angle - instead, it would be horizontal and be pointing only in the direction the rifle was rotated.

This is important to understand when shooting the rifle on its side. This is an advanced technique that has some practical applications. For example when there is not a tall enough hole to shoot through and see through at the same time. Because this is an advanced technique, however, we will not cover it in this book.

13.3 Rifle Manipulation

It always amazes me when shooters who take shooting other firearms so seriously neglect their manipulation of a precision bolt action rifle. For example, "tactical" shooters usually work hard to keep their carbine or pistol running. It is rare to see one of these shooters shoot until their pistol is empty and then stand there with an empty pistol with the slide locked back. They usually perform a magazine change and then holster a loaded pistol (they might even throw in some extra tactical moves throughout the process). These same shooters, however, more often than not, will sit there on a bolt action precision rifle after shooting a drill with the bolt to the rear and the rifle empty. Something they'd never do with a carbine or a pistol, they almost always do with a bolt action rifle. Instead of keeping the gun up and running, they are either looking through the scope trying to figure out why they missed or high-fiving their buddy because they hit.

So, why do these "tactical" shooters have multiple practiced methods of reloading a pistol and clearing malfunctions but they have never even spent time thinking about either of those activities with a bolt action rifle? I think this is due, in part, to the mystique of long range shooting. To many, shooting a precision bolt action rifle is so different that they don't put it in the same category as other "tactical" shooting disciplines. It also is a result of the relatively low entry threshold to this romanticized style of shooting. Without training, a shooter can purchase an expensive rifle system and shoot decent groups in paper at 100 yards. Just as with pistol training, however, proper manipulation and use requires learning and practice.

My description above may lead you to think that only "tactical" shooters need to know how to properly manipulate their rifles. This isn't true. Confident rifle manipulation and fast follow-up shots are useful when hunting and many shooting competitions now reward speed along with accuracy.

13.3.1 Mounting the Rifle

Long range shooting should be ritualistic. If consistency is the key to accuracy (it is), then you should make it a habit to be consistent in how you shoot.

When the circumstance allows, you should get into the same position and mount the rifle the same way each and every time.

I ritualistically set my pack down first, lay my rifle on my pack, drop into position, open my scope caps, load my rifle (or ensure it is loaded), adjust my magnification and target focus, and then start to determine the necessary adjustments I need to make for windage and elevation.

13.3.2 Loading the Rifle

You should load your rifle without looking at the rifle. You should be looking through the scope at your target or looking for targets. You can also be spending this time looking at the wind to help make your wind call later.

If you have a rifle with an internal magazine, you should be able to grab and load one round at a time with the bolt to the rear. If you need to shoot during loading, you can simply push the bolt forward and shoot.

Your ammunition should be somewhere where you can easily access it without moving your position. I recommend using a shooting bag to support the front of the rifle and keeping your ammunition accessible in the bag from your position. This way, you can just reach forward and grab your ammo.

At any time during your shooting, you can top-off the rifle with a few more rounds the same way you did while loading. When I am training students, especially those who will use the skills professionally, I make them reload their rifles to their full capacity before unloading at the end of a drill.

13.3.3 Running the Bolt

When it's time to cycle the action of your bolt action rifle, you should do it with authority. Just like you wouldn't gently pull the slide of a pistol to the rear and let is slowly close to reload a pistol, don't do it with a bolt action rifle.

A solid and quick movement to run the bolt isn't just about speed - it also helps prevent malfunctions. If the bolt doesn't come all the way to the rear, it may not come back far enough to strip another round from the magazine. Also, if you aren't in the habit of running your bolt, you will catch yourself trying to shoot a rifle that still has the previous empty shell case in the chamber or you'll have a fresh round in the chamber but the bolt handle won't be down. Either way, you may have just missed your opportunity to shoot the target.

13.3.4 Clearing a Malfunction

When you experience a malfunction on a bolt action rifle, such as a failure to eject, extract, or feed, there is an immediate action solution I recommend:

1. Pull the bolt to the rear
2. Remove the source of ammunition
    a. For internal magazines with hinged floorplates, open the floor plate and let the rounds spill out. If you cannot get the rounds out of your gun without cycling the action for each round, upgrade your system to one that can.
    b. For detachable magazines, remove the magazine
3. Run the bolt through its full cycle twice and leave the bolt in the open position
4. Replace the ammunition source
    a. For internal magazines with hinged floorplates, pinch the spring at the front while closing the floor plate to help align the follower and keep it from binding, then lay a round on top of the follower
    b. For detachable magazines, insert a fresh magazine
5. Chamber a round by closing the bolt

This method tends to clear most malfunctions with bolt action rifles. If this doesn't solve the problem, then your problem deserves more attention. At this point, stop and diagnose the issue.

13.4 Scope Manipulation

The scope should be adjusted while looking through the scope. There are only four adjustments that you should be making on your scope after it is set up.

13.4.1 Magnification

You should store and carry your rifle on the lowest magnification setting. This way, if a close target presents itself while you are walking, you can pick up the rifle and engage the target easily because of the low magnification setting. If the target is far away, and thereby requires more magnification, you generally have enough time to turn the magnification up. Also, it is often easier for new shooters to find their target on low magnification and then turn they power up only as needed.

When you are done shooting, and before getting off the rifle, always turn the power setting back down and close your scope's caps. This should be a habit.

13.4.2 Target Focus / Parallax

Once I've found my target, I adjust the target focus while looking at the target. I do not think it is necessary to move my head back and forth to ensure the absence of parallax. Instead, because I know that I set my scope up properly, I just adjust the target focus until the target image is crisp along with the reticle.

Do not look at the target focus knob for this. It is irrelevant what the markings on the knob say. I do, however, like to remember which direction to turn the knob for closer or further targets so I can get to the right focus adjustment. On many scopes, you roll the knob away for closer target and roll the knob back towards you for further targets. This is a trick I use to remember the correct direction: If a target is too far, I roll the knob back to bring it closer and if it is too close, I roll the knob out to get it further away. Of course, this isn't really what is happening, it is just a mnemonic device.

Every time you change target distance, you should reconfirm your target's focus.

13.4.3 Elevation Turret

You should be able to adjust your elevation turret without looking at it. If your target moves while you are adjusting your scope, I'm sure you'd like to know where it went.

If you do need to look at the turret, however, you should be able to quickly glance up without moving your head.

Always ensure your turret is on the proper zero before you start shooting. If your turret is one revolution off, the "0" may still be line up with the hash-mark even though you are already one revolution too high. If this happens, you may be sending your bullet way over the target. This isn't safe.

As soon as you are done engaging your target, and you don't have an emergency to engage another target, you should be dialing your turret back to zero. This is a good habit and it should also be confirmed before you get up off of your rifle.

13.4.4 Windage Turret

Unless I am adjusting for spin drift or Coriolis (and even then, it's rare), I don't generally touch my windage turret after my rifle is zeroed.

14 SPOTTING

Spotting is more difficult than shooting. This is why the senior member on a sniper team is usually the spotter. For example, when I became sniper team leader, I could spot for my shooter as well as focus on running the team (big picture) while he could focus on running the gun. The fact that the more experienced sniper isn't on the rifle is a surprise to most people.

The less experienced sniper is usually the one actually shooting because all that is needed is to employ the proper fundamentals of shooting. It should be completely irrelevant to the shooter how far away the target is or even how fast the wind is blowing. The shooter's job is to make the adjustments the spotter tells him and to make a good shot. The bullet leaves the gun on a certain path and it flies until it hits something - it doesn't know how far it is being shot. For example, the shooter doesn't shoot a 100 yard target any differently than a 1000 yard target. Each time, the shooter is able to focus on sight picture/sight alignment, having a stable platform, and applying proper trigger control.

When starting out, it is very likely that you'll be spotting for yourself or that your spotter will have the same experience and knowledge as you do. And even as you gain experience, there are many times where you'll be shooting by yourself. Therefore, even though I'd rather you focus on becoming the best shooter you can be and worry about learning how to spot properly later, you'll need a crash-course in spotting now.

14.1 Making Initial Adjustments

Refer to *Chapters 17, 18,* and *19* for information on how to determine what adjustments are needed for distance, wind, and angle. Don't forget to incorporate what you learned in *Chapter 10* into your calculations!

Determine the amount to adjust for a particular target in a particular situation in an angular measurement (MOA or Mils) and not in "clicks."

Before making an adjustment on a scope, ensure that the scope is at its proper zero, or at least that the actual settings on the scope are known. Double check to confirm.

14.1.1 Be Honest

If your spotter tells you to adjust up 12 MOA and hold 1/2 Mil left, then do exactly that. Even if you are your own spotter and those are the calculations you decided upon - use them! You are never going to get better at shooting or spotting if the adjustments are second guessed. If the shooter decides that 1 Mil left is a better wind call and uses that instead and hits the target, then the spotter will mistakenly think that 1/2 Mil was the right call. Also, if the shooter uses 1 Mil left and misses the target to the left, the spotter will think the 1/2 Mil left was too much wind correction and he will bring the shooter's point of aim further to the right. Then, when the shooter obeys the spotters adjusted wind call, there's a good chance he will miss to the right.

If the shooter isn't honest with the spotter, neither will be successful. This is true even if you are your own spotter - if you don't pick an adjustment and try it, you're never going to learn what the correct adjustment is.

14.2 Determining Bullet Impact

The shot missed. You need to know where the miss was so you can adjust correctly in order to hit the target. The easiest way to know where the bullet missed is to see its impact.

When you are shooting into a dirt backstop, this can be easy to determine. If you see the bullet impact in the dirt, it should kick up some dirt in the air. But be careful when using the cloud of dirt as a reference point for the bullet impact. Often, the bullet impacts well below where you see the dirt kicked up. Make sure you are seeing the bottom point of the dirt cloud where the bullet actually impacted. Also, just because you see dirt kick up doesn't mean you've missed. For example, if you are shooting at steel targets, the bullet splashes off of the steel and sends fragments of the bullet in all directions. These fragments will impact the dirt in a line across the bottom of the target and kick up dirt. To the untrained eye, this line of kicked up dirt can look like a miss even though it is actually the fragments from the "splash" of the hit.

If you have no idea where the bullet missed, and you aren't concerned that it travelled to an unsafe location, then don't be afraid to shoot again to try and see the impact. Also, bold corrections in any direction can sometimes help you to know where it is impacting.

14.2.1 Trace

Targets aren't always in front of backstops that help you identify where a bullet went. So you might have to rely on seeing the bullet during flight. I know that this sounds like something out of the Matrix, but trust me, it's possible. And, when someone sees it for the first time, they get more excited than the person who just made the shot.

As the bullet flies through the air at supersonic speed, there is a small turbulent bubble around the bullet. If you know how to look for it, and the conditions are right, you can see this bubble around the bullet as it flies through the air.   This bubble and its path are called "trace" because it traces the path of the bullet.

You can best see trace through a quality spotting scope.   You don't need high magnification, actually as with many other things it can be more difficult with higher magnification, but you do need quality glass.   My trick to seeing trace involves backing-off the focus of the spotting scope to about 2/3 of the way to the target.[15]   Then, relax your eye and look above the target to where the bullet will be at its highest on its path to the target.

Relaxing your eye is the most difficult part.   This involves physically relaxing your muscles in and around your eye and not flinching from the sound of the rifle.   If you can do this, you might see the small bubble around the bullet as it peaks on its path and drops down into the target.   It takes lots of practice and the right conditions, but just like those 3D pictures that were popular in the '90s, once you learn how to see it the first time, it gets much easier to pick up.

Trace is a wonderful thing because it not only lets you know where the bullet ended up, it also helps you to see how it got there.   In the right conditions, I've seen the trace of a bullet move with the wind one direction and then back the other way.   It is nice to get real feedback of the wind's effect on a bullet.

14.3 Adjusting Bullet Impact

Be careful when adjusting the impact of a bullet based off of the feedback from a previously fired bullet.   If you're not careful, you can have a bad day of "chasing your bullets" all over the target.   The trick is to make sure you know that the previous impact you just witnessed was an accurate representation of the conditions.   For example, if the bullet missed low because the shooter jerked the trigger, it isn't wise to add an elevation adjustment to the scope to bring the impact up. If you do, and the shooter makes a good second shot, the bullet will now be too high.   You can see how this can turn into a vicious cycle.

---

[15] This is similar to the method discussed in *Section 18.1.3*

It is up to the spotter to determine if the bullet's impact can be trusted. If an impact doesn't make sense, don't be afraid to have the shooter do the exact same thing again. If you get the exact same result, then the result can be trusted and you can make an adjustment. For example, imagine a shooter barely misses below the target and I, as the spotter, determine that they need to adjust up 2 MOA. Then I have them shoot again. If the bullet impacts 6 MOA higher on the second shot, I know something is wrong. However, I don't know whether the first or second round was bad feedback. Their first shot could've been too low and the second shot could've been too high because of a shooter or equipment error. If this happens, I'll immediately have the shooter shoot a third time with the same settings as the second shot. If the bullet impacts in the same high location, then I know exactly how much to adjust down. If the bullet impacts somewhere else, however, there's something wrong with the shooter or the rifle system. Stop and diagnose it before you waste ammunition.

14.3.1 Calling Shots

Make the shooter call their shots. After all, you need to know if the shot went left because they pulled it left or because the wind blew it over there. As discussed above, it is up to the spotter to decide whether they believe the shooter. All "good" shots aren't really good. However, if the shooter says "I don't know" or they tell the spotter that the shot was bad, the bullet impact can't be trusted and the spotter should have the shooter shoot again.

14.3.2 Adjust to Center

When making adjustments, always adjust to the center of the target. It is a common mistake to adjust only to the target's edge. For example, imagine that we are shooting at a 18 inch tall target 600 yards away. As the spotter, you should immediately determine that 1 MOA at that distance is a 6 inch chunk and start thinking in those increments. If the shooter's first shot misses 6 inches below the target, it is common to adjust up 1 MOA because that is a 6 inch adjustment at that distance. If you do this, however, you will only be adjusting to the bottom edge of the target. Instead, you need to realize that a miss 6 inches below an 18 inch tall target is actually a miss 15 inches low from the center. This is because it is 9 inches from the center to the bottom edge (half the height) and the additional 6 inches below the target is 15 inches total. Therefore, the proper adjustment is to come up 2.5 MOA because two and a half 6" "chunks" fit into 15 inches.

14.3.3 Be Bold

Another lesson that can be learned from the above example is to not be afraid to make bold adjustments. Don't be afraid of over-correcting, especially while you are learning. If you over correct and miss on the other side of the target, at least you know exactly how much to come back for a hit. Conversely, if you slowly inch your rounds in closer and closer, you'll never learn to have an eye for the correct adjustment and you might waste ammo walking your way in.

14.3.4 Focus on Hits, not Misses

When a shooter misses a target, the most common response I hear from a new spotter is them telling the shooter how far they missed and in which direction they missed. Stop talking about misses! Focusing on your hits is not a "think positive" theory - it's a method to get you on target faster.

If the shooter is told where they missed, one of two things can happen. First, time is wasted because now the shooter and the spotter are going to work together to determine what the appropriate adjustment is. Second, the shooter may inadvertently favor the opposite direction in the hope for a hit. This ruins the integrity of the spotter's calls.

If a shooter misses and it seems as though it was an error on their part, I will refuse to tell them where they missed. After all, that round is down-range and there's nothing they can do to bring it back.

Instead they should focus only on making the next shot a good one. As a note, this is a good life motto: "That round is down range, forget it and make the next one count." By telling them where they missed, they are likely to favor the other direction without telling me.

If the shooter missed because of an adjustment issue (wind, gravity, etc.), then I'll tell them what they need to do to hit the target - not where they missed. From the example above, I'll tell the shooter, "Up 2.5 MOA." I won't get into a discussion about where they missed.

15   ZEROING YOUR RIFLE

Without a proper zero on your rifle and scope, you will not be able to effectively hit targets at longer ranges. A good zero is so important that I start most visits to the range confirming the zero before I start shooting other targets.

A "zero" is a baseline setting of the scope from which adjustments can be made. A scope and rifle are considered to be "zeroed" when the point of aim in the scope equals the point of impact of the bullet at a set distance when the scope turrets are set to zero.   I recommend that you use a 100 yard zero (or meter, depending on which unit of measurement you want to use).   This means that when your scope's turrets are both turned to zero, your bullet will impact exactly where your reticle is aimed at 100 yards.

When zeroing a rifle and scope, especially for the first time, I recommend bore-sighting and shooting at 25 yards to confirm your impacts before shooting at a 100 yard target.   It is not absolutely necessary to follow those steps, however, they may save you time and ammunition because they're the best way of ensuring that your impacts will be on target at 100 yards. I've seen countless shooters trying to zero at 100 yards first and waste time and ammunition while they try to figure out which direction they are missing the 100 yard target.

With quality scopes, there is no change in the scope's zero throughout the magnification range. On cheaper scopes, however, you should zero at the highest power setting.

15.1 Bore-Sighting

Bore-sighting a rifle and scope is the process of adjusting the reticle in the scope to line-up with where the bore (barrel) is pointing. It's an imprecise adjustment which merely gets you close to being zeroed. Even though it is a rough adjustment, you may be surprised by how much you'll need to adjust your turrets to get close to zeroed - especially on a brand new scope. (Note: On some semi-automatic rifles, it is impossible to see down the barrel to bore-sight it. For example, with M1/M14 style rifles, this step must be skipped.)

> To ensure you are looking straight down the barrel, center the circle shape of the end of the barrel viewed through the circle shape of the chamber.

A rifle must be stable to bore-sight properly. Bolt-action rifles are easier to stabilize and bore sight than semi-automatic rifles. On all rifles, the bolt must be removed so that you can see through the barrel. With bolt-actions rifles, the stock of the rifles can be used to rest and stabilize the rifle. With semi-automatic rifles, the action usually must be opened in such a way that the stock can't be used to rest and stabilize the rifle. For AR-style rifles, it's easiest to take the upper receiver completely off of the lower receiver and rest it on a table while bore-sighting.

To bore-sight a rifle to a scope, look down and through the rear of the barrel and out the front of the barrel to a target 100 yards, or less, away. Special care must be taken to ensure that you are looking straight down the barrel and that the target is in the center of the

> **To move the reticle in a certain direction, move the turrets in the opposite direction. For example, to bring the reticle down, rotate the elevation turret in the "up" direction.**

image through the barrel. While not disturbing the rifle's position, raise your head to look through the scope and move the turrets to adjust the reticle so that it lines up with the target.

It is usually necessary to repeat this process a few times because it is easy to accidentally disturb the rifle's position while moving your head from the barrel to the scope and while adjusting the turrets. If you get good at bore-sighting, you can get very close to zeroing a rifle.

15.2 25-yard Confirmation

A 25-yard confirmation is only intended to confirm that your impacts will be on target when you zero your rifle at 100 yards. This is why it is called a "confirmation" and not a "zero."

As discussed in Section 4.2, the variation in the impact of a bullet from its intended location can be measured with an angular measurement like Mils or MOA. At 100 yards, a 12 MOA error to the right will be about 12 inches right from where the rifle was aimed. That error is enough to completely miss a standard 8.5x11" sheet of paper. At 25 yards, however, that same 12 MOA error will only be 3 inches

> **Quick Tip: Adjust the impact of the bullet to be about an inch low at 25 yards. When properly zeroed at 100 yards, most rifles will shoot about 1 inch low at 25 yards.**

from the center of the target. By shooting at 25 yards first, you will be able to adjust the impact of the bullet 12 MOA left before moving to the 100 yard target. This will ensure that your first round will at least be on the sheet of paper at 100 yards. For help making angular adjustments at 25 yards (or meters), *see Figure 15.2-1.*

Although you can shoot a group of rounds to ensure that the impacts on the target are reliable, it's not necessary for this 2 5 - y a r d confirmation. If you shoot one round and feel confident that it was a good shot, feel free to adjust your scope. After all, you'll be shooting groups for precision at 100 yards.

Distance to Target:	Unit of Adjustment:	Adjustment on Target:
25 yards	1 MOA	about 0.25 in
25 yards	1 Mil	0.36 in
25 meters	1 MOA	about 0.27 in
25 meters	1 Mil	2.5 cm

Figure 15.2-1

15.3 100 yard zero

This is the distance I recommend for a true zero on a rifle. If you prefer to use meters instead of yards, you can use a 100 meter zero. If you are zeroing a rifle for hunting, it is common to zero the rifle at a different distance, like 200 yards, so that the bullet will impact within the kill-zone of an animal at any distance from 25 yards to 250 yards. For precision rifles, however, you need a solid baseline 100 yard (or meter) zero from which you can adjust for precise impacts at all distances your rifle is capable of shooting.

For free targets with guides to help you make the appropriate adjustments at different distances, visit this book's website.

Additionally, with a 100 yard (or meter) zero, you'll likely never have to adjust below "zero" on your elevation turret to hit a target. This is because the impact of most bullets rises from 0 to 100 yards (or meters) where the impact meets the line of sight through the scope and then the impacts start to lower after 100 yards (or meters). If the impacts are always lower than or at the aiming point with a 100 yard zero, then the scope never needs to adjust lower than "zero" on the elevation turret.

When zeroing your rifle, only adjust the scope based off of the location of good groups. What I mean is this, if your shot group size is not at most 1 MOA with at least 3 rounds, do not try to adjust for a zero. Without a good group, you do not know which impacts on the target are due to a misaligned reticle and which rounds are due to improper trigger control or bad accuracy. By adjusting off of bad groups, you will "chase the rounds" around the target by adjusting too far one way and then back the other. Save yourself time and ammunition by taking care to shoot a good group before adjusting your scope. With a good group and a quality rifle, scope, and ammunition, you can zero your rifle with just one scope adjustment.

15.4 Slipping Scales

Once you have zeroed your scope by adjusting the reticle so that it matches the point of impact of the bullet at your "zero" distance, the next step is to "slip your scales." Slipping a scope's scales involves adjusting the numbers on the outside of the turrets (the scales) in a way that doesn't allow the turrets to grab the adjustment mechanism inside the scope (the turret slips by).

Upon zeroing your scope, it is very likely that the "0" on the scope's turrets will not line up with the indicator marks on your scope. To "slip the scales," you must loosen the turret from the adjustment mechanism in the scope. Depending on which scope you have, this can be achieved by loosening a set of Allen-type screws, lifting the turret, or other

> **On scopes with adjustment screws, take care to not strip the screws!**

methods. Please refer to your scope's manual to determine the correct method for your scope. Once the turret is disengaged from the internal adjustment mechanism, turn the turret so that the "0" lines up with the indicator mark and reattach the turret to the internal mechanism.

This process is similar to using a wrench on a nut. When the wrench is attached to the nut, a turn of the wrench also turns the nut.

But, when the wrench is disengaged from the nut, it can be turned and repositioned without turning the nut. Once the wrench is in the new position, it can reengage the nut so that subsequent turns of the wrench also turn the nut.

When slipping a turret, be careful to ensure that the turret is still not attached to the internal adjustment mechanism. If you feel or hear the scope "click," stop moving the turret, reattach it to the mechanism, turn back the appropriate amount of "clicks" you accidentally adjusted, re-disengage the turret and try again.

Once this process is complete, you should be able to adjust the scope back to its zero by turning the turrets so that the "0" aligns with the indicator mark.

15.5 Mechanical Zero

Obtaining a mechanical zero is the most overlooked step of zeroing a rifle. In my experience, most shooters don't know their mechanical zero. Knowing your mechanical zero means knowing how far away your actual zero is from the mechanical limits of the scope. This is important information to know in case your turret ever becomes loose and slips itself.

For example, from your zero, for your particular scope and rifle combination, you might be able to come up 30 MOA and down 40 MOA before the scope physically can't adjust further. This means that your mechanical zero would be either 30 MOA down from the top limit of the scope or up 40 MOA from the bottom limit of the scope. This information should be written down and stored with the rifle.

The process of finding your mechanical zero also lets you know the limits of your scope. If the scope settings from the sample above applied to a scope on a 308 Winchester rifle, you wouldn't be able to adjust the scope to shoot past 850 yards. Upon finding out my scope only had 30 MOA of adjustment, I'd swap the scope base for one with elevation built-in.

16 ALTERNATE POSITIONS

The lower you are to the ground (or a stable shooting bench as a platform), the more stable you get. The prone position (laying flat on the ground on your front) is much more stable, and therefore much easier to be accurate, than trying to shoot while standing. Unfortunately, when you're trying to shoot in the real world (as in, not at a perfectly flat and manicured shooting range), you'll find it difficult to always shoot in the prone position due to the obstacles that will block your view to the target.

Although you can lie in the prone (or use a shooting bench) to zero your rifle and gather data, you absolutely must shoot in other positions if you're going to be effective with your rifle when you are not at the range. I don't know of any hunters who have been able to take every shot at an animal while in the prone position. Often, grass, rocks, logs, or minor terrain features make it impossible to lie in the prone position and see the target. Also, it may be difficult for hunters to move from the position they are in when they see the animal to the prone position to shoot without being spotted by the game. Most hunting shots are taken from a knee, from resting on something (sticks, a tree, etc.) or from the standing position.

Likewise, military or police snipers who try to shoot in the prone position often find their view from the prone position is also blocked. Even though these hunters and snipers know that the prone position is an unlikely position while they are using their rifles, it amazes me that they often still practice only the prone (or bench-rest) position while at the range.

Yes, it's important to remove as many variables as possible when gathering data or zeroing your rifle. After all, I want to be sure of what my rifle system can do. However, if I want to know *what I can do with my rifle*, I need to challenge myself and get up off the ground.

There are five major positions I am going to cover, namely: seated, kneeling, kneeling supporting, standing, and standing supported. I'll finish this chapter with my best tip for shooting in an "alternate" position - allow for an "acceptable amount of error."

16.1 Sling Use

In some of these positions, a sling should be used to help stabilize you and your rifle. A rifle sling is an important part of your shooting system. It's not just useful as a method to hold your rifle, it's also a tool to help you stabilize an otherwise unsteady position.

The best and most-stable type of sling is a cuff-style sling. Unfortunately, a cuff-style sling can also be uncomfortable and difficult to put on. This makes cuff-style slings great for shooting competitions but not ideal for hunting or taking a shot under a hurried condition. For this reason, I recommend using a "hasty" sling. No, it isn't as stable as a cuff-style sling, but it's much faster and easier to use. Also, just about any standard rifle sling (perhaps

the one you already have on your rifle) will work for this method.

No matter which style sling you use, the sling should be adjusted so that it is tight while you are in your shooting position. Once you're in position, the sling's tension should keep you from lowering the rifle (the tension around the back of your support arm should be helping to hold up the front end of the stock). Take care to ensure that the sling is properly adjusted for you and your rifle in whichever position you intend to shoot in. For me, my slings need to be a little longer in the prone position than they need to be in the seating or kneeling positions. For competition style shooting, I've placed marks on my sling so that I could adjust it to the proper tension for each position. For all-around use, however, I've found it best to adjust the sling so it is barely too tight in the prone position and use that setting for each position. It's not perfect this way, but it sure is faster.

When using a sling in a shooting position, try to allow the sling to hold the front end of the rifle and only use your support hand as a "support" - try not to grab the rifle with your support hand. As I mention in other places in this book, the less you manipulate the rifle, the more accurate you can be.

When I couldn't find exactly what I wanted in a sling, I developed my own design that blends the best of both worlds. I worked with the Wilderness Tactical Products after I left the military in 2003 to design the sling and I've used it in some of  my YouTube instructional videos. The sling looks like (and can be used like) a standard rifle sling. However, it has some features that allow it to be quickly used like a cuff-style sling. The quick-cuff feature can be adjusted for your arm so that you can quickly put your arm through the cuff and pull it to the pre-determined tightness by simply adding tension to the sling. Also, you can use a quick detach buckle to disconnect the rear portion of the sling if you choose - you'll likely find that having the rear of the sling attached in a cuff-style setup will put unwanted tension on the rear of the rifle. Personally, I also like the quick detach feature in case the rifle is across my back and I need to get it off quickly. The sling is available directly from the manufacturer at www.TheWilderness.com and also through this book's website.

	Pros	Cons
Cuff-Style Sling	• Very Stable	• Slow to use • Uncomfortable • Often can't be used as a regular sling
Hasty Sling	• Quick to use • Can be used as a regular sling	• Less stable
Wilderness Cleckner Cuff Sling	• Can be used as cuff-style or hasty to take advantage of all of the "Pros" above	• None (Can be used as cuff-style or hasty to avoid all of the "Cons" above)

16.1.1 Cuff-Style Sling

A cuff-style sling is the standard military sniper/competition shooter-style sling. This style of sling attaches to the support arm via a "cuff" that wraps tightly around the upper part of the support arm (above the tricep). The cuff must be tight enough that it does not pull down your support arm under tension. From the cuff, the sling wraps around the far side of your support arm's wrist (pinky side), across the back of your support arm's hand, and attaches to the front of the rifle's stock. The sling should pin your support hand against the stock while in use.

The cuff can be uncomfortable when it is adjusted as tight as it should be. Because of this, many shooters using this style of sling will wear a shirt with some padding in the sleeves. In SOTIC, most of us wore sweatshirts, even in hot weather, to provide some padding for the cuff of the sling. The cuff-style sling is extremely stable but it takes some time to get into (and out of). This makes it ideal when you have the time to use it but often, situations for hunters and military/police shooters require use of a rifle, and movement after use of a rifle, faster than a cuff-style sling will allow. I've seen some attempts to minimize the time burden by attaching the cuff to the arm and then allowing the sling to attach via a method that allows quick connection and removal of the sling. This makes it quicker, but I'm too much of a wimp to wear a cuff longer than I need to.

16.1.2 Hasty Sling

A hasty sling is the name used for when you use a standard rifle sling in an expedient manner to stabilize your position. It is not as stable as a cuff-style sling but it is surely quicker to use and it allows you to take advantage of just about any rifle sling as long as it is sturdy enough.

In order to use a hasty sling, you must place your support arm far

enough through the sling so that the sling lines up with the upper part of your arm (above your tricep). Wrap your support arm around the sling and place your hand onto the front of the rifle. Right handed shooters will move their arm in a clockwise motion once around the sling (left-handed shooters will go counter clock-wise). The sling should go from the rifle's buttstock, around behind the support arm high above the

tricep, then across and through the "V" made by the support arm's bent elbow, and then wrap around the far side of the support arm's wrist and across the hand to the fore-end of the stock. Just like with the cuff-style sling, the sling should be holding your support hand tight against the stock so that your hand can't move while in your shooting position.

There are plenty of people who doubt that the hasty sling is useful. All I can say is this, if you try it and don't like it, you don't have to use it. However, I think that if you give it an honest try (or ten), you will find it useful. As with other techniques in this book, it should be a tool that you can keep handy and use when appropriate (not necessarily all the time).

To prove that the hasty sling is helping to hold and stabilize the rifle, you can try one of two things. First, you can have a friend grab a part of the sling in their hand while you are in a shooting position. Then, have the friend twist their hand thereby making the sling tighter. You should feel the rifle pull tighter into your body. Tension on the sling = connection

> Quick Tip: Disconnect the rear of your sling and give it a half twist counter-clockwise and re-attach it to the rifle. For a right-handed shooter, this will allow the sling to curve naturally along your wrist and hand while using a hasty sling. Reverse for lefties.

and stability with your body. Also, you can get into position and have a friend extend or disconnect the sling. Upon doing either of these, you should see the front end of the rifle immediately fall. This means that the sling's tension was helping to hold the rifle up.

16.1.3 Wilderness Cleckner Cuff Sling

The sling I designed is an attempt to take advantage of the benefits of both the cuff-style and hasty slings. Most of the time, it stays on the rifle and will operate like any other rifle sling. But if you choose, you can use it like a cuff-style sling.

Just like the choice of which shooting position to use, the choice of how to use the sling will be determined by each particular situation. If you need to shoot quickly, you'll want to use a hasty sling (or no sling support at all if you're resting on something else). If time allows, however, you can slide your arm through the quick adjust cuff, pull the sling tight to cinch the cuff down to the predetermined position, and if you desire, detach the rear of the sling from the rifle with the quick detach clip.

Just remember, once you are done shooting, you will need to take the time to remove your arm from the cuff. It will be faster than using a typical cuff sling, but it will still take slightly longer than removing your arm from a hasty sling.

16.2 Seated Position

The seated position is the lowest of the "alternate" positions (those other than prone). Remember, lower is more stable and stable is more accurate. The only reason we want to raise our position is because the terrain requires us to. Therefore, you should use the lowest position that time and terrain allow. This means that if you have enough time to get into the prone position and you will be able to clearly see the target, then you should use the prone position.

If, however, you won't be able to see the target or you don't have time, then an "alternate" position should be used.

Of course, the other time you should use an alternate position is when you are practicing! I know you like shooting good groups in the prone – everyone does - but you need to get out of your comfort zone and practice these alternate positions. It is the rare real-world shot that is taken in the prone.

There are two variations on the seated position that I recommend, the crossed leg and crossed ankle methods.

16.2.1 Crossed Leg Method

The crossed leg method is the standard seated position used in NRA-style competitions and it is what is taught in many precision rifle schools. I'll note now that although it's popular, I don't like it, and neither do most of my students.

To get into the crossed leg position, the shooter sits on the ground, crosses their legs "indian-style," and faces their body 45 degrees to whichever side is their dominant hand/ shooting hand side. If the target is at 12:00, then a right-handed shooter's belt buckle is pointing to 1:30. This is just a starting point, some shooters find that it is easier to rotate even more from the target - you'll only find out what works for you when you try it.

Once in the seated position, place the elbow of each arm in the pocket made in the bend of the knee on each

> If you don't understand why this position is not enjoyable, you haven't tried it. Even while in SOTIC, when we were "professional" snipers, we moaned and groaned about having to shoot in this position. Also, we learned to unbuckle our belts and undo the top button on our pants to help relieve the pressure on our stomachs (and this was while my stomach was a bit smaller than it is today).

respective side. Whenever possible, you want to avoid bone to bone contact because it's easy for your elbow to slip around within your skin. By placing your elbows in the pockets made by your knees, you are ensuring that they're locked into place and can't slip around.

You'll notice that your head and rifle has a tendency to cant or roll away from you. It can be difficult to keep the rifle and scope level - especially when using a hasty sling. This is because a hasty sling pulls tight around the back of your support arm and is attached to the bottom of the buttstock at the rear of the rifle. The tighter the sling pulls at the bottom of the buttstock, the more it pulls the bottom of the rifle towards you. Even without a hasty sling pulling on the rear of the rifle, the rifle can still roll away because your upper body is also rolling over to rest your elbows on your legs.

As you work to master this position and keep the rifle level, pay special attention to how close your eye is to your scope. It is easy to lose track of your head position when you're also fighting so many other variables. By ignoring your head position, you run the risk of having improper sight alignment within your scope and, even worse, you run the risk of getting "scope bite" when the scope smacks your eyebrow during recoil. If this does happen to you, don't worry - it's a self-correcting problem and you'll only do it once.

In addition to learning to shoot in this position, you should also practice manipulating your rifle, reloading your rifle, and clearing malfunctions while in this position. You might find that you have to make some changes to your technique once you are "slung up."

16.2.2 Crossed Ankle Method

Of the two methods of shooting in the seated position that I cover, this is my favorite. Like the crossed leg method, it will take some practice but I think if you try it, you might like it better.

For the crossed ankle method, your body will be facing the target more straight on. Start by sitting on the ground with both legs straight in front of you. Next, angle your legs slightly to the side of your dominant hand. By slightly, I mean only a degree or two. If you are shooting at a target 100 yards away, try starting with your feet pointed about 5 feet to the appropriate side of the target. Next, bend your knees slightly as you cross your ankles.

You should now be facing slightly off to one side of the target with your ankles crossed and your knees slightly bent. Allow your legs to naturally fall to the side. Don't worry that your legs aren't likely flexible enough to lay completely flat - this position, in part, relies upon you not being completely flexible, which is great if your wardrobe contains more cargo than yoga pants.

Sling-up with either a cuff or hasty sling and allow your upper body to fall forward. Your hamstrings will probably keep you from folding completely flat. Again, this is good. Let the weight of your body rest and be held up by the natural tension in your legs. Next, "hook" your non-dominant elbow just beyond your non-dominant kneecap. Right about now you should be asking yourself, "didn't he say that this was the preferred position?"

By placing your elbow just beyond your kneecap, it should allow your elbow to "hook" in place and keep your upper body from bouncing back up once you've relaxed into the proper position.

You should notice that the rifle doesn't have the same cant/"roll" problem that it has when you are using the crossed leg method. Don't try too hard to get too low to the ground. After all, you should be using this position because you need to get higher up off the ground than the prone position allows. If you are able to get too low, you might as well save yourself the hassle and get in the prone. Practice getting this position to allow you to shoot with the rifle higher than prone, but lower than kneeling.

16.3 Kneeling

The kneeling position is the best mix of speed and stability. It is definitely not as stable as either the prone or seated positions, because it's higher off the ground and it has less contact with mother earth for stability. However, it is extremely quick to shoot from the kneeling position and it offers much more stability than the slightly quicker standing position. When a quick shot is called for and I have enough time that I don't have to take the shot standing, I'll drop down to a knee every time.

There are two methods I use when shooting in the kneeling position. They are very similar, and I honestly don't have a preference for either. I call the two methods the heel rest method and the side of foot rest method. These extremely creative names for each method come from whether your are sitting on your heel or the side of your foot.

Another variable here dependent on time is whether or not to use a sling. A sling makes this position more stable and I personally prefer to use one whenever I can. However, the kneeling position can be used without using a sling.

16.3.1 Heel Rest Method

With the heel rest method of shooting in the kneeling position, place your non-dominant side foot in front (towards the target) and drop down on to your dominant side knee. Curl your dominant side foot's toes under slightly and sit on your heel.   This method is useful when you need to get into the kneeling position quickly and when you need a few extra inches of height.

Once kneeling, rest your non-dominant arm on your knee by placing your elbow just past your knee. You do not want to place the point of your elbow on your knee. Just as with the seated position, you want to avoid bone to bone contact because it is easy for your elbow to slip around. By placing your elbow past your knee, you are ensuring that the meat on the back of your arm just above your elbow is acting as a good platform on your knee.

16.3.2 Side-of-Foot Rest Method

It's best to start with trying the heel rest method described above. From that position, you can easily transition to the side-of-foot rest method by allowing your dominant side foot to lay flat on its side on the ground. By laying your foot flat on the ground and then lowering down to sit directly on the side of your foot, you are able to get a few inches lower and, in my experience, you can gain stability.

Because this method lowers your body, you may find it necessary to extend your non-dominant foot farther out in front of you. By sliding the non-dominant foot forward, your knee should get lower to the ground. If your non-dominant knee stays the same height and you lower your body, then you'll be pointing your rifle higher than you were in the heel rest method.

16.4 Kneeling Supported

If you're able to rest your rifle on something and kneel behind it, then you should use the kneeling supported method. It's important to note that you should never rest your barrel on an object - instead, only rest the stock so that you don't affect the harmonics of the barrel. It would make no sense to spend extra money on a free-floated barrel only to negate the benefit by resting your barrel on a low tree branch.

In the kneeling supported method, you can use either of the two kneeling methods described above. And because the object you're using for support may be more steady than you could ever be, you may not need to rest your butt on your foot at all.

When you are using something else for support, you no longer need a knee out front for support. Therefore you may switch which knee is up and down. I've found that it's sometimes helpful to have my dominant knee up and my non-dominant knee down when I'm able to rest my rifle on something. This is because I can now rest my dominant arm on my dominant knee, and now the rifle has something to steady it both up front and in the rear.

It is not as important to use a sling in this position, if at all. The sling is helpful when I'm using my body for support, but if I have something more stable to rely upon, I'll just use that instead.

16.5 Standing

All I need to say here is, "good luck." Just kidding. But, if you already have trouble accurately engaging targets in the other positions, then trying to shoot from the standing position will be an exercise in frustration.

There are two types of standing shooting: target-style shooting where you take your time and shoot standing for the challenge, or real-world situations where you don't have enough time to do anything else.

I understand that many (most?) of shooting occurs while standing. For example, most pistol, non-precision rifle, and shotgun shooting happens while the shooter is standing. However, when it comes to precision shooting, some form of support is generally used.

If you are shooting in the standing position for target-shooting style practice, I recommend using a small-bore style hold. In this position, you face the non-dominant side of your body towards the target and lean away from the target (bend sideways at the waist).

> Shooting from "alternate" (less stable) positions is a true test of marksmanship.

The purpose of this position is to stick your non-dominant side of your hip out towards the target and use it as a rest for your non-dominant elbow.

This is an awkward position that can not be used by everybody. Don't worry if you're unable to use this position. Shooting while standing in this position is mostly useful for shooting competitions, practicing trigger control, and often for no other reason than to see if you can do it.

If you're shooting from the standing position because the situation requires it (as in you need to take the shot immediately) and you are not able to drop into a more stable position, then the best advice I can give is to practice allowing for an "acceptable error."

If I have time to get into the small-bore style shooting position described above, I surely have time to drop to a knee for a more stable position. If you must shoot standing because of your circumstance, then you probably aren't worried too much about MOA accuracy.

Despite everything I wrote above, I absolutely love to shoot while standing. It is truly the ultimate test of marksmanship ability and its a fun way to show-off. Most people can hit a 5 MOA target in the prone, but very few can hit it while standing.

16.6 Standing Supported

The standing supported position, unlike the unsupported position above, is a decent position to use for precision shooting. Similar to the kneeling supported position, this position allows for the resting of your rifle's stock (never the barrel, remember?) on something for stability.

If possible, depending on the height of the support and the target's location, a wider base with your feet spread apart is usually helpful. Also, if the object you are using for support allows, leaning into the object can be a great way to add some stability. Unlike using a knee for your arm to rest the rear of the rifle in the kneeling supported position above, this position relies solely on your body for support. This means that all of your breathing and movement will be noticeable while you are trying to aim at the target.

Horizontal support objects aren't the only useful supports. You can also use vertical supports and even your shooting buddy's shoulder if you like (and he lets you).

16.6.1 Vertical Support

Vertical supports are fairly common for both tactical shooters and hunters alike. For example, in the "real world," shooting benches are hard to come across but trees, corners of buildings, and poles/posts are common.

It is usually easiest for a right handed shooter to shoot off the left side of a vertical support but it's easier for them to stay concealed and/or covered while shooting off of the right side. It is generally easier off of the left side for a right handed shooter because the support hand can both hold the rifle up and also press it against the vertical support for stability.

When shooting off of the right side of a vertical support, a right handed shooter must try to hold both the vertical support and the rifle with their left hand - this can be difficult. Except for the trick I'm going to share next, I usually end up with some variation of the following grip: left hand pressing against the vertical support, pinky side up, while my thumb and/or index finger provide a shelf for the rifle. This method works, but it does not provide near as much control or stability as pressing the rifle into the vertical support from the left side.

Here's my trick for shooting off of a vertical support from the same side as your dominant hand: fold down the bipod leg that is on the side of the vertical support (for shooting off of the right side of a support, this is the left bipod leg) and use your support hand in a thumb down position to press and hold the bipod leg against the vertical support.

16.6.2 Buddy Support

I am including the "buddy" support method only because I am often asked about it. I don't think it is a desirable method and if you never end up trying it, you probably won't be missing out on much.

The "buddy" support method involves shooting while using somebody else as support. I put "buddy" in quotes because this person may not actually be your friend and even if they were, they may not be after you use them as a shooting bench.

The best method I've seen involves positioning the person in front of and facing the shooter. This can be done seated, kneeling or standing but I include it in the standing section because it's actually an improvement in stability over trying to stand with the rifle on your own. The rifle's stock is rested on the support person's shoulder, who places both hands on the rifle's extended bipod legs to pull the rifle down firmly onto their shoulder.

By facing the shooter, the support person's face is shielded from any muzzle blast and communication with the shooter is much easier. If possible, it is ideal to time the breathing of the support person with the shooter. While looking at the shooter, the support person can get visual cues on timing without requiring the shooter to speak while they are trying to shoot.

16.7 Acceptable Error

If I had to pick only one section of this book as the section that is most likely to make someone a better shooter, this section would surely be a finalist. Read this section twice, think about it, practice it, and repeat as necessary. Once I was able to embrace this theory, my shooting evolved from technical proficiency (knowing what to do) to tactical proficiency (knowing how to do it).

In addition to being powerful, this section will also be controversial. Perhaps those two qualities go hand in hand. I am not a bullseye shooter. It's not difficult to find a shooter that can shoot prettier, smaller groups than I can. I, instead, pride myself on my ability to see a target and hit a target under real-world conditions. I would rather shoot 1 MOA groups at 100 yards and be able to engage and hit targets at different distances on demand, and quickly, than shoot 1/4 MOA groups at 100 yards but take forever to hit a target at a distance because I have to get everything situated and calculated "just right."

Many of you will disagree with me and instead want extreme accuracy over functional accuracy (good enough to hit the target) even if it takes you 5 times longer to hit the target and you'd only consider taking the shot in a perfect prone or bench-rest position, That's OK. I see both expectations of shooting as different *styles* of shooting - neither one is "better."

Shooting groups gets boring for me. I want to know that I can hit a pie-plate sized target at 500 yards while I'm freezing cold, leaning up against a tree, and I need to shoot quickly. My style of shooting won't win bullseye competitions, but it's useful when hunting or in tactical environments. Your mileage may vary.

Shooting from alternate, less stable positions is a true test of marksmanship. Once my students start becoming proficient at maintaining 1 MOA of accuracy out to medium distances, I have them try shooting from "alternate positions." Unstable positions do two things - they magnify errors in the fundamentals of shooting and they wreck whatever confidence was built up in the students.

Although my intent is never to make a student feel bad about their abilities, the rude-awakening from unstable positions does help me teach. First, by magnifying their errors, I am able to easier diagnose what they need to fix. For example, a shooter who is jerking the trigger or who has bad follow through might be able to hide their bad habits (even from themselves) when their rifle is stable on the ground and locked into place with sandbags. When they're in an unstable position, however, it's very easy for us both to see when they flinch or do something else they shouldn't do.

Second, by wrecking their confidence, they're more willing to improve. I know that this sounds harsh, but there's a predictable learning curve when it comes to shooting. Many of us think that we are already experts and are unwilling to listen – it's a guy thing. Shooters can get to 80% of their ability/capacity fairly easily. If they are never taken out of their steady and prone comfort zone, they'll never see how much they have to improve. And without knowing how much they can improve, they're less likely to go back to the basics and focus on the fundamentals.

16.7.1 Perfection Isn't Always Good

I bet I can read your mind while you are shooting. You probably have a monologue that goes something like this in your head while you're trying to make an accurate shot:

> "Ok, a little bit higher. A little bit higher. A little left. Is that the center? Ok, a little bit more. Right . . . nope, wait . . right . . . now!"

That last part, the "now!" followed by the subsequent jerk of the trigger is why you're missing. You know that you're supposed to allow the pressure to build on the trigger until it breaks and then apply proper follow-through. However, when you're trying so hard to get the sights or reticle lined up on the target while they keep moving because of your unstable position, you're very likely to want to pull a "now!" when the sights or reticle happened to get close to the center of the target.

By trying to be too perfect, you missed. For an example of this phenomenon, take a look at *Figure 16.7-1*. Imagine that the dotted line is the path of your sights as they move around on the target. As you get them lined up with the center, your brain thinks, "Now!" and you jerk the trigger and miss the target.

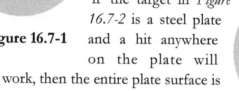

"Now!"

Figure 16.7-1

Miss

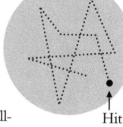

Hit

Figure 16.7-2

Instead, consider embracing the "error" and allow the movement to happen while you apply proper trigger control. As long as the error is acceptable (and the sights stay on the target), then when the bullet fires, it will hit the target. It is up to you to decide what "acceptable" means for a particular situation. For example, if the target in *Figure 16.7-2* is a steel plate and a hit anywhere on the plate will work, then the entire plate surface is an "acceptable" area. If, however, you are hunting, then just the animal's kill-zone will be the "acceptable" area.

Let's take a look at the "acceptable error" method. If you apply proper trigger control and focus only on keeping the sights within the acceptable error, you are much less likely to jerk the trigger. If your scope isn't set up properly, then the bullet is going to impact wherever the rifle was aimed when the bullet fired. If the rifle was always aiming in an "acceptable" area in the target, then you'll hit it. It may seem counter-intuitive that I'm telling you to be ok with less than perfection in a precision shooting book. But which would you rather have, a hit on the edge or a miss?

Don't forget, it is up to you to define the acceptable area. If the acceptable area is a smaller section in the center of the target, then it might be tougher for you to do this, but it will still work if you try it.

Another reason this method works so well is because it allows you to focus where you should - on your front sight post or reticle. It is very common for shooters to look past their front sight or reticle and instead look at the target when they are trying to be too perfect. When shooters do this, it's because they are trying to find the exact center of the target. If you are focusing on the target instead of your front sight post or reticle, you're less likely to get good results.

By using the "acceptable error" method, you can keep a crisp and clear front sight post or reticle somewhere within the acceptable zone of a target in the background. This is also why "calling your shots" works so well. It requires you to focus on what you and the rifle are doing instead of focusing only on the center of the target and losing track of where your front sight post or reticle is.

Try this method. Then, try it again until it clicks. Once you are able to do this, your shooting is going to improve. You will be faster and more confident on a rifle and you will get hits.

17 ESTIMATING AND ADJUSTING FOR TARGET DISTANCE

There are multiple methods for determining the distance to a target. Although using a laser rangefinder is the most precise method of determining a target's distance, electronic devices can fail, and some target surfaces do not easily reflect the laser.

I strongly encourage learning how to read a map before relying on a GPS and learning how to add before using a calculator, so it should come as no surprise that I also strongly encourage learning and practicing to estimate a target's distance with angular measurements by using the Mil or MOA marks in a scope.

17.1 Angular Measurements ("Milling")

There's an inverse relationship between how big an object appears and how far away it is. As the distance to an object increases, the size of the object appears to decrease. For example, imagine a target at

100 yds as a starting point. *See Figure 17.1-1.* If that target was moved to half the distance (50 yds) it would appear twice as big. Likewise, if that 100 yd target was moved twice as far away (200 yds) it would appear to be half the original size, and if it was moved four times as far away, (400 yds) then the target would appear to be one quarter the size.

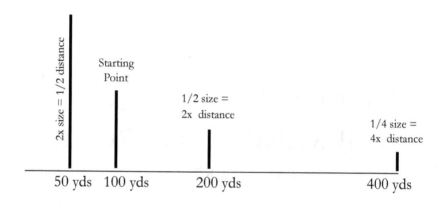

Figure 17.1-1

This predictable relationship allows us to estimate a target's distance based on how big or small the target appears. A target's size can be measured in a scope using the marks in your reticle (MOA or Mil). Using the apparent measurement of the target, the distance to the target can be determined. In order for this to work, of course, the actual size of the target must be known.

17.1.1 Calculating Distance with Mils

To calculate a target's distance with Mils, multiply the known size of the target by 1000 and then divide that number by the size of the target measured in Mils through your scope *(See Figure 17.1-2).* It's important to note that the distance to the target will be in whatever unit of measurement was used for the actual size of the target.   If the target's size in yards is used in the calculation, then the distance determined from the formula will be in yards. The same is true if meters or

If you want to use inches for the target size and still get a distance in yards, use "27.77" instead of "1000" in the formula below.

any other linear measurement is used. This is based on the concept that a Milliradian is 1/1000th of any distance *(See Chapter 9)*.

Mil Formula

$$\frac{(\text{Actual size of target}) \times 1000}{\text{Measured size in Mils}} = \text{Distance to target}$$

Figure 17.1-2

17.1.2 Calculating Distance with MOA

To calculate a target's distance with MOA, multiply the known size of the target in inches by 95.5 and then divide that number by the size of the target measured in MOA through your scope *(See Figure 17.1-3)*. Unlike the Mil formula, this formula should only be used when working with target sizes in inches and distances in yards. If needed, however, there are alternate numbers that can be used in the formula *(See Figure 17.1-5)*.

MOA Formula

$$\frac{(\text{Actual size of target in inches}) \times 95.5}{\text{Measured size in MOA}} = \text{Distance to target in yards}$$

Figure 17.1-3

17.1.3 Alternate Units with Mil and MOA Calculations

Sometimes it's useful to use one unit of measurement for the actual size of the target and have the distance to the target be in a non-standard unit of measurement. For example, you may have a scope which measures in Mils and a target size in yards but you need your distance in meters (instead of yards). Or you may have a scope which measures in MOA and a target size in inches but you need your distance in meters (instead of yards).

If you're trying to determine the distance of a target in a non-standard size and distance unit combination, you have a few options: 1) Convert the actual size of the target into a different unit, 2) alter the formula, or 3) convert the calculated final distance into the

The 95.5 figure from the formula in *Figure 17.1-3* accounts for the almost 5% variation from rounding 1.047 inches per 100 yards for MOA to 1 inch per 100 yards. The 5% may also be accounted for after your calculation if you would like to use 100 instead of 95.5 in the formula. Just remember to subtract 5% from your answer if you choose to use 100 instead of 95.5!

desired unit. To try out each of these options, let's use the following hypothetical:

> You have a target that is **12 inches** tall which measures **1 Mil** tall in your scope and you need your distance in **yards**.

Option 1: Convert the size of the target into a different unit. In our hypothetical above, we can convert the target size from inches to yards to get a distance calculation in yards. The linear unit conversion chart in *Section 9.2* of this book (*Figure 9.1-3*) shows that to convert from inches to yards, you divide the size in inches by 36 (the number of inches in a yard). (12/36=0.333). After converting to yards, we can use the standard Mil formula:

$$\frac{12 \text{ inches}}{36} = 0.333 \text{ yds}$$

$$\frac{0.333 \text{ yds x } 1000}{1 \text{ Mil}} = 333 \text{ yds}$$

Option 2: Alter the formula. In our hypothetical above, we need to alter the Mil formula to allow us to start with a target size in inches and end up with a distance in yards. The chart in *Figure 17.1-4* below shows that in order to input inches into the Mil formula and end up with yards, you replace the "1000" in the Mil formula with "27.77". Now we can use the altered formula:

$$\frac{12 \text{ inches x } 27.77}{1 \text{ Mil}} = 333 \text{ yds}$$

Option 3: Convert the distance into the needed unit. If we used a target size in inches from our hypothetical and we used the standard Mil formula, our target distance would be in inches and need to be converted to yards. The linear unit conversion chart in *Section 9.2* of this book (*Figure 9.1-3*) shows that to convert from inches to yards, you divide the size in inches by 36:

$$\frac{12 \text{ inches x } 1000}{1 \text{ Mil}} = 12{,}000 \text{ inches}$$

$$\frac{12{,}000 \text{ inches}}{36} = 333 \text{ yds}$$

In each of the three options, we can calculate that a 12 inch target measuring 1 Mil tall in a scope is 333 yards away. It is up to you to determine which method is easiest or best for your needs. Generally, I prefer the first option because you won't always be converting target sizes in inches to distances in yards. In fact, you may want a distance in meters or you may have target size in centimeters, feet, or any other unit of linear measurement. Although it is easy to convert feet to inches, you're still converting units prior to using the formula. If you're already converting from one unit to another, then why not just convert to yards, so that you can use the standard formula with "1000"? I will admit that if I am in a situation

> **ADVANCED NOTE:**
> I calculated the alternate formula numbers by dividing 1000 by the number of starting units that fit into the ending unit. For example, 36 inches fit into a yard. Therefore, I divided 1000 by 36 and ended up with 27.77.

where all of my target sizes are known in inches and I want all of my results in yards, I will make an exception and alter the formula to use "27.77" instead of 1000.

To help you with entering one target size unit into the Mil formula in *Figure 17.1-2 or the MOA formula in* Figure 17.1-3, and calculating a target distance in another unit, see *Figures 17.1-4 and 17.1-5.*

Mil Formula Conversions

To start with a size in:	and end with a distance in:	Instead of "1000," use:
Inches	Yards	27.77
Inches	Meters	25.4
Centimeters	Yards	10.93
Centimeters	Meters	10

Figure 17.1-4

MOA Formula Conversions

To start with a size in:	and end with a distance in:	Instead of "95.5," use:
Inches	Meters	87.3
Centimeters	Yards	37.6
Centimeters	Meters	34.4

Figure 17.1-5

17.1.4 Measuring Target Size with Mils and MOA

As targets get further away, they get harder to calculate range using Mils or MOA. This is because smaller appearing targets are harder to measure, and also because a small percentage error can magnify the result. For example, when a 1 meter tall target measures 10 Mils tall in your scope, it is 100 meters away. At this distance, a 10% error is difficult to make. Even if a 10% error was made, however, and you mistakenly measured the target to be 11 Mils tall, then you'd think the target is 91 meters away. Even with this 10% error, there would be negligible effect on your ability to hit the target. On the other hand, if the 1 meter target was 1000 meters away, it would measure 1 Mil tall in your scope. At this distance, when the target appears so small in your scope, a 10% error is much easier to make. Additionally, the 10% error also has a much bigger effect. For example, if you mistakenly measured the target as 1.1 Mils tall, you would think the target is 910 meters away. If you tried to shoot a 1 meter tall target at 1000 meters with the elevation adjustment on your scope set for 910 meters, you'll completely miss.

In order to get the most accurate measurement possible from your scope, you must have a stable platform for your rifle. The most difficult part of measuring a target with your reticle will be holding the rifle steady enough to line up one part of the reticle with one edge of the target and then shifting your focus to the other edge of the target to see where it measures on the reticle.   It is difficult to ensure that one edge is lined up properly while looking at the other. A trick I use to help with this is to use the edge of a mil-dot, instead of the middle of the dot, as a starting point whenever possible. By doing this, I can better keep track of its alignment while I'm looking at the other edge of the target because

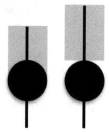

Figure 17.1-6

it is easier to ensure a specific edge is aligned versus trying to make sure the edge of the target is still exactly in the middle of the dot. See *Figure 17.1-6*.

Also, some targets are narrower than the mil-dot. By using the edge of the mil-dot, you won't have to keep moving the mil-dot to confirm where the edge of the target is.

Get creative with your measurements. For example, it might be easier to measure a

1 Mil

1 Mil

Figure 17.1-7

certain target's width rather than its height. In the military, we often used "E-type" targets which measured 1 meter tall and 1/2 meter wide. It was sometime difficult to determine whether one of these targets measured 1.6 or 1.7 Mils tall in a mil-dot scope. Therefore, it was necessary to get creative and use the width of the target and the dimensions of the mil-dots in our scope to our advantage.

0.2 Mil

0.8 Mil

Figure 17.1-8

Our mil-dot scope on our rifles had dots that measured 0.2 Mils in diameter and they were spaced 1 Mil apart. This meant that from a particular spot on one dot (e.g. bottom, middle, or top) to the same spot on an adjacent dot was 1 Mil. See *Figure 17.1-7.* However, by using the width of the dots to our advantage, we could also precisely measure 0.8, 0.9, 1.1, and 1.2 Mils.

From the outside edge of one dot (e.g. the bottom) to the outside edge (e.g. the top) of an adjacent dot was 1.2 Mils. This is because from the bottom of one dot to the bottom of the next dot is 1 Mil plus the width of the top dot is 1.2 Mils.

Using the same math, we also knew that the inside edges of two dots were 0.8 Mils apart. See *Figure 17.1-8.* By combining the edge of one dot with the center of another, we could measure 0.9 and 1.1 Mils. See *Figure 17.1-9.*

Now, back to the example above of not knowing whether an "E-type" target was 1.6 or 1.7 Mils tall. We knew the width of these targets was half their height. Therefore, if we used the edges of the dots to our

1.1 Mil

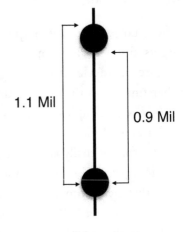

0.9 Mil

Figure 17.1-9

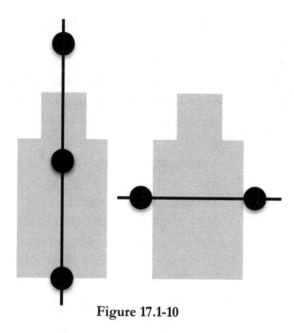

Figure 17.1-10

advantage and measured the width, we could see whether the target was exactly 0.8 Mils wide which would mean that it must be 1.6 Mils tall. See *Figure 17.1-10*.

Angled Target Measurements

Often, targets are not perpendicular to your line of sight. That is, targets don't always appear perfectly flat towards you. Sometimes you are at an elevated vantage point looking down at a target and other times you may be looking at a target from the side. See *Figure 17.1-11* for examples.

An angled view of a target makes at least one dimension appear smaller than it really is. For example, assume that the targets "A" and "B" in *Figure 17.1-11* are both 25 inches tall and they are both the same distance from your position. Target "A" is directly in front of you while target "B" is below you and you are looking down at it. You measure target "A" to be 1.1 Mils tall and you measure target "B" to be 0.9 Mils tall.

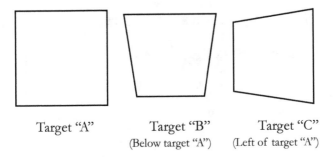

Target "A"   Target "B"   Target "C"
             (Below target "A")   (Left of target "A")

Figure 17.1-11

If we don't compensate for the angled view, then our Mil calculation based on the height of the target may lead us to think that target "B" is further away than target "A". This is because targets appear smaller the farther away they are. For example, a 25 inch target measured at 1.1 Mils tall would be 631 yards away and the same target measured at 0.9 Mils tall would be 730 yards away.

There are two methods of compensating for angled targets: mathematically compensating for the smaller-appearing dimension and using a non-skewed dimension for measurement.

To mathematically compensate for an angled view, multiply the angle's cosine by the distance calculated by the Mil or MOA formula. *See Figure 17.1-12* for a table of angles and their corresponding cosines.

In our example, target "B" is 30 degrees below us. The cosine for 30 degrees is 0.866. The 730 yards calculated from the angled view of target "B" multiplied by the cosine for the 30 degree angle of target "B"

> **Cosine is an "angle killer." Whenever there's an angle problem, whether from measuring size in Mils or MOA or from shooting up or downhill (Chapter 19), multiply the distance by the angle's cosine to get rid of the angle problem.**

Cosines for Angles			
Angle	Cosign	Angle	Cosign
5°	0.999	50°	0.642
10°	0.984	55°	0.573
15°	0.965	60°	0.5
20°	0.939	65°	0.422
25°	0.906	70°	0.342
30°	0.866	75°	0.258
35°	0.819	80°	0.173
40°	0.766	85°	0.087
45°	0.707	90°	0

Figure 17.1-12

equals 632 yards. Although the corrected distance for target "B" of 632 yards is not exactly the 631 yard target distance of target "A", it's nothing more than a rounding error and won't have an effect on hitting the target.

It is important to note that this will only work if the target is straight up and down from the ground. If a target is 30 degrees below you and it is also angled back 30 degrees, then you would see the full size of the target and an angled-view compensation is not required.

The other method for compensating for an angled view of a target is to use a non-skewed dimension. For example, although the height of target "B" and the width of target "C" appear smaller, the width of target "B" and the height of target "C" are unaffected by their angles. If the target is angled forward or back because it's not level with the ground or it's above or below you, use the target's width for your Mil or MOA calculation and no adjustment to the formula or result is needed. Likewise, if a target is twisted to one side or it is angled away left or right, then use its height. This method only works if you know both the height and width dimensions

For information on how to measure the angle of a target and how to shoot targets at angles, *see Chapter 19.*

18 ESTIMATING AND ADJUSTING FOR WIND

Wind is the second biggest effect on a bullet in flight. It is also the hardest to account for. Determining the wind's speed and direction at different distances, or "reading wind," is truly an art and can take a lifetime to master. As I used to say in the military, "If it wasn't for wind, everybody could be a sniper."

This chapter will only explore the basics - this is a beginner's book, after all. In a subsequent and more advanced book on the topic, wind will be discussed in more detail. This doesn't mean that wind isn't important. On the contrary, it is supremely important. However, you should master the other topics of this book with a basic understanding of wind and its effects before delving into advanced topics.

There are three reasons why wind is difficult to compensate for. First, it is hard to determine exactly how fast the wind is blowing and in which direction. Second, it is difficult to calculate how varying wind speeds and directions at different distances will effect the bullet. Third, even if you have figured the first two out, wind often changes as it gusts stronger or dies completely.

Similar to gravity, the bullet is affected more by the wind the longer it is exposed. As an example, the bullet will be affected by the wind only a fraction of a second between the shooter and a target on the 100 yard line. On the other hand, between the 700 and 800 yard lines, the slower bullet will be exposed to the wind for a longer amount of time.

I am often asked whether wind matters more at the shooter, at the target, or somewhere in between. The answer to that question is, "all of the above." Wind at every distance matters.

But, a bullet that is slightly moved off its original path near the shooter will stay on this new path all the way to the target. This does not mean that wind at the shooter matters most, however. The faster bullet near the shooter is not exposed very long to the wind so it is less likely to be blown off course. This means that wind at the shooter doesn't move the bullet much, but any change can have a magnified effect down range. And conversely, although the movement of a bullet off its path downrange won't have much time to keep moving off it's path, it is easier for the wind to move the bullet when downrange.

18.1 Determining Wind Speed and Direction

Wind meters can be useful tools but they do not tell the whole story because they only measure wind at the shooter's position. In order to see what the wind is doing all the way to the target, you must learn to interpret the movement of objects, such as vegetation or flags, or heat waves - "mirage."

18.1.1 Wind Flags

Wind flags are the easiest way to determine what the wind is doing all the way to the target. Unfortunately, wind flags are usually only found at shooting ranges and are very rare in the real world. Also, wind flags can vary greatly in material and size making it difficult to translate the various angles of wind flags into certain wind speeds.

18.1.2 Vegetation

Vegetation can also be a difficult tool to use to measure wind speed. For example, grass in Arizona or Texas behaves different than grass in Tennessee in the same wind conditions. It is useful to see that the wind is blowing and even what direction it is blowing in, but it is difficult to use vegetation to determine the wind's speed.

18.1.3 Mirage

"Mirage" is the distortion of light caused by rising heat waves. Mirage is useful for judging wind because it is sensitive to slight changes in wind speed and you can see it almost everywhere. With appropriate optics, I have even seen it in the French Alps in the snow.

When the heat waves are rising straight up from the ground, there is either no wind at all, or it is blowing straight at or away from you. This vertical pattern is often called a "boiling mirage." As the heat waves start to drift to one side or another, the wind speed is increasing. In my experience, 3-5 mph wind causes the mirage to shift about 30 degrees in the direction the wind is blowing. A 7-10 mph wind causes a little over 45 degrees shift in the mirage and any wind over 12 mph causes the mirage to appear straight side to side.

With strong wind it can be difficult to tell the direction the mirage is blowing because the image is so distorted. You may think it is obvious to know the wind's direction but trust me – when there is too much mirage traveling straight side-to-side, it is easy to be wrong.

The best way to see mirage is through a quality spotting scope on medium to low power. With the magnification set too high, you will be "looking through" much of the mirage you want to see. A trick I use to ensure that I am seeing the wind between me and the target is to focus first on the target with the spotting scope and then back the focus out to about 2/3rd of the way to the target. When you do this, you should clearly see the mirage in front of a slightly blurry target.

The take away here is to use all of these methods in conjunction with one another to determine what direction and speed the wind is blowing at different distances.

18.2 Determining the Effect of the Wind

The wind will blow the bullet off of its original path in the direction the wind is blowing. For example, wind blowing from the right (3 o'clock) to the left (9 o'clock) will blow a bullet to the left with the wind. *See Figure 18.2-1.*

There are multiple formulas people use to calculate the effect of the wind on their bullet. The problem with these formulas is that they usually rely on certain pre-determined "constants" that change with distance (which I suppose isn't really a constant). Another reason I don't like the formulas is that they give a false sense of accuracy. When you are first learning to read wind, you are going to have a difficult time seeing the difference between 6 and 8 mph wind downrange. By

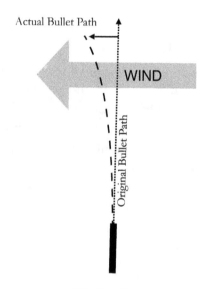

Figure 18.2–1

entering the wrong number into the formula, you are going to calculate an incorrect answer.

As an example, here is the wind formula we were taught in SOTIC: Distance to target in 100s of yards multiplied by the wind speed in mph and then divided by a "constant" gives you the wind drift in MOA. The "constants" we used were "12" out to 600 yards and "10" out to 1000 yards for our ammunition. Depending on where you look you will find different "constants" for different projectiles.

This is one of the rare times I think you should just start with a chart or ballistic software. See what a 10 mph wind will do to your projectile and follow the guidance below to turn it into meaningful info.

18.2.1 Wind Value

As we've discussed above, the longer amount of time the wind can make contact on a bullet, the more it will be able to affect the bullet. In addition, the angle of the wind on the bullet can play a large role.

Wind coming 90 degrees from the left or right will have the greatest effect on a bullet and is therefore referred to as "full value." When the wind is blowing at other angles, the effect of the wind is lessened. *See Figure 18.2-2.*

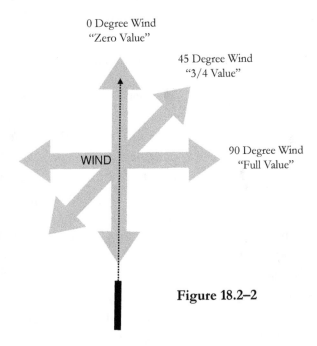

0 Degree Wind
"Zero Value"

45 Degree Wind
"3/4 Value"

90 Degree Wind
"Full Value"

WIND

Figure 18.2–2

Figure 18.2-3 is a chart showing the estimated effect of a full-value (90 degree) 10 mph wind on a 175 grain 308 Win. bullet. If the wind is blowing at a different angle and therefore it has a lesser value, modify the listed effect as needed. For example, if the wind is blowing at 45 degrees, multiply the listed effect by 0.75 because the wind will only have 75% of the effect.

308 Win 175gr BTHP 10mph / 90 Degree Wind	
Yards	Inches of Shift
0	0
100	0.75
200	3
300	7
400	12.75
500	20.75
600	31
700	44.25
800	60.5
900	80.25
1000	104.25

Figure 18.2–3

18.2.2 *Wind Speed*

Of course, faster wind will have a greater effect than slower wind. The good news is that the effect from the wind's speed is linear. This means that if the wind speed is cut in half, then the effect is also cut in half. Similarly, if the wind speed is doubled, then the effect on the bullet is also doubled. Therefore, if the wind is only blowing at 5 mph, divide the listed value in *Figure 18.2-3* by 2 because it will only have half the effect.

18.2.3 *Additive Effect*

The wind's value and speed are calculated together. From the examples above, the 75% effect from the "value" and the 50% effect from the speed combine to a net effect of about 37%. This is because the 45 degree angle makes the 10 mph wind value from the chart effect the bullet as if it were only 7.5 mph (75% of 10 mph). And, the 5 mph actual wind speed cuts the value of the effect in half so that the bullet is only affected half as much as it would if it were 10mph. Therefore, the 7.5 mph effect above is cut in half to about 3.7 mph.

If that method is confusing to you, just take the result from the chart for 10 mph at whatever distance you are shooting. Then, adjust the value proportionately to whatever the wind's actual speed is. For example, if the wind's speed is 7 mph, then multiply the value by 0.7. If the speed is 12 mph, then multiply the value by 1.2.

Next, decrease the value as necessary to compensate for the direction of the wind. If the wind is full-value, then you already have your answer after adjusting for the wind's speed from the chart. If it is blowing at a lesser value, then you need to multiply your calculated value from the wind speed by the appropriate percentage. For example, if the wind is ¾ value because it is blowing at 45 degrees, then you take your adjusted value and multiply it by 0.75.

Let's put this all together in a couple of examples:

Example 1. Using *Figure 18.2-3*, let's determine the effect on our bullet from a 14 mph full-value wind at a 500 yard target. First, we see that the effect from a 10 mph full value wind in the chart is 20.75 inches at 500 yards. Next, we multiply 20.75 inches by 1.4 to convert the 10 mph value to 14 mph and we end up with 29.05 inches. Next, we decrease the effect by any decrease in wind value. Because the wind is full-value, we don't decrease the effect in this example. Therefore our bullet will drift 29.05 inches in the direction the wind is blowing.

Example 2. Using *Figure 18.2-3*, let's determine the effect on our bullet from a 7 mph wind blowing at 45 degrees for a 500 yard target. First, we see that the effect from a 10 mph full value wind in the chart is 20.75 inches. Next, we multiply 20.75 inches by 0.7 to convert the 10 mph value to 7 mph and we end up with 14.52 inches. Next, we decrease the effect by any decrease in wind "value." Because the wind is blowing at 45 degrees and therefore has a ¾ value, we multiply 14.52 inches by 0.75 for a net effect of 10.89 inches on the bullet in the direction the wind is blowing.

18.2.4 *"Seeing" the Wind*

This might be the most difficult section of the book to write because it is surely the most difficult to explain. Once you get good enough at "reading" the wind, you won't be doing calculations. Instead, you will look at the wind and "see" the right amount of compensation for your rifle. Only experience will allow you the ability to do this. I am so accustomed to shooting .308 Win. that I look at some wind and "see" a ¾ Mil left hold.

This sounds corny, but I've explained to students as being able to see the "Matrix." At the beginning it might look like a big jumble of information. But, once you master it, you'll see the wind calls in front of you.

18.3 Adjusting for Wind

Great, we know how to figure out how fast the wind is blowing, what angle the wind is blowing, and we know how much of an effect each of those variables will have. But, what do we do with that information? We aim our rifle in the opposite direction of the effect so that the wind blows our bullet into the center of the target.

18.3.1 Holding for Wind

The first step is to calculate the effect of the wind in a unit we can use in our scopes. I wrote "in" instead of "on" because I do not like dialing for wind corrections with turrets on my scope. Instead, I like to "hold" into the wind using my reticle.

I like "holding" because it is faster than dialing. By "holding" to the left or the right of the target it allows me the chance to shoot before the wind changes. If you've ever sat and watched the wind, you know that its speed is not constant. It can gust, die-down, and even change direction in seconds. Therefore, if you have taken the time to calculate the wind's effect, you must shoot before the wind changes, or you'll need to start all over again.

Using the Target

When holding for wind using the target as a reference point, you aim into the wind using the target's width as a reference point. The benefit to this system is it's very fast and can be used to ensure a hit somewhere on the target without calculating the wind precisely. The downside to this method is that the amount of compensation for the wind changes with distance.

Let me explain. When you hold for wind using the target's width, you either hold on the edge of the target or some variation of the edge. For example, a "hold left" means you will aim at the left edge of the target to compensate for wind blowing left to right. See *Figure 18.3-1*. A "favor left" means that you are going to hold halfway between the center of the target and the left edge. Also, you can increase the hold by holding a "half target width left," or a "full target width left" which means you are aiming to the left of the target a distance equal to half the width or the full width of the target.

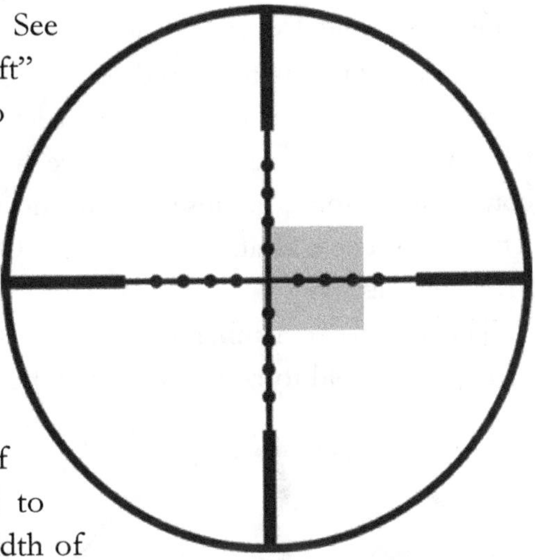

Figure 18.3-1

These might sound complicated but they are fast and can be useful in some situations. For example, if I need to make a quick shot at a 12 inch steel target at 300 yards and there is a steady wind blowing from the left, I can just "hold left" and shoot.

It doesn't make sense to hold in the center of the target because I know the wind is going to have some effect on the bullet. By aiming in the center I am effectively cutting the target in half because I can only hit the center or the right 6 inches because of the wind. Instead, by holding left, I give myself the full 12 inches of the target to get a hit. If the wind only affects the bullet 1 inch, it's still a hit. Also, if it blows the bullet 11.5 inches, it's also a hit. This is surely a lot faster than doing a wind calculation and then holding a precise amount.

The problem with this method is that holding on the edge is a smaller adjustment the farther the target is. For example, if the same 12 inch target is at 600 yards, a "hold left" only compensates for the wind half as much. This is doubly bad because at 600 yards, you'll need to compensate even more than you do at 300 yards.

Using the Reticle

When you hold for wind using a reticle, you aim into the wind a specified amount as measured on the reticle. This can be confusing to a new shooter. For example, see *Figure 18.3-2* which represents what you should see when you are holding "2 Mils right." It is confusing to some because you are using the second mil-dot to the left of the reticle as an aiming point. Of course, this can work with MOA reticles too.

The way to remember it is to first ask yourself which direction you need to hold to compensate for the wind, then ask yourself how far you need to go that direction. In effect, you are using the reticle only as a ruler. No matter which way you measure a piece of paper, it is 8 1/2" inches wide regardless of which direction the numbers on the ruler are going. The same is true for a wind hold. *Figure 18.3-2* shows "2 Mils right" because you are aiming which way? To the right. How far? 2 Mils. Therefore, move the reticle to the right until you reach the 2 Mil mark.

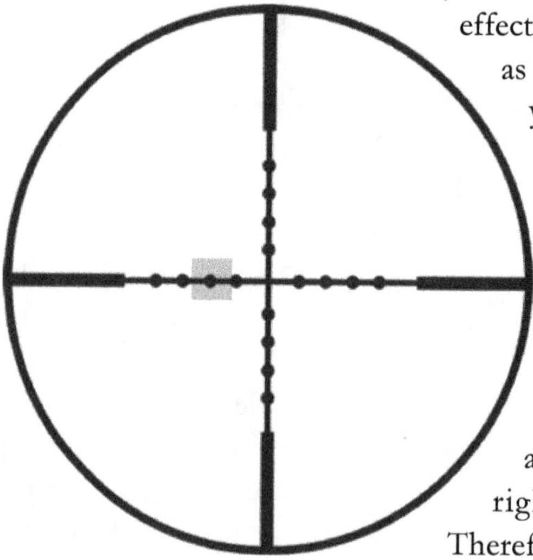

Figure 18.3-2

Don't worry too much when you mess this up. It's all part of learning this system and most people mess this up at least once. It's obvious to me as an instructor when the bullet goes double the distance in the wrong direction.

Holding isn't just faster on the initial shot, it's also faster for follow-up shots. If my wind call was wrong and the bullet misses, I can just move the spot on the reticle where the bullet impacted and shoot again. This is because the wind just showed me how far it is going to blow the bullet off of its original path. For example, if I hold 1 Mil right for wind and the bullet's impact lines up with the second Mil-dot to the right of the reticle, I now know that the wind actually moved the bullet off of its original path 2 Mils to the right instead of 1 Mil left like I thought it would (that's a 3 Mil miss!). See *Figure 18.3-3*.

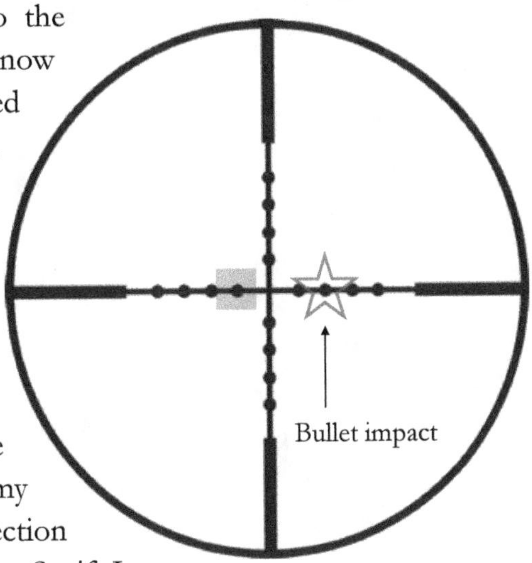

Remember that my barrel is pointed in the direction of the center of my reticle, which is also the direction of the bullet's original path. So if I change my wind hold to 2 Mils left instead, before the wind changes, I will hit the target. Of course, this is only true if my first shot was a good one.

Bullet impact

Figure 18.3-3

Remember the discussion earlier about calling your shots? If I accidentally jerked the trigger and caused a miss 3 Mils to the right, then I might think the wind is responsible for the miss instead of myself. In this scenario, if I didn't call my shot, I could adjust my wind hold, make a good shot the second time, and still miss because now the bullet will impact where it should've for the first time. As you can imagine, this can be a frustrating endeavor.

19 ESTIMATING AND ADJUSTING FOR ANGLES

When shooting at either an upward or downward angle, your bullet will impact higher than it would if you were shooting a target the same distance away across flat ground. This is because a bullet does not fall as far away from its original path. Therefore, when shooting up or down, you need to treat the target as if it were closer than it really is when accounting for gravity, but you still need to treat it as its actual distance for wind.

The steeper the angle, the greater the effect. This is because a bullet drops off of its original path most when gravity is pulling perpendicular to its path, i.e., when traveling flat across the ground, and it drops off of its original path least when it is traveling straight up or down.

With moderate angles (20 to 30 degrees) and close distances (100 to 200 yards), the change in impact may only be a couple of inches. With greater angles and longer distances however, the change can be significant.

19.1 Measuring Angle

There are a few ways to measure the angle to a target. At a basic level, you can use a card with angled measurements on it or a protractor such as the one found on the back of a Mil-Dot master. Also, some compasses, and devices with compass features (to include watches and iPhones) have the ability to measure angles. You can either look down the edge of one of these devices to see the angle from you to the target or you can measure off the top of your turret while you look through your scope at the target.

There are also devices which mount directly to your rifle. One of my favorites is called the Angle Cosine Indicator. What's nice about this is it gives you the cosine of the angle (which as you'll read later is what you want), instead of giving you the angle measurement.

Of course, there are now laser rangefinders which have angle measurements and compensation built-in. These are the simplest solution for determining the angle of the target and the "angle distance" (discussed below) you should use to engage the target. However, just like with using laser rangefinders for estimating distance, I strongly encourage you to learn how to measure and compensate for angle manually before you rely upon an electronic gadget.

Whichever method you use, go out and guess with your naked eye first. You might be surprised how far off you are. For example, if you're looking up or down a mountain, it's rare to see an angle steeper than 30 degrees. This is because the angle of repose (the angle at which dirt naturally starts to slough off itself) is about 30 degrees. If you've ever noticed, this is why mountains and mounds of dirt have uniform angles.

19.2 Calculating the Effect on Elevation

To understand how to calculate for an angled shot, we need to go back to trigonometry. For these examples, I'll use a shooter shooting downhill, but it's the same when shooting uphill. Just trust me.

In the simplest terms possible, the bullet will cover more distance to the target at an angle than it would cover side-to-side across the ground. In *Figure 19.2-1* you can see a triangle made from the elevation of a shooter on a hill (X), the distance to the target down the hill (Y), and the line of sight to the target (Z). Note that the line of sight is longer than the horizontal distance across the ground. Even though the bullet will travel the full distance to the target (Z), gravity will only affect it as if it traveled the shorter horizontal distance (Y). The trick, then is to figure out the length of the horizontal side of the triangle.

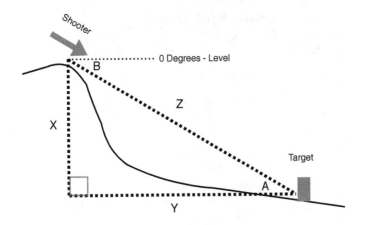

Figure 19.2-1

19.2.1 Cosine

The corner of the vertical and horizontal sides of the triangle make a right angle (90 degrees) so we can use some common trigonometric functions – specifically cosine. This also means that the line of sight side of the triangle is the "hypotenuse." If you remember the mnemonic, "soh cah toa," you're off to a good start. If you don't, don't worry, I'll walk you through it.

All you need to know for our purposes is that the "cah" from the mnemonic which stands for "cosine, adjacent hypotenuse." For our purposes, it means that you can find the length of the side of a triangle if you first know (1) the angle where it connects to the hypotenuse and (2) the length of the hypotenuse (you can do it the other way too).

To keep the example simple, let's just say that we used a laser rangefinder and determined that the target is exactly 800 yards away from us at a downward angle. We know that we can't put our normal 800 yard elevation on our scope or we'll impact too high. We need to figure out the horizontal distance across the ground and use that corresponding elevation for our scope.

Cosines for Angles			
Angle	Cosign	Angle	Cosign
5°	0.999	50°	0.642
10°	0.984	55°	0.573
15°	0.965	60°	0.5
20°	0.939	65°	0.422
25°	0.906	70°	0.342
30°	0.866	75°	0.258
35°	0.819	80°	0.173
40°	0.766	85°	0.087
45°	0.707	90°	0

Figure 19.2-2

Another trigonometric rule to remember is that alternate angles are equal. All you need to know for this is that angle B in *Figure 19.2-1* is the same as angle A. You've measured angle B to be 30 degrees. Now, with knowing the actual distance to the target and the angle, we can figure out the horizontal distance. This distance is the shorter distance that we use for elevation instead of the real distance; I call this the "angle distance."

Because we know the hypotenuse and the angle, we can use the cosine of the angle to find the adjacent triangle side. In this case, the adjacent side is the horizontal distance. Therefore, if we multiply the hypotenuse by the respective cosine, we'll get the horizontal distance. In *Figure 19.2-2* we see that the cosine for 30 degrees is 0.866. Therefore, we multiply the actual distance of 800 yards by the cosine to get an "angle distance" of 692.8 yards. Therefore, we put the elevation data for 692.8 yards on our scope. As you can see, if we used the data for 800 yards, we'd probably have missed the target entirely.

You don't need to remember how all the math works, you just have to remember this formula:

Angle Formula:

Actual distance to target * Cosine for the angle = Angle distance

Let's try another example. You have a target that is 500 yards away and it is 35 degrees uphill. First, we find that the cosine for 35 degrees is 0.819. Next, we multiply that cosine by the actual distance for an "angle distance" of 409.5 yards.

19.3 Calculating for Wind

When shooting at up or downhill angles, the angle is irrelevant when calculating for wind and other environmental variables.   This is because the angle only changes how *gravity* affects the bullet's flight.

The bullet still needs to travel the full distance to the target. Therefore, it's still exposed to the same wind and other environmental effects as if it were traveling across flat ground.

Here's the takeaway – use the "angle distance" for elevation but the actual distance for wind.

20 CLEANING YOUR RIFLE

It is crucial to properly clean the barrel of your precision rifle. I have an entire cleaning regimen that I go through when it comes to my precision rifles. Other guns? Not so much.

When it comes to most firearms, I'm a fan of keeping them functionally clean. Pretty guns with wood stocks get wiped down and oiled so that they're clean and they look nice. "Working" guns such as my competition pistols and rifles (not precision) and tactical-style guns get wiped down with a rag and re-oiled. It might not be a popular approach but I find that my hard-use guns run best when slightly dirty but properly lubed. Besides, if I was as particular about my other guns as I was about my precision rifle barrels, I'd never have time to do anything else – I'd be cleaning all the time!

On a Glock pistol for example, I don't notice an accuracy or performance difference depending on the level of cleanliness. Of course, if it is too gunked up, it'll start to malfunction. Precision rifle barrels, on the other hand, perform better when properly clean. The difficult part is determining what it means for your barrel to be "properly clean."

As you'll read, a lot of these techniques or theories are subjective. This might be due to that fact that nobody really knows what works best or perhaps its just that each barrel is different. I believe it is the latter.

However, there is a certain amount of gun voodoo that accompanies precision rifle shooting. There are some things shooters do for no reason other than that the process is ritualistic. There may be no proof that it works, but because long range shooting had been an unattainable (or at least difficult) goal for so long, shooters are eager to follow whatever rituals they are told.

If you want to stir up a debate on an online forum about guns, bring up one of the following theories you'll read. If I write that barrel break-in is crucial, I'll get feedback from readers that say I'm crazy. If I write that barrel break-in isn't necessary, I'll get feedback from the other half saying that I'm crazy. All I can do in this book is tell you what I've experienced and works well for me – you'll need to determine what works best for you.

This means that there is NO standard rule. Some barrels need to be "broke in," some barrels don't. Some barrels shoot better perfectly clean, some shoot better dirty.

20.1 Barrel "Break-In"

Some argue that a barrel could be ruined if you don't break it in properly. Personally, I think that this is hogwash. I do like to break-in a barrel, but I don't think that permanent damage can occur.

The practice of breaking in a barrel involves shooting a small number of rounds and then cleaning the barrel, and I've heard many variations on this. Shoot one round and clean, for ten rounds total, shoot 1 round and clean, then shoot two and clean, and so on until you get to 10 rounds at a time, and many more.

One theory of breaking in the barrel is that you'll help fill the pores of the metal in the barrel with the copper from the bullet jackets and not from the carbon that you clean out. This may be true, but it sounds like you'd have to do it every time you completely cleaned your barrel. Survey high-end barrel makers and you'll find that some recommend this type of break-in and others don't. If you like to do it, it sure isn't going to hurt anything.

The other theory is that if there are any burs or imperfections in the barrel, these initial rounds will help wear them down and smooth things out. This not only makes more sense to me, I have also seen this happen first hand. Some barrels, especially from large factories, can be very rough on the inside. This is due to the speed at which some manufacturers make their barrels and the emphasis they put into quantity over quality. With these rough barrels, I've seen dramatic improvements after a couple hundred rounds.

By shooting many rounds through these rough barrels, the shooter is effectively lapping the barrel. Lapping involves polishing to make something smooth. A high-end barrel might be hand-lapped to ensure it is smooth. With these rough factory barrels, you are lapping it by firing the gun which is sometimes called "fire lapping."

I don't think that you should take an abrasive to the inside of your barrel to try to lap it yourself – especially while you are still new to shooting. Personally, I don't do this either but I know a few shooters (some of whom are better shots than me) who do this and swear by it. My advice is to be careful. Barrels have a limited life – the more you wear yours down, the sooner you'll have to start over with a new barrel.

20.2 Fouling Equilibrium

The fact of the matter is that a perfectly clean (bare metal) barrel usually shoots different than that same barrel after it has had 500 rounds of fouling in it. Fouling from firing will fill the pores in the metal, can build up copper from the bullets, and surely will build up carbon from the gunpowder residue.

If the barrel behaves differently depending on the time since it has been cleaned, then how is it ever going to be consistent or reliable? After all, once you spend a day at the range, shoot 100 rounds through your barrel, and get it shooting exactly like you want it to, you're going to go home and clean it and start over again with a barrel with no rounds through it since it's last cleaning.

There is a theory that you should allow the barrel to continually get dirtier only until you see accuracy degradation. This is partly true, but if you're not careful, this theory can be taken too far.

For example, I have heard some people say that they won't clean their barrels at all until accuracy degrades and that the barrels shoot better the dirtier they are.   They often cite a theory of carbon or copper fouling equilibrium. While this sounds like it might work, and it has a certain amount of unorthodox style to it that new shooters are likely to rush to adopt it, there is a problem with the logic. First, when taken to the extreme, this means that your barrel would shoot its best when it has over 500 rounds through it.   Imagine your accuracy starts to degrade at 600 (and I'd be impressed to see a barrel go this far). So you'll clean your barrel and get the count back down to 0. Does this mean that you have to go shoot 500 rounds through your barrel again until it's accurate?   Surely, if your barrel shoots differently depending on how dirty it is and you collect and use the data between the 500 and 600 round marks, then you'll be starting from scratch again at 0. In a sense, you are ensuring is that you experience most the extreme ends of clean and dirty. And this sounds like the worst idea to me.

I do believe there is something to the theory – just not when taken to the extreme. In my experience, bare metal in a barrel and extreme filth from fouling are both ends of the spectrum I like to avoid. Instead, I like to clean my barrel after every time I shoot it.

There are so many opinions on this topic. And I wasn't afraid to give someone else a call for their opinion – you shouldn't be either. I called my friend, Tony Shankle, a shooting world record holder, and he agreed with my middle-ground approach. Tony explained that he has seen every technique from extreme clean bare metal bench rest shooters to guys who refuse to clean their barrels. What he's found is that a happy-medium approach works best but that no particular answer will work for every barrel.

He brought up the idea that there are different levels of cleaning when it comes to barrels. I liked the idea enough to include it here. Most of the time, I do what would be considered a medium cleaning. This means that I don't take the barrel all the way down to virgin metal but I do clean out the fouling that I added during my last range trip.

By doing this, I keep my barrel constantly in a state of somewhere between 20-200 rounds of fouling.

The take away here? Clean your barrel. Yes, some fouling might help, but you're going to have to clean it sometime – you might as well keep the barrel closer to the clean end of the spectrum. Remember, consistency is the key to accuracy. Minimizing the variations in the barrel is more consistent than shooting in both extremes (0 and 500+).

20.3 Clean-bore/Cold-bore

There is a theory that the first bullet (or two) out of a clean barrel will impact in a different location on a target than the subsequent bullets which are fired out of the barrel. Yes, I've seen a difference on some barrels between bullet impacts when the barrel is perfectly clean and when it is a little dirty. However, I don't subscribe to the theory that this "clean-bore" shot should be recorded in a DOPE book because it will go to this alternate location each time.

What I see, more often than not, is that the effect on the first flyer is caused by "cold-shooter" and not a cold or clean barrel. Shooters like to blame something other than themselves for non-perfect shots.

It's reasonable to think that a shooter who got to the range and just plopped down behind the rifle might not employ the proper fundamentals and might make a bad first shot or two until they have warmed-up. I analogize this to a baseball pitcher blaming the performance of his first thrown ball of the day on the fact that the ball is too new. After all, once the ball is used a bit (and he warms up), the pitches are usually better.

When I used to teach full-time, every single morning started with making the students dry fire before they shot their first group of the day. I would have them call their shots and I wouldn't allow them to shoot live ammo until they were able to have at least 5 perfect dry fires. Amazingly, once the students started doing this, the effects of their cold or clean barrels went away!

Wait a minute, didn't I just say that there's a noticeable effect on barrel performance based on whether it is raw metal or completely fouled? Yes. The difference is in the overall accuracy. I believe it is a fallacy to think that the cold-barrel shot always goes to the same spot. Instead, a raw barrel might shoot 1 MOA and an adequately broken-in/fouled barrel might shoot ½ MOA. You might end up with a flyer, but it won't be in the same spot every time. If it is, I'd be willing to bet it's you doing something wrong until you warm up, and not the barrel.

The best shooters I know blame themselves before they blame their equipment. Chances are, you are the weakest link in the system if you have appropriate equipment. If you stop looking for something else to blame, you have a chance to identify and improve something about your skill.

After I can trust that students are shooting good groups and they're starting to get their fundamentals down, I've sometimes used a method to disprove this theory. I put up a piece of paper at 100 yards that has 2 separate one MOA targets on it. I have them clean their barrels and shoot at one target for their cold/clean bore shot. Then, I have them shoot a 5 round group at the other target. In the hundreds of times I have done this with students, I have never seen a cold bore shot that wasn't within the same area of the target as the five round group. Except for when students admitted to making a bad shot, the cold bore shot could always be superimposed into the group.

The takeaway? Learn your rifle and be honest with your shooting ability. The cold bore shot might just be a cold shooter. And, if you aren't warming up before you shoot, you are just as wrong as a pitcher who doesn't warm up before he steps onto the mound.

20.4 Cleaning Instructions

As mentioned above, I generally do a "medium clean" of my barrel after every trip to the range. Only after I've shot enough rounds to require a heavy cleaning, do I do a full cleaning. The amount of rounds required depends on the chambering of the rifle. For a 300 Win. Mag. and other cartridges which burn off a lot of copper in the barrel and have short barrel lives, I won't go past 500 rounds before a full cleaning. For my 308 Win., I'll do a full cleaning once its been long enough that I can't remember the last time I did one.

The faster the bullet, the more you'll need to do a full cleaning to get the copper out. Fast bullets literally melt the copper off the bullet as it goes down the barrel.

If you are shooting bullets lubed with Moly B, you can go longer between cleaning and each cleaning process will be easier. This is one of the reasons some shooters like coated bullets.

20.4.1 Cleaning Equipment

You need, at a minimum, a good quality cleaning rod, appropriate solvent, patches, and a set of brushes and jags for each caliber.

Cleaning Rod

Personally, my favorite cleaning rods are the nylon coated rods from J. Dewey. Get one for each caliber you need – don't try to get one for your .223 and also try to use it on your .300. I recommend getting the rods with a male thread. If you accidentally break off the threaded portion of a brush or a jag in a female ended cleaning rod, you're in for a bad time. You can still use male ended brushes and jags with the male rod because J. Dewey includes an adapter. Buying a new adapter is much cheaper than buying a new rod.

Brushes

As long as you are getting quality bronze brushes for the appropriate caliber, you'll be fine. Buy extras! Honestly, I have no brand preference on brushes. Even if I did, I'd forget the name before the next time I needed more.

Jags

Unlike brushes, I do have a clear preference for jags. I absolutely hate to use the eyelet or "poke" style jags. Somehow, I always manage to get them stuck and they don't clean as well as they should.

I solely recommend Parker Hale style jags. With these jags, you wrap the patch around the jag, maximizing the cleaning surface area of the patch, which allows for a firm steady push through the barrel without binding. After you try them for the first time, you'll see what I mean.

The only trick to the Parker Hale style jags is getting accustomed to wrapping the patch on the jag. It takes some practice with dry patches, but you'll get the hang of it. You can start with one edge of the patch along the jag and roll the patch around the jag as if you were trying to roll a cigarette. Also, depending on the size of your patches, you can get a slightly tighter fit in the barrel if you start with the corner of a patch on the jag – this method is like wrapping a diamond from the corner, instead of a square from the edge.

Patches

I have yet to find my favorite cleaning patches. I do, however, try to use a patch that is the same width as my jag is long.

Solvent

I'm a sucker for Shooter's Choice solvent. It's what I used in the military and what I've stuck with. For me, it is the best there is.

For copper remover, I like Sweet's 7.62 solvent. Be careful with this stuff – it is effectively ammonia jelly. It has a very strong odor (no, it doesn't smell sweet) and can destroy certain materials that come in contact with it. If you chew tobacco, put in your dip prior to touching this stuff!

Solvent Jar

A solvent jar? Yes, this is another one of those "Aha!" moments you're likely to have.

I recommend using a clean baby food jar (or similar sized glass jar – I use an old green chilies jar myself) to store your patches and solvent. The idea is to have a jar that can hold a stack of patches about an inch thick while having an opening wide enough that it is easy to grab a patch.

Put a stack of patches in the jar and pour in enough solvent to soak the patches but not enough that you have more than a ¼" of solvent in the bottom of the jar. Effectively, you want to reach in and grab a patch like grabbing a moist baby-wipe. You don't want to dip your fingers in the solvent each time to grab a patch.

Using this system allows you to reach down and grab a solvent-soaked patch whenever you need one. When you run low on patches, just stuff a few more in. You shouldn't ever run low on solvent, however, because I have another trick up my sleeve.

Whenever you need to get solvent on your brush, just hold the brush over the opening of your solvent jar and pour some solvent over it. This not only covers the brush, it also helps to replenish the solvent in your jar. Also, it keeps you from spilling solvent on the ground or contaminating your solvent bottle by sticking in a dirty brush.

Everybody loves this idea so much I wish I could take credit for it. But, the idea came from a SOTIC instructor. Mind you, he didn't share it with me during the course to make my life easier – I picked it up from him as we both were part of a testing program for sniper rifle equipment. Unfortunately, I can't remember his name. I believe he was the NCOIC of the school after I graduated – if I find out his name, I'll surely include it in future editions of this book.

Specialty Tools

A chamber guide is a nice tool to have. It is a device that inserts into your rifle's chamber and helps to guide the patch into the barrel. This will help keep your patches wrapped on your jag and it will help keep solvent and crud out of your rifle's action.

Depending on what rifle you have, a bolt disassembly tool is also handy. However, if you're inclined to watch me struggle through the process, I show you how to use your shoelace to disassemble a Remington 700 bolt in the video posted on this chapter's webpage.

I like to grease my bolt's lugs to allow for smoother operation of the bolt and to minimize wear of the parts. I keep a syringe of Shooter's Choice grease handy for this purpose. I'm still using the same one that I've had for 10 years.

20.4.2 Regular Cleaning Instructions

1. Remove the bolt from the firearm and insert your chamber guide.
2. Pour some solvent on a brush (over your solvent jar) and pass the brush back and forth through the barrel a few times with your cleaning rod.
   a. No, it doesn't hurt the barrel to go both directions. The bullet is putting way more stress on the barrel than a bronze brush ever will. If you insist on only going the same direction as the bullet travels because you heard somewhere that it matters, by all means do what you think is best for your rifle.
3. Remove the brush from the rod and wipe the rod down with a rag – it'll likely be coated in dirty solvent.
4. Screw your jag into the rod and wrap it with a dry patch.
5. Pass the dry patch through the barrel, mopping up the gunk you scrubbed off with your brush. Remove the dirty patch before pulling the rod back through the barrel.
   a. If you like, you can also unscrew the jag from the end of the rod before pulling it back through the barrel to prevent

the jag from scraping against the crown of your barrel.

6.   Take a wet patch from your solvent jar and wrap it around the jag (and re-attach the jag if you removed it).

7.   Pass the wet jag through the barrel. I like to push the rod until the jag and patch barely stick out the end of the barrel and then pass it back and forth a few times. I believe that this helps scrub the barrel. After all, if you are trying to wipe a stubborn spot off a surface with a rag, you probably don't just give one pass per rag – you scrub back and forth.

8.   Repeat steps 2-7.

9.   Wrap a dry patch around your jag and push it through the barrel once. Repeat this process until the patch comes out dry.

10. If the patches are still dirty, you can continue cleaning by alternating between wet and dry patches until they're clean. You will need to use your judgment on how many wet patches or brushings you'll need. There's no magic number of times for each.

11. Once clean, run one last wet patch or a patch with a light coat of oil down the barrel to protect the barrel in storage.

12. Clean the chamber with some patches wrapped around your finger.

13. Use a wet patch on your thumb to twist on and clean your barrel's crown.

14. Wipe down the bolt and apply a small amount of grease to the lugs and bolt body. Too much grease will attract unwanted dirt.

15. Wipe out the inside of the action and you're done.

20.4.3 Heavy Cleaning Instructions

1.   Complete steps 1-9 of the medium cleaning instructions above.

2.   Wrap a patch with copper remover around your jag and pass it slowly through the barrel.

3.   Wait 10 minutes. Copper solvent can corrode your barrel if

you leave it in too long. 15 minutes won't destroy your barrel, but leaving it in overnight can.

4. Pass a dry patch through the barrel on your jag. You should notice a blue-green color. This color is because of oxidization and removal of the copper.

5. Run a solvent soaked brush through your barrel to clean out the copper remover.

6. Use dry patches on your jag to clean out the solvent.

7. If your barrel is heavily fouled, you can repeat steps 2-6.

8. Continue with steps 10-15 of the medium cleaning instructions above.

Appendix

The Appendix includes the following sections:

Ballistic Tables - This section includes sample ballistics table for common cartridge comparison.

Log Book - This section includes sample log book pages.

Targets - This section includes sample targets available for download on this book's website.

BALLISTIC TABLES

I have included some sample ballistics charts for common long-range cartridges for your comparison. These should only be used as a starting point - each rifle, scope, and brand of ammunition will behave uniquely.

For each of the calculations, I used the following ballistic calculator software app for my iPhone: *Ballistic* by Peak Studios, LLC. For environmental conditions, I used the following settings: 29.92 inHg, 59 degrees F, 0 ft altitude, 78% humidity, and a 10 mph wind at 90 degrees.

Included cartridges are:
◆ 223 Remington
◆ 6.5 Creedmoor
◆ 308 Winchester
◆ 300 Winchester Magnum
◆ 338 Lapua Magnum

223 Remington - 77gr Sierra HPBT

Range (yards)	Drop (in)	Drop (moa)	Drop (Mil)	Wind. (in)	Wind. (moa)	Wind (Mil)	Veloc. (fps)	Energy (ft-lbs)	Time (sec)
25	-0.65	-2.49	-0.72	0.06	0.21	0.06	2666	1215	0.03
50	-0.11	-0.21	-0.06	0.23	0.43	0.13	2605	1160	0.06
75	0.11	0.14	0.04	0.51	0.66	0.19	2545	1107	0.09
100	0.00	0.00	0.00	0.93	0.88	0.26	2485	1056	0.12
125	-0.46	-0.35	-0.10	1.46	1.12	0.32	2427	1007	0.15
150	-1.30	-0.83	-0.24	2.13	1.36	0.39	2369	959	0.18
175	-2.52	-1.37	-0.40	2.93	1.60	0.47	2312	913	0.21
200	-4.15	-1.98	-0.58	3.88	1.85	0.54	2255	869	0.24
211	-5.08	-2.29	-0.67	4.38	1.97	0.57	2231	849	0.26
225	-6.20	-2.63	-0.77	4.96	2.11	0.61	2200	827	0.28
250	-8.70	-3.32	-0.97	6.20	2.37	0.69	2145	786	0.31
275	-11.68	-4.06	-1.18	7.60	2.64	0.77	2091	747	0.35
300	-15.15	-4.82	-1.40	9.16	2.91	0.85	2037	710	0.38
325	-19.15	-5.63	-1.64	10.88	3.20	0.93	1985	673	0.42
350	-23.70	-6.47	-1.88	12.78	3.49	1.01	1933	639	0.46
375	-28.82	-7.34	-2.14	14.87	3.79	1.10	1882	606	0.50
400	-34.57	-8.25	-2.40	17.14	4.09	1.19	1832	574	0.54
425	-40.96	-9.20	-2.68	19.60	4.40	1.28	1783	544	0.58
450	-48.03	-10.19	-2.96	22.27	4.72	1.37	1735	515	0.62
475	-55.82	-11.22	-3.26	25.14	5.05	1.47	1688	487	0.67
500	-64.38	-12.30	-3.58	28.23	5.39	1.57	1642	461	0.71

223 Remington - 77gr Sierra HPBT (cont)

Range (yards)	Drop (in)	Drop (moa)	Drop (Mil)	Wind. (in)	Wind. (moa)	Wind (Mil)	Veloc. (fps)	Energy (ft-lbs)	Time (sec)
525	-73.74	-13.41	-3.90	31.54	5.74	1.67	1597	436	0.76
550	-83.95	-14.58	-4.24	35.09	6.09	1.77	1553	412	0.80
575	-95.07	-15.79	-4.59	38.87	6.45	1.88	1511	390	0.85
600	-107.13	-17.05	-4.96	42.89	6.83	1.99	1469	369	0.90
625	-120.20	-18.37	-5.34	47.16	7.21	2.10	1429	349	0.96
650	-134.34	-19.74	-5.74	51.69	7.59	2.21	1391	331	1.01
675	-149.60	-21.16	-6.16	56.47	7.99	2.32	1353	313	1.06
700	-166.04	-22.65	-6.59	61.52	8.39	2.44	1318	297	1.12
725	-183.74	-24.20	-7.04	66.84	8.80	2.56	1283	282	1.18
750	-202.76	-25.82	-7.51	72.42	9.22	2.68	1251	267	1.24
775	-223.16	-27.50	-8.00	78.27	9.64	2.81	1220	254	1.30
800	-245.03	-29.25	-8.51	84.39	10.07	2.93	1191	243	1.36
825	-268.42	-31.07	-9.04	90.76	10.51	3.06	1164	232	1.42
850	-293.42	-32.96	-9.59	97.40	10.94	3.18	1139	222	1.49
875	-320.10	-34.93	-10.16	104.27	11.38	3.31	1117	213	1.55
900	-321.20	-35.01	-10.18	104.55	11.40	3.32	1116	212	1.56
925	-348.52	-36.98	-10.76	111.39	11.82	3.44	1094	205	1.62
950	-378.76	-39.10	-11.37	118.74	12.26	3.57	1074	197	1.69
975	-410.88	-41.30	-12.01	126.30	12.70	3.69	1056	191	1.76
1000	-444.95	-43.58	-12.68	134.08	13.13	3.82	1039	184	1.83

6.5 Creedmoor - 140gr Hornady A-Max

Range (yards)	Drop (in)	Drop (moa)	Drop (Mil)	Wind. (in)	Wind. (moa)	Wind (Mil)	Veloc. (fps)	Energy (ft-lbs)	Time (sec)
25	-0.70	-2.66	-0.77	0.00	0.00	0.00	2785	2411	0.03
50	-0.17	-0.33	-0.10	0.00	0.01	0.00	2745	2343	0.05
75	0.06	0.08	0.02	0.02	0.02	0.01	2706	2276	0.08
100	0.00	0.00	0.00	0.04	0.04	0.01	2667	2210	0.11
125	-0.37	-0.28	-0.08	0.07	0.06	0.02	2628	2146	0.14
150	-1.05	-0.67	-0.19	0.13	0.08	0.02	2589	2084	0.17
175	-2.05	-1.12	-0.33	0.20	0.11	0.03	2551	2023	0.20
200	-3.39	-1.62	-0.47	0.30	0.15	0.04	2514	1964	0.23
207	-5.00	-2.13	-0.62	0.43	0.18	0.05	2479	1908	0.25
225	-5.08	-2.15	-0.63	0.44	0.19	0.05	2476	1906	0.26
250	-7.11	-2.72	-0.79	0.61	0.23	0.07	2439	1849	0.29
275	-9.52	-3.30	-0.96	0.81	0.28	0.08	2402	1793	0.32
300	-12.29	-3.91	-1.14	1.07	0.34	0.10	2366	1739	0.35
325	-15.46	-4.54	-1.32	1.37	0.40	0.12	2329	1686	0.38
350	-19.03	-5.19	-1.51	1.73	0.47	0.14	2293	1635	0.41
375	-23.01	-5.86	-1.70	2.15	0.55	0.16	2258	1584	0.45
400	-27.41	-6.54	-1.90	2.64	0.63	0.18	2222	1535	0.48
425	-32.26	-7.25	-2.11	3.20	0.72	0.21	2187	1487	0.51
450	-37.56	-7.97	-2.32	3.84	0.81	0.24	2153	1440	0.55
475	-43.33	-8.71	-2.53	4.56	0.92	0.27	2118	1395	0.58
500	-49.58	-9.47	-2.75	5.38	1.03	0.30	2084	1350	0.62

6.5 Creedmoor - 140gr Hornady A-Max (cont)

Range (yards)	Drop (in)	Drop (moa)	Drop (Mil)	Wind. (in)	Wind. (moa)	Wind (Mil)	Veloc. (fps)	Energy (ft-lbs)	Time (sec)
525	-56.33	-10.25	-2.98	6.30	1.15	0.33	2051	1307	0.65
550	-63.60	-11.04	-3.21	7.32	1.27	0.37	2017	1265	0.69
575	-71.40	-11.86	-3.45	8.45	1.40	0.41	1984	1223	0.73
600	-79.76	-12.69	-3.69	9.66	1.54	0.45	1951	1183	0.77
625	-88.68	-13.55	-3.94	10.98	1.68	0.49	1919	1144	0.81
650	-98.20	-14.43	-4.20	12.38	1.82	0.53	1887	1106	0.85
675	-108.33	-15.32	-4.46	13.86	1.96	0.57	1855	1070	0.89
700	-119.08	-16.25	-4.73	15.43	2.11	0.61	1824	1034	0.93
725	-130.49	-17.19	-5.00	17.08	2.25	0.65	1793	999	0.97
750	-142.58	-18.15	-5.28	18.79	2.39	0.70	1762	965	1.01
775	-155.36	-19.14	-5.57	20.57	2.54	0.74	1732	932	1.05
800	-168.87	-20.16	-5.86	22.42	2.68	0.78	1702	900	1.10
825	-183.13	-21.20	-6.17	24.32	2.81	0.82	1672	869	1.14
850	-198.17	-22.26	-6.48	26.27	2.95	0.86	1643	839	1.19
875	-214.01	-23.36	-6.79	28.26	3.08	0.90	1615	811	1.23
900	-230.69	-24.48	-7.12	30.29	3.21	0.93	1587	783	1.28
925	-248.22	-25.63	-7.45	32.35	3.34	0.97	1559	755	1.33
950	-266.66	-26.80	-7.80	34.44	3.46	1.01	1532	729	1.38
975	-286.01	-28.01	-8.15	36.54	3.58	1.04	1505	704	1.42
1000	-306.33	-29.25	-8.51	38.64	3.69	1.07	1479	680	1.48

308 Winchester - 175gr Sierra HPBT

Range (yards)	Drop (in)	Drop (moa)	Drop (Mil)	Wind. (in)	Wind. (moa)	Wind (Mil)	Veloc. (fps)	Energy (ft-lbs)	Time (sec)
25	-0.62	-2.36	-0.68	0.04	0.17	0.02	2561	2549	0.03
50	-0.06	-0.12	-0.04	0.18	0.34	0.04	2517	2462	0.06
75	0.15	0.19	0.05	0.40	0.51	0.06	2474	2377	0.09
100	0.00	0.00	0.00	0.72	0.69	0.09	2431	2295	0.12
125	-0.51	-0.39	-0.11	1.13	0.87	0.11	2388	2215	0.15
150	-1.41	-0.90	-0.26	1.65	1.05	0.13	2345	2137	0.18
175	-2.70	-1.47	-0.43	2.26	1.23	0.16	2303	2061	0.21
200	-4.39	-2.10	-0.61	2.98	1.42	0.18	2262	1988	0.25
207	-5.03	-2.31	-0.67	3.23	1.48	0.19	2250	1965	0.26
225	-6.52	-2.77	-0.81	3.80	1.61	0.20	2221	1916	0.28
250	-9.08	-3.47	-1.01	4.74	1.81	0.23	2180	1846	0.31
275	-12.10	-4.20	-1.23	5.78	2.01	0.25	2140	1779	0.35
300	-15.59	-4.96	-1.45	6.94	2.21	0.28	2100	1713	0.38
325	-19.58	-5.75	-1.68	8.22	2.42	0.31	2060	1649	0.42
350	-24.08	-6.57	-1.92	9.63	2.63	0.33	2021	1588	0.46
375	-29.11	-7.41	-2.17	11.15	2.84	0.36	1983	1528	0.50
400	-34.69	-8.28	-2.42	12.81	3.06	0.39	1945	1469	0.53
425	-40.85	-9.18	-2.69	14.60	3.28	0.42	1907	1413	0.57
450	-47.61	-10.10	-2.96	16.53	3.51	0.45	1870	1359	0.61
475	-54.98	-11.05	-3.24	18.59	3.74	0.47	1833	1306	0.65
500	-63.00	-12.03	-3.53	20.80	3.97	0.50	1797	1255	0.69

308 Winchester - 175gr Sierra HPBT (cont.)

Range (yards)	Drop (in)	Drop (moa)	Drop (Mil)	Wind. (in)	Wind. (moa)	Wind (Mil)	Veloc. (fps)	Energy (ft-lbs)	Time (sec)
525	-71.70	-13.04	-3.83	23.15	4.21	0.53	1761	1205	0.74
550	-81.09	-14.08	-4.13	25.66	4.45	0.57	1726	1158	0.78
575	-91.22	-15.15	-4.45	28.32	4.70	0.60	1692	1112	0.82
600	-102.10	-16.25	-4.77	31.14	4.96	0.63	1657	1067	0.87
625	-113.77	-17.38	-5.11	34.12	5.21	0.66	1624	1025	0.91
650	-126.27	-18.55	-5.45	37.26	5.47	0.70	1591	984	0.96
675	-139.63	-19.75	-5.81	40.58	5.74	0.73	1559	944	1.01
700	-153.88	-20.99	-6.18	44.07	6.01	0.77	1527	906	1.06
725	-169.06	-22.27	-6.55	47.74	6.29	0.80	1496	870	1.11
750	-185.21	-23.58	-6.94	51.59	6.57	0.84	1466	835	1.16
775	-202.37	-24.94	-7.35	55.62	6.85	0.87	1436	802	1.21
800	-220.59	-26.33	-7.76	59.84	7.14	0.91	1408	770	1.26
825	-239.90	-27.77	-8.19	64.25	7.44	0.95	1379	739	1.31
850	-260.36	-29.25	-8.63	68.86	7.74	0.99	1352	710	1.37
875	-282.00	-30.78	-9.09	73.65	8.04	1.03	1326	683	1.43
900	-304.88	-32.35	-9.56	78.65	8.34	1.07	1300	657	1.48
925	-329.04	-33.97	-10.04	83.83	8.65	1.11	1276	632	1.54
950	-354.55	-35.64	-10.54	89.22	8.97	1.15	1252	609	1.60
975	-381.43	-37.36	-11.06	94.80	9.29	1.19	1229	587	1.66
1000	-409.76	-39.13	-11.59	100.58	9.60	1.23	1207	566	1.72

300 Win Mag - 190gr Sierra HPBT

Range (yards)	Drop (in)	Drop (moa)	Drop (Mil)	Wind. (in)	Wind. (moa)	Wind (Mil)	Veloc. (fps)	Energy (ft-lbs)	Time (sec)
25	-0.72	-2.74	-0.80	0.04	0.14	0.04	2861	3453	0.03
50	-0.20	-0.39	-0.11	0.14	0.27	0.08	2816	3346	0.05
75	0.04	0.05	0.01	0.33	0.41	0.12	2772	3242	0.08
100	0.00	0.00	0.00	0.58	0.56	0.16	2728	3140	0.11
125	-0.33	-0.25	-0.07	0.92	0.70	0.20	2685	3041	0.13
150	-0.97	-0.61	-0.18	1.33	0.85	0.25	2642	2945	0.16
175	-1.91	-1.04	-0.30	1.82	1.00	0.29	2600	2851	0.19
200	-3.18	-1.52	-0.44	2.40	1.15	0.33	2558	2760	0.22
207	-4.77	-2.03	-0.59	3.06	1.30	0.38	2516	2671	0.25
225	-5.06	-2.11	-0.61	3.18	1.32	0.39	2511	2656	0.25
250	-6.71	-2.56	-0.75	3.81	1.46	0.42	2475	2584	0.28
275	-9.01	-3.13	-0.91	4.65	1.61	0.47	2434	2499	0.31
300	-11.67	-3.71	-1.08	5.57	1.77	0.52	2394	2417	0.34
325	-14.71	-4.32	-1.26	6.59	1.94	0.56	2353	2336	0.37
350	-18.14	-4.95	-1.44	7.71	2.10	0.61	2314	2258	0.41
375	-21.98	-5.60	-1.63	8.92	2.27	0.66	2274	2182	0.44
400	-26.24	-6.27	-1.82	10.23	2.44	0.71	2235	2108	0.47
425	-30.94	-6.95	-2.02	11.65	2.62	0.76	2197	2035	0.50
450	-36.08	-7.66	-2.23	13.17	2.79	0.81	2158	1965	0.54
475	-41.69	-8.38	-2.44	14.79	2.97	0.87	2120	1897	0.57
500	-47.78	-9.13	-2.65	16.53	3.16	0.92	2083	1830	0.61

300 Win Mag - 190gr Sierra HPBT (cont)

Range (yards)	Drop (in)	Drop (moa)	Drop (Mil)	Wind. (in)	Wind. (moa)	Wind (Mil)	Veloc. (fps)	Energy (ft-lbs)	Time (sec)
525	-54.38	-9.89	-2.88	18.39	3.34	0.97	2046	1765	0.65
550	-61.49	-10.68	-3.11	20.35	3.53	1.03	2009	1703	0.68
575	-69.14	-11.48	-3.34	22.44	3.73	1.08	1973	1642	0.72
600	-77.35	-12.31	-3.58	24.65	3.92	1.14	1937	1582	0.76
625	-86.14	-13.16	-3.83	26.99	4.12	1.20	1901	1525	0.80
650	-95.53	-14.03	-4.08	29.46	4.33	1.26	1866	1469	0.84
675	-105.54	-14.93	-4.34	32.05	4.53	1.32	1831	1415	0.88
700	-116.20	-15.85	-4.61	34.79	4.75	1.38	1797	1363	0.92
725	-127.53	-16.80	-4.89	37.66	4.96	1.44	1763	1312	0.96
750	-139.57	-17.77	-5.17	40.68	5.18	1.51	1730	1263	1.01
775	-152.32	-18.77	-5.46	43.84	5.40	1.57	1697	1215	1.05
800	-165.84	-19.80	-5.76	47.15	5.63	1.64	1665	1169	1.09
825	-180.13	-20.85	-6.06	50.61	5.86	1.70	1633	1125	1.14
850	-195.24	-21.93	-6.38	54.23	6.09	1.77	1602	1082	1.19
875	-211.20	-23.05	-6.70	58.01	6.33	1.84	1571	1041	1.23
900	-228.03	-24.20	-7.04	61.95	6.57	1.91	1541	1002	1.28
925	-245.78	-25.37	-7.38	66.06	6.82	1.98	1511	964	1.33
950	-264.49	-26.59	-7.73	70.34	7.07	2.06	1483	927	1.38
975	-284.18	-27.83	-8.10	74.79	7.33	2.13	1454	892	1.43
1000	-304.90	-29.12	-8.47	79.42	7.58	2.21	1426	858	1.48

338 Lapua Mag - 250gr Sierra HPBT

Range (yards)	Drop (in)	Drop (moa)	Drop (Mil)	Wind. (in)	Wind. (moa)	Wind (Mil)	Veloc. (fps)	Energy (ft-lbs)	Time (sec)
25	-0.73	-2.80	-0.80	0.03	0.12	0.04	2914	4713	0.03
50	-0.22	-0.43	-0.11	0.13	0.24	0.08	2873	4581	0.05
75	0.02	0.03	0.01	0.29	0.37	0.12	2832	4452	0.08
100	0.00	0.00	0.00	0.52	0.49	0.16	2792	4326	0.10
125	-0.30	-0.23	-0.07	0.81	0.62	0.20	2752	4203	0.13
150	-0.89	-0.57	-0.18	1.18	0.75	0.25	2712	4083	0.16
175	-1.78	-0.97	-0.30	1.61	0.88	0.29	2673	3966	0.19
200	-2.96	-1.42	-0.44	2.12	1.01	0.33	2634	3851	0.22
207	-4.46	-1.89	-0.59	2.70	1.15	0.38	2596	3739	0.24
225	-5.01	-2.05	-0.61	2.91	1.19	0.39	2585	3704	0.25
250	-6.29	-2.40	-0.75	3.36	1.28	0.42	2557	3630	0.27
275	-8.44	-2.93	-0.91	4.10	1.42	0.47	2519	3523	0.30
300	-10.94	-3.48	-1.08	4.91	1.56	0.52	2482	3419	0.33
325	-13.79	-4.05	-1.26	5.80	1.70	0.56	2445	3317	0.36
350	-17.01	-4.64	-1.44	6.78	1.85	0.61	2408	3217	0.39
375	-20.60	-5.24	-1.63	7.83	2.00	0.66	2371	3120	0.43
400	-24.57	-5.87	-1.82	8.98	2.14	0.71	2335	3025	0.46
425	-28.94	-6.50	-2.02	10.21	2.29	0.76	2299	2933	0.49
450	-33.73	-7.16	-2.23	11.53	2.45	0.81	2263	2842	0.52
475	-38.94	-7.83	-2.44	12.95	2.60	0.87	2228	2754	0.56
500	-44.58	-8.51	-2.65	14.45	2.76	0.92	2192	2668	0.59

338 Lapua Mag - 250gr Sierra HPBT (cont)

Range (yards)	Drop (in)	Drop (moa)	Drop (Mil)	Wind. (in)	Wind. (moa)	Wind (Mil)	Veloc. (fps)	Energy (ft-lbs)	Time (sec)
525	-50.68	-9.22	-2.88	16.06	2.92	0.97	2158	2584	0.62
550	-57.25	-9.94	-3.11	17.76	3.08	1.03	2123	2502	0.66
575	-64.29	-10.68	-3.34	19.56	3.25	1.08	2089	2422	0.69
600	-71.84	-11.43	-3.58	21.46	3.42	1.14	2055	2344	0.73
625	-79.90	-12.21	-3.83	23.47	3.59	1.20	2022	2268	0.77
650	-88.49	-13.00	-4.08	25.59	3.76	1.26	1988	2195	0.81
675	-97.62	-13.81	-4.34	27.82	3.94	1.32	1956	2123	0.84
700	-107.33	-14.64	-4.61	30.16	4.11	1.38	1923	2053	0.88
725	-117.63	-15.49	-4.89	32.62	4.30	1.44	1891	1984	0.92
750	-128.53	-16.36	-5.17	35.19	4.48	1.51	1859	1918	0.96
775	-140.06	-17.26	-5.46	37.89	4.67	1.57	1828	1854	1.00
800	-152.24	-18.17	-5.76	40.71	4.86	1.64	1796	1791	1.04
825	-165.10	-19.11	-6.06	43.65	5.05	1.70	1766	1730	1.09
850	-178.65	-20.07	-6.38	46.73	5.25	1.77	1735	1671	1.13
875	-192.92	-21.05	-6.70	49.94	5.45	1.84	1705	1614	1.17
900	-207.94	-22.06	-7.04	53.28	5.65	1.91	1676	1559	1.22
925	-223.73	-23.10	-7.38	56.76	5.86	1.98	1647	1505	1.26
950	-240.33	-24.16	-7.73	60.38	6.07	2.06	1618	1453	1.31
975	-257.75	-25.24	-8.10	64.15	6.28	2.13	1590	1403	1.35
1000	-276.04	-26.36	-8.47	68.06	6.50	2.21	1562	1354	1.40

LOG BOOK

In this section, I have included some sample log book pages for you to use. The sample pages that I have included should not necessarily replace whatever system you use or think is best. Instead, if you bring this book to the range with you for reference and you'd like a handy place to keep your information, please feel free to use the included pages. If you run out of space, I'm sure that you can see that they're easy to replicate on your own. I have also included files for each of these on this book's website.

The included pages are for: DOPE Cards to record your data for various rifles and Round Count Logs to keep track of your barrel life.

DOPE Card for Rifle:_____

Distance	Temperature								
	30	40	50	60	70	80	90	100	110
50									
100									
150									
200									
250									
300									
350									
400									
450									
500									
550									
600									
650									
700									
750									
800									
850									
900									
950									
1000									

DOPE Card for Rifle:_____

Distance	\<br\>				Temperature				
	30	40	50	60	70	80	90	100	110
50									
100									
150									
200									
250									
300									
350									
400									
450									
500									
550									
600									
650									
700									
750									
800									
850									
900									
950									
1000									

DOPE Card for Rifle:_____

Distance	Temperature								
	30	40	50	60	70	80	90	100	110
50									
100									
150									
200									
250									
300									
350									
400									
450									
500									
550									
600									
650									
700									
750									
800									
850									
900									
950									
1000									

DOPE Card for Rifle:_____

Distance	Temperature								
	30	40	50	60	70	80	90	100	110
50									
100									
150									
200									
250									
300									
350									
400									
450									
500									
550									
600									
650									
700									
750									
800									
850									
900									
950									
1000									

DOPE Card for Rifle:_____

Distance	Temperature								
	30	40	50	60	70	80	90	100	110
50									
100									
150									
200									
250									
300									
350									
400									
450									
500									
550									
600									
650									
700									
750									
800									
850									
900									
950									
1000									

DOPE Card for Rifle:_____

Distance	Temperature								
	30	40	50	60	70	80	90	100	110
50									
100									
150									
200									
250									
300									
350									
400									
450									
500									
550									
600									
650									
700									
750									
800									
850									
900									
950									
1000									

Round Count Log for Rifle:_____

Date	Ammunition	Fired	Total

Round Count Log for Rifle:_____			
Date	**Ammunition**	**Fired**	**Total**

Round Count Log for Rifle:_____

Date	Ammunition	Fired	Total

Round Count Log for Rifle:_____

Date	Ammunition	Fired	Total

Round Count Log for Rifle:_____			
Date	Ammunition	Fired	Total

Date	Ammunition	Fired	Total

Round Count Log for Rifle:_____

Round Count Log for Rifle:_____

Date	Ammunition	Fired	Total

Round Count Log for Rifle:_____

Date	Ammunition	Fired	Total

TARGETS

The following targets are a couple examples of the targets that are available for download on this book's webpage here: https:// ryancleckner.com/long-range-shooting-handbook/ Two examples are included here for your reference.

The first target in this section is intended to help you zero your rifle. It includes the MOA adjustments needed to adjust your group for different distances along each line. For example, if the center of your group is one inch to the left of center at 100 yards, the target shows that you must adjust right 1 MOA. If the group was on the same spot on the paper at 25 yards, the target shows that you must adjust right 4 MOA. Additionally, the target includes 3 circles in the center to help calculate 1, 2, and 3 MOA size groups at 100 yards. The included target is optimized for at least a 10x scope at 100 yards. Other targets are available on this book's website that are better suited for lower power scopes and iron sights.

The second target is useful for learning to shoot good groups. The background makes it difficult for the shooter to see where their impacts are. This prevents the shooter from making adjustments while they are shooting the group.

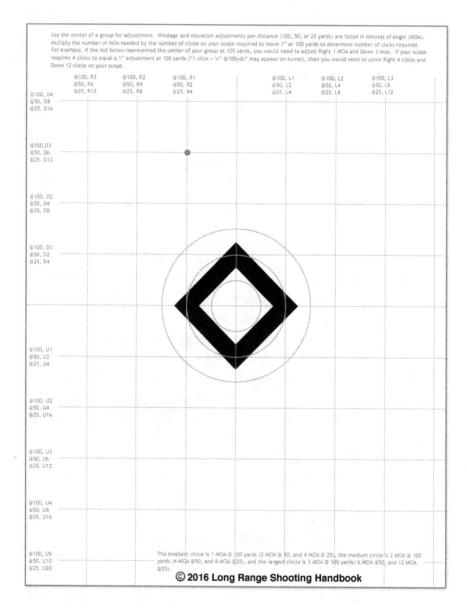

Use the center of a group for adjustment. Windage and elevation adjustments per distance (100, 50, or 25 yards) are listed in Minutes of Angle (MOA). Multiply the number of MOA needed by the number of clicks on your scope required to move 1" at 100 yards to determine number of clicks required. For example, if the dot below represented the center of your group at 100 yards, you would need to adjust Right 1 MOA and Down 3 moa. If your scope requires 4 clicks to equal a 1" adjustment at 100 yards ("1 click = ¼" @100yds" may appear on turret), then you would need to come Right 4 clicks and Down 12 clicks on your scope.

@100, R3   @100, R2   @100, R1   @100, L1   @100, L2   @100, L3
@50, R6   @50, R4   @50, R2   @50, L2   @50, L4   @50, L6
@25, R12   @25, R8   @25, R4   @25, L4   @25, L8   @25, L12

@100, D4
@50, D8
@25, D16

@100,D3
@50, D6
@25, D12

@100, D2
@50, D4
@25, D8

@100, D1
@50, D2
@25, D4

@100, U1
@50, U2
@25, U4

@100, U2
@50, U4
@25, U16

@100, U3
@50, U6
@25, U12

@100, U4
@50, U8
@25, U16

@100, U5
@50, U10
@25, U20

The smallest circle is 1 MOA @ 100 yards (2 MOA @ 50, and 4 MOA @ 25), the medium circle is 2 MOA @ 100 yards (4 MOA @50, and 8 MOA @25), and the largest circle is 3 MOA @ 100 yards(6 MOA @50, and 12 MOA @25).

© 2016 Long Range Shooting Handbook

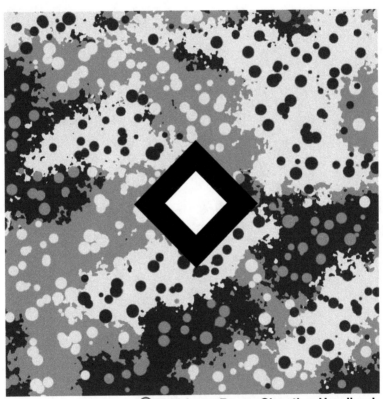

© 2016 Long Range Shooting Handbook

ABOUT THE AUTHOR

Ryan Cleckner was born in Phoenix, AZ where he grew up hunting, shooting, and learning to love the outdoors. Shortly after graduating High School, he enlisted in the Army where he served in the 1st Ranger Battalion of the 75th Ranger Regiment. He graduated from the premier sniper training program, the Special Operations Target Interdiction Course. Ryan first deployed as a sniper, and then later as a sniper team leader, in support of the Global War on Terror in Afghanistan.

Upon returning home to Arizona, Ryan received his Bachelor of Science degree from Arizona State University while he taught at a local Community College and at a government contracted sniper school. Ryan and his wife moved to Connecticut for law school where they had two wonderful children. He received his Juris Doctorate degree from Quinnipiac University School of Law as a Dean's Fellow Scholar.

Ryan managed federal government affairs for the firearm industry's trade association, the NSSF, where he created a series of YouTube training videos - the popularity of which prompted the creation of this book. Ryan also appeared on multiple seasons of History Channel's Top Shot television program as a sniper expert.

Ryan subsequently served as a Vice President for the Freedom Group, later Remington Outdoor Company, before teaching Constitutional law at the University of Alabama in Huntsville, and starting his own law practice, building custom rifles (https://cleckner.co), and starting RocketFFL to help people get their own FFLs and help FFLs stay compliant (https://www.rocketffl.com).

CONNECT WITH RYAN:
https://www.facebook.com/ryan.cleckner/
https://www.instagram.com/cleckner/

Printed in the USA
CPSIA information can be obtained
at www.ICGtesting.com
LVHW011747271123
765049LV00005B/10